The History of Christian Theology
Part I

Professor Phillip Cary

THE TEACHING COMPANY ®

PUBLISHED BY:

THE TEACHING COMPANY
4840 Westfields Boulevard, Suite 500
Chantilly, Virginia 20151-2299
1-800-TEACH-12
Fax—703-378-3819
www.teach12.com

Copyright © The Teaching Company, 2008

Printed in the United States of America

This book is in copyright. All rights reserved.

Without limiting the rights under copyright reserved above,
no part of this publication may be reproduced, stored in
or introduced into a retrieval system, or transmitted,
in any form, or by any means
(electronic, mechanical, photocopying, recording, or otherwise),
without the prior written permission of
The Teaching Company.

ISBN 1-59803-488-X

Scripture quotations are from Professor Cary's own translations and from The Holy Bible, English Standard Version ®, Copyright © 2001 by Crossway Bibles, a publishing ministry of Good News Publishers. Used by permission. All rights reserved.

Phillip Cary, Ph.D.

Professor of Philosophy, Eastern University

Professor Phillip Cary is Director of the Philosophy Program at Eastern University in St. Davids, Pennsylvania, where he is also Scholar-in-Residence at the Templeton Honors College. He earned his B.A. in both English Literature and Philosophy at Washington University in St. Louis, then earned an M.A. in Philosophy and a Ph.D. in both Philosophy and Religious Studies at Yale University. Professor Cary has taught at Yale University, the University of Hartford, the University of Connecticut, and Villanova University. He was an Arthur J. Ennis Post-Doctoral Fellow at Villanova University, where he taught in Villanova's nationally acclaimed Core Humanities program.

At Eastern University, he is a recent winner of the Lindback Award for excellence in undergraduate teaching. His specialty is the thought of Augustine, on whom he has written three scholarly books for Oxford University Press: *Augustine's Invention of the Inner Self* (2000), *Inner Grace* (2008) and *Outward Signs* (2008). He has also written *Jonah* for the Brazos Press series, Theological Commentary on the Bible, as well as numerous articles for philosophical and theological publications. Professor Cary has published scholarly articles on Augustine, Luther, the doctrine of the Trinity, and interpersonal knowledge. Professor Cary produced the following popular courses for The Teaching Company: *Augustine: Philosopher and Saint* and *Philosophy and Religion in the West*. He also contributed to The Teaching Company's third edition of the course titled *Great Minds of the Western Intellectual Tradition*.

Table of Contents
The History of Christian Theology
Part I

Professor Biography	i
Course Scope	1
Lecture One	What Is Theology? 3
Lecture Two	Early Christian Proclamation 19
Lecture Three	Pauline Eschatology 34
Lecture Four	The Synoptic Gospels 48
Lecture Five	The Gospel of John 64
Lecture Six	Varieties of Early Christianity 79
Lecture Seven	The Emergence of Christian Doctrine 95
Lecture Eight	Christian Reading 112
Lecture Nine	The Uses of Philosophy 129
Lecture Ten	The Doctrine of the Trinity 146
Lecture Eleven	The Doctrine of the Incarnation 164
Lecture Twelve	The Doctrine of Grace 180
Timeline	197
Glossary	209
Biographical Notes	249
Bibliography	260

The History of Christian Theology

Scope:

This course surveys major developments in the history of Christian theology, which is the tradition of critical reasoning about how to teach the faith of Christ. Taking the centrality of Jesus Christ as the distinctive feature of Christianity, it focuses on theological concepts by relating them to Christian life and experience, including especially practices of worship.

The course begins with the first Christian theological writings, the books of the New Testament, the earliest of which, the letters of Paul, reflect a worship of the exalted Christ at the right hand of God, in light of which later documents, such as the Four Gospels, tell the story of the historical Jesus, his earthly life, death, and resurrection. The course proceeds to examine the theology of the early church, how it read the Jewish scriptures and how it used Greek philosophy, as well as how the very idea of official Christian doctrine and its opposite, heresy, arose in response to the large variety of early Christianities. The survey of ancient Christian theology concludes in Part I by presenting three key doctrines: Trinity, Incarnation, and grace.

Part II covers medieval and Reformation theology. The distinctive features of Eastern Orthodox theology are discussed, including the use of icons, the theology of the Transfiguration, the distinction between divine essence and energies, and the disagreement with the Western churches about whether the Holy Spirit proceeds from the Father "and the Son." Key developments in medieval Catholicism are examined, including scholastic theology, the use of logic and analogy, the seven sacraments, and the soul's existence in heaven, hell, or purgatory in the time between death and resurrection. Reformation theology begins with the doctrine of justification by faith alone and the Lutheran distinction between Law and Gospel, followed by the Reformed tradition and the development of Calvinism, with its distinctive commitment to the knowledge of eternal salvation, from which flows its embrace of the doctrine of predestination. The Anabaptists, such as the Mennonites, form a third and radical wing of the Reformation, while the Anglican tradition of the English Reformation aims for a middle way between Reformed theology and Catholicism.

Part III begins by tracing the course of Protestant theology through the modern period. Modernity means a gradual secularization of Western Christendom, as can be seen in the theology of Baptists and Quakers, both of which offer an alternative to state churches and advocate religious liberty for all. True religion comes to be seen increasingly as a private inner experience rather than outward conformity to an institutional church, as can be seen in the Puritan emphasis on conversion, which leads to the Pietist emphasis on true Christianity as well as to the tradition of revivalism that is so strong in America, including the Methodist emphasis on holiness and its offshoot, Pentecostalism. On the other hand, the increasing secularization of modern culture and especially of historical scholarship on the Bible poses new problems for Christian theology, to which deism, liberal theology, neo-Orthodoxy, evangelicalism, and Fundamentalism are responses.

The course concludes by treating the history of Roman Catholic theology in modernity, beginning with the doctrine of grace formulated by the 16th-century Council of Trent in response to Protestant challenges, proceeding to the high point of mystical and devotional theology in early modern Spain and France, and concluding with the first and second Vatican councils, the doctrine of papal infallibility, and questions about how the church's teaching may legitimately change. A final lecture examines the ecumenical theology that opens up after Vatican II, drawing Catholics, Orthodox, and Protestants into ongoing conversation about the boundaries of the tradition of Christian theology and its center in Jesus Christ.

Lecture One
What Is Theology?

Scope:

For purposes of this course, Christian theology will be defined as the tradition of critical reflection on what should be taught as Christian doctrine. The central focus of Christian doctrine as presented here is not salvation, Christian life, or the Kingdom of God (important as these themes are) but the identity of Jesus Christ. From this vantage point, the lectures will aim to bring key disagreements within the theological tradition into focus, so listeners may have a better understanding of the diversity of Christianity today. We will begin not with research into the historical Jesus but with the early church's faith in Christ.

Outline

I. This course arose in part as a response to the many e-mailed questions received as a result of previous Teaching Company courses on Christian thought.
  - **A.** Many Christians want to know where their particular form of Christianity (Catholic, Lutheran, Presbyterian, etc.) fits in with or contrasts with others.
  - **B.** By the same token, people from outside the Christian tradition (Jews, Muslims, agnostics, atheists, etc.) want to know what and how Christians think.
  - **C.** In both cases, one finds out about oneself by coming to a deeper understanding of others and how they are different.

II. Christian theology is the central intellectual activity of the Christian tradition, consisting of critical reasoning about what should be taught in the Christian community, the church.
  - **A.** The major world religions are all intellectual traditions, involving both the handing down of specific wisdom and critical reasoning about that wisdom.
    - **1.** "Tradition" means the "handing down" of wisdom (both practical and theoretical) from one generation to the next.
    - **2.** Both sciences and religions are traditions in this sense.

3. Both sciences and religions are intellectual traditions, in that what they pass on is a form of wisdom that requires critical reasoning.
4. Whereas sciences are oriented toward discovery of new knowledge, religions are oriented toward fidelity, obedience, and propagation of a message or revelation already received.

B. Christian theology is a tradition of critical reasoning about Christian doctrine, that is, about what should be taught in the church about Jesus Christ and life in him.
1. Christian theology focuses on doctrine rather than law, because Christianity is a faith more than a way of life, so the question of what people should be taught to believe is of the essence.
2. Unlike other religions, Christianity is essentially a faith because it is not fundamentally about how to live but about the life of another person, Jesus Christ.
3. Theology is a normative discipline because it concerns not just what is taught in the church, but what ought to be.
4. The wisdom and message at the heart of Christianity is not primarily a revelation about how to live but primarily the story about who Jesus is, called the Gospel.

C. The key concepts of Christian theology should be understood in terms of their relation to Christianity's central focus on Jesus Christ.
1. In Christian theology, even the crucial theme of Jesus's own teaching, the Kingdom of God, is subordinated to teaching about who Jesus is—the Christ, which means the king in the Kingdom of God.
2. Similarly, for Christian theology all other questions (including very important ones like "How do I get saved?") are subordinate to the question, "Who is Jesus?"
3. For Christianity, what is parallel to the Torah as the fundamental revelation of God in Judaism or to the Koran in Islam, is not the Bible but Jesus Christ himself (of whom the Bible functions as a kind of witness).

- **D.** Theology concerns concepts that cannot be understood apart from the way they shape Christian life.
    1. Although theological concepts can become quite abstract, they have meaning only as they relate believers to Christ and thereby give shape to Christian life.
    2. Once formed, theological concepts are used to guide and correct Christian practice, teachings, and storytelling.
    3. To understand what is at stake in Christian theological concepts is to see how they form Christian life and practices and their relation to Christ.

III. The focus of this course will be on theological arguments where something important is at stake for those involved.
- **A.** The aim is for listeners to understand the diversity of Christian theology today, where it comes from, and what is at stake for participants in the tradition.
- **B.** The lectures will aim not for neutrality but for fairness and generosity.
    1. Though there is much common ground, there is no purely neutral ground between rival Christian traditions, such as Catholicism and Lutheranism.
    2. Hence a better metaphor than "neutral territory" is "hospitality," which is what happens when the people you disagree with are visiting your home turf and must be welcomed with generosity.
    3. Accordingly, these lectures will not aim for a neutral objectivity (which is not really possible) but a generous engagement with rival traditions—the kind of interest you take in friends with whom you enjoy a good argument.

IV. The course will start with the New Testament documents, then will explore the early church and its relation to philosophy. We will move on to examine the fundamental issues of the Reformation, and then we will trace both Protestant and Catholic theologies through modernity and beyond.

V. Interestingly, Christianity does not start with what some scholars call the "historical Jesus."
- **A.** The history of Christian theology begins with the Christ of faith, which the earliest Christian theology understands to be no different than the historical Jesus.
- **B.** This means that the history of Christian theology does not begin with the New Testament Gospels, which tell the earthly life of Jesus, but with earlier New Testament documents, which tell us how the early church worshiped Christ exalted at God's right hand.
- **C.** To begin with accounts of the historical Jesus is to begin with modern historical research rather than with ancient Christian theology.

Suggested Reading:

Buschcart, *Exploring Protestant Traditions*.

Foster, *Streams of Living Water*.

Willis, *The Teachings of the Church Fathers*.

Questions to Consider:

1. What interests you about Christian theology enough to be listening to these lectures?
2. Do you think theology is worth arguing about?

Lecture One—Transcript
What Is Theology?

Welcome to a course on the history of Christian theology. I am your professor Phillip Cary. I teach at Eastern University outside of Philadelphia and I also teach for The Teaching Company in this Great Courses series. I have taught for The Teaching Company, courses on Augustine, on Luther, and on the history of philosophy and religion in the West.

One of the things that happened to me as a result of this teaching is that I got a lot of e-mails from Teaching Company customers who wanted to find out what did Augustine, this ancient church father from the 5th century, have to do with Protestantism? What did he have to do with Catholicism? What did Luther have to do with Catholicism? We know that there's a conflict there but what do Lutherans and Catholics think about each other? What do Lutherans and other Protestants think about each other? A deluge of e-mails. They were fascinating. I loved them. I love being able to think about these things and to respond to them and to articulate what goes on in the whole history of the Christian tradition—Augustine, Luther, Catholics, Protestants, Eastern Orthodox and as a result, I found myself thinking, wouldn't it be good to have a course where we talk about how all of these diverse strands of the Christian theological tradition arise, intersect with each other, pull apart, and maybe join back together. So, we have a course on the history of Christian theology.

Many of the people who wrote to me were Christians of one kind or another—Presbyterians, Catholics, and so on—wondering about other kinds of Christians and their relationship to other kinds of Christians. To know the history of "the other" is to know something about your own history. By the same token, there are lots of folks who are not Christians—Jews or Muslims or atheists—who want to know what makes Christians tick. How do they think? What holds this project called Christian thought together? That's another way in which, another context in which, learning about the other is a way of coming to understand, in a deeper way, yourself. Jews and Christians in particular have a history together that we need to understand, so that the history might go better than it has in the past. But, there are similar histories between Jews, Christians, and Muslims, Christians and atheists, and so on. This course should help you get situated on the map of Christian theology and also in its long history, showing where that map came from.

When we think about the history of Christian theology, what are we thinking about? I've already used the word tradition. I would suggest to you that we could have as a preliminary definition of Christian theology a definition of a tradition of intellectual activity in the context of the Christian Church, the community of those who believe in Christ, and that this intellectual activity is focused on the issue of what to teach, how to teach within the Christian community about the faith of the Christian Church, which is another name for the Christian community.

Let's start with this notion of tradition, though. This is a general term. You don't have to be Christian to have a tradition. Every religion has a tradition. "Tradition" is an English word that comes from a Latin word, *traditio* meaning "to hand down." In a tradition, you have some kind of wisdom or knowledge or skill that is passed down from one generation to another. Broadly defined, in that sense, I think every science as well as every religion is a tradition. You learn to become a scientist, for instance, by going to graduate school learning the skills of becoming a physicist designing physical experiments and so on. You learn to become a Christian or a Jew or a Muslim by being initiated into the Christian tradition or the Muslim or Jewish traditions usually as a child, sometimes by conversion.

One of the things that sciences and religions have in common, I think, are that they are both traditions of reasoning, of critical discussion. They both have forms of wisdom and knowledge to hand down and they both think about the best ways to hand those down and sometimes criticize what they are handing down. The sciences are about learning new knowledge and therefore the criticism of old knowledge is a crucial and inevitable part of the sciences. The religions are more about handing down an ancient wisdom and therefore they're not fundamentally about discovering new things. But, the future is always there for all of us. We always have to learn new things to face the future and I think the religious traditions end up learning a lot through critical reasoning.

In other words, if you think of traditions the way I do here in this course, you will find that faith and reason naturally belong together. Religions are intellectual traditions. They have faith commitments. They have doctrines that they teach. But, in order to teach well, they're constantly thinking about the truth of these doctrines in a critical fashion. Is this teaching really true? That's what I mean by critical reasoning, which is a fundamental function of every healthy intellectual tradition whether religious, scientific, or whatever.

By the way, let me mention to think about how deep a tradition is. One of the most fundamental traditions of all is a particular language. We learn our language at our mother's knee. It's handed down to us—English, Chinese, French and notice how once you master a language, you can use it to think critically. You can use it even to think critically about the people who taught it to you. Traditions are like that. You go to graduate school in science, you end up criticizing the views of your teachers. You become a theologian, you end up criticizing the tradition you come from. Traditions can do that. Traditions are not sort of rigid and unthinking. They are precisely, I think, the context of thinking.

In a tradition, you try to hand down a wisdom from one generation to another. It is not just theoretical, but also practical. How do you live like a Christian? How do you conduct experiments like a physicist? Practical and theoretical wisdom. I would suggest that in fact the practical wisdom typically comes first, especially in religions. First you learn how to worship like a Christian or a Jew and then you ask questions like, what are we doing when we worship in this way? What does it mean, for instance, when Christians cross themselves and says "in the name of the Father, Son, and Holy Spirit"? What's going on there? What does it mean when Christians call upon the name of Jesus as Lord, which is a fundamental act of Christian worship? We will start with those fundamental acts of worship, of Christian practice, which already have a theology embedded in them. They already have faith commitments, commitments about what ought to be taught.

Here's another focus of Christian theology and the focus is precisely Christian doctrine. Doctrine is a word coming from a Latin term *doctrina* meaning "teaching." Doctrine is what is taught and theology is critical reflection on what you should teach. It's a little bit like parents getting together and having a discussion with other parents, saying how do we raise our children? If you're thinking of Christian parents raising Christian kids, well then you've got something close to theology already. If you think about pastors talking with each other about how they should teach people to believe in Jesus, then you've got theology.

Christian theology is this ancient centuries long tradition of people arguing with each other, reasoning with each other, thinking with each other about how the Christian faith ought to be taught. It is a doctrine, but not just an abstraction. Christianity's actually fascinated by doctrine in a way that other religions, aren't I think and it's a doctrine because it's a faith and it's a faith because it's focused on a person. Other religions might be described primarily as a way of life. I think that's a good description for most religions. Christianity, I think, is not fundamentally a way of life and that's an interesting feature of it. Christianity is fundamentally a faith, which is to say a belief in a particular person. At the heart of Christianity is not a law or rule or way of life, but a particular individual human being, Jesus of Nazareth. What is taught in Christianity, what is the doctrine of Christianity, is the faith in Christ. Christian theology is about how shall we teach our children to believe in this man. What do we teach them to believe? What's the right thing to teach? What's the wrong thing to teach? How ought we to teach? It's a normative discipline where people try to think what should we teach, like parents getting together thinking about what they should teach their children. The name for what is taught, in addition to doctrine, is this lovely old word Gospel meaning "good news." The Gospel is this story about who Jesus is. What needs to be taught for Christians is the story about Jesus. Everything else in theology grows from the kind of Christian obsession with the question who Jesus is and the Gospel is a story meant to answer that question.

Christian theology is a doctrine or argues about doctrine, thinks about doctrine, how to teach doctrine. The doctrines are often highly conceptual, but the concepts are about Christ and how this is linked to the life of Christians. This focus on Christ, which is so characteristic of Christian religion and Christian faith, is I think an important thing to bear in mind as you think about what Christian theology is all about. There are some very, very important and central concepts of Christian theology, which are not essential as this one person. For instance, it's fairly clear from the historical evidence that we have that at the center of Jesus's own teaching, when he was teaching in Galilee and Jerusalem in the 1st century A.D., was the concept of the Kingdom of God, an enormously important concept. Scholars had been focusing a great deal of attention on what Jesus meant when he spoke about the Kingdom of God and its coming. But, the Christian theological tradition says all, right, that's very important, but nothing is more important than the king of the Kingdom of God, the Christ. That is Jesus. Christ meaning the King of the Jews, the king of the Kingdom of God. The theme of the Kingdom of God, which is at the center of Jesus's teaching, becomes secondary to the theme of who Jesus himself is in early Christian theology. Early Christian theology is not simply about what Jesus taught. It's about who Jesus is. That's why it's a faith. That's why it's doctrine. Christians, I will argue in a later lecture, more or less invent the notion of religious doctrine because they're so intent on getting it right when they teach people what to believe about Jesus. Theology in Christianity is doctrinal because it's about a faith, because it's about a person. It's not fundamentally about a way of life, not even fundamentally about the Kingdom of God. That's second. The person of Christ, who Jesus is, is primary. That's what Christian theology's all about.

Likewise, there are very important questions like, how shall I get saved? A deep and important question for Christian theology, but not the most important question. For Christian theology the most important question is who is Jesus? We'll run into that question when we examine the New Testament Gospels. We will see how Christian doctrine emerges out of that question. How do we teach people to believe the truth about who Jesus is? What is the truth about who Jesus is? What are we doing, we ancient Christians, when we call upon the name of the Lord and we mean the name of this man, Jesus?

Another way of putting this centrality of Christ in Christian theology is to say that for Christianity, Christ plays the role that, say, the Torah does in Judaism or the Koran does in Islam. Christianity does, of course, have a Bible consisting in part of the Jewish Torah and then lots of other stuff, but the Bible for Christianity is not as central as the one person Jesus Christ. When Christians talk about the word of God, the most important word of God they have in mind is not the Bible, but Jesus himself. Jesus the person plays the role that the Torah does or the Koran does. He is the fundamental revelation and communication and presentation of God to humanity. Christian theology can almost be defined as an ongoing tradition of obsession with this one man, Jesus.

It's important I think to get that sense of obsession in order to see that Christian theological concepts are not just abstractions. We will deal with some theological concepts that are really quite abstract. We'll be talking about whether Christ is *homoousios* with the Father, of one essence with the Father, whether he is two natures, whether there are three persons in the Trinity, whether there is one essence or two essences, one essence or two natures in Christ. Lots of very complicated language. It's all a way of trying to get clear who Jesus is and then relate it to the Christian life. There is, of course, a Christian way of life. That second—what's first is the identity of Christ—but then Christian theological concepts aiming to teach people who Jesus is are aiming to shape Christian life by linking the life of Christians with this one man, Jesus Christ. That is why I think it's very important to recognize Christian theological concepts are meant to shape Christian life. They're not just abstractions and they shape Christian experience.

I'm someone who thinks that we don't get our concepts from our experience. It's not like we have this deep inner experience and then we express it outwardly in words. I think it's more likely the other way around. We've got these words. We learn the language. We learn the language, we learn how to talk as kids, and that shapes our experience. We learn how to talk like Christians or Jews or Muslims, and that gives us a kind of Christian or Muslim or Jewish experience. The outward words shape our inner hearts. What we believe shapes us. The words that we hold dear, the words that we pray and sing, the words that express our longings, the words that give shape to our longings give shape to our hearts. Instead of a model of an experience that we then express, I would suggest the model of a tradition of wisdom and words, of prayer and practices, which shape the heart. Theological concepts result in a distinctively shaped heart.

I'll suggest in a later lecture that because of the particular theological concepts you have, you'll have a particular set of anxieties. Catholics are anxious about different things than Protestants are and indeed Lutheran Protestants are probably going to be anxious about different things from what Calvinist Protestants are. Many Protestants are anxious about whether they have true faith. Catholics, in effect, can't be anxious about that because Catholics have a different set of theological issues on their mind. Catholics will worry about whether they are in a state of grace or a state of mortal sin. That's an anxiety that Protestants can't have. Why? Because they have a different set of theological concepts that shape their hearts, shape their experience and feelings and anxieties too. These theological concepts, as abstract as they might appear at first, have deep implications for how people feel about their lives, who they think they are, and how they experience their whole lives.

That's why if you're a member of one Christian tradition—and in a later lecture we're talking about some other Christian tradition that's quite foreign to you, quite unfamiliar—say you're a Catholic listening to a lecture about Baptists. Or, you're a Baptist listening to lectures about Eastern Orthodoxy. Be aware that these concepts, which may seem at first a bit foreign and strange to you, are in fact deeply implied, deeply formative, deeply shaping the experience and lives of these other Christians. I will always try in these lectures to make clear how these concepts shape people's lives and experience and hearts. But, always the aim is, in Christian theology, to link these life-shaping concepts to the identity of Jesus.

Because there is so much genuine conflict within the Christian tradition between Protestants and Catholics, between actually Catholics and the Eastern Orthodox as well, it's important to think about how disagreement works in the Christian tradition and how in a course of lectures one deals with disagreement and arguments. I suggested that traditions involve critical reasoning. It involves disagreements. That's not such a bad thing, but there are bad ways and good ways to disagree.

Let me suggest that one of our problems as historians—whether we're doing history of politics or history of theology—is that it's very hard to be neutral, maybe impossible. Imagine trying to tell a neutrally objective story about American politics. That doesn't work. If you're reading a book about American politics, a book about Bill Clinton or George Bush, you want to have some idea whether the author is a Republican or a Democrat. Not that Democrats have to be unfair to Bush or Republicans have to be unfair to Clinton, but you want to know their perspective. We're all located in a particular place within our traditions and it's important to be able to be generous and fair to these other traditions that are not your own traditions.

Disagreement does not have to mean unfairness. I think it does mean that we're never in a position simply to be neutral. These lectures will not aim at a kind of neutral objectivity. What they will aim at is something that I will call "hospitality." Think of the metaphor of hospitality and how it works. When you are being hospitable, you're not on neutral ground. You're on your own home turf and precisely because you're on your own home turf, you have to be generous and hospitable and gracious to a person who doesn't particularly belong in your home, who may be someone you disagree with.

Let us practice not an impossible neutral objectivity, but a generosity and hospitality—indeed a kind of friendship. I love the fact that the more you get to know someone, the more freely you can disagree with them. When you don't really know someone very well, you have to be very careful how you disagree. You won't say oh you're wrong, you're just wrong. You'll say something like I beg to differ or I disagree with that one or let me tell you what I think about that. You'll be very courteous with people you hardly know. But, with your friends, you can just argue all night saying you're wrong. No, no, you're wrong. Because you trust each other, you can go ahead and say you're wrong and it's not going to bother you.

Think of these lectures as both an attempt to practice hospitality and an attempt to begin the process of forming friendships. Inviting you to form friendships across the dividing barriers from one tradition to another, so that from having a passing acquaintance with an alternative tradition—say a Baptist knowing something about Catholics and maybe being a bit suspicious about it—you might end up being able to have a deeper acquaintance with this tradition that is not your own and begin to form a kind of intellectual friendship with that tradition. Which might be not only helpful for your relationships with people who come from that tradition—maybe Baptists and Catholics can be friends—but also will be helpful for your own understanding of your own Christian life. Or, indeed, for that matter, your own life as an atheist or a Jew or someone who has to deal with these Christians and their obsession with Christ and their obsession with theology.

As we go forward in this course, I do want us to think about these traditions and their disagreements in a context where we're looking to be hospitable and friendly. We can only begin that process in these lectures; we only have 30 minutes to talk about a deep and rich tradition, for instance, like Anabaptism. Wonderful set of people, deep set of theologies, a practice of Christian love and community that is worth deep study and we'll spend less than 30 minutes on it.

Not enough. But, what I'll try to do in all these lectures is to get at something that's close to the heart of the thinking of each of these traditions. It'll be somewhat simplified because I only have 30 minutes, but it should properly be like a key that opens a door. The simplification, the simple overview of these traditions should be close enough to the heart of these traditions that you can use it as a key, open the door, and enter into a deeper study of these traditions. I hope that these lectures will provide a good introduction to deeper study as sort of like an invitation to friendship, to cross these boundaries and learn about these other traditions.

Now let's get to the précis. Now let's get to the issue of where we're going. The structure of the course is going to look something like this. We'll start in the next few lectures—the next four lectures in fact—looking at documents from the New Testament. The New Testament being, of course, the specifically Christian part of the Bible, the part of the Bible, which contains really the earliest Christian theology. The earliest Christian theology in written form is the New Testament. We'll look through that, then we'll move on to other features of the early church in the 2nd, 3rd, 4th, 5th centuries. We'll look at how early Christian practices worked, things like how Christians read the Bible, how they read the Jewish part of the Bible later called the Old Testament. What's happening when Christians read the Jewish Bible? How do they do it?

Also, how Christians interacted with philosophy. Christianity, like other religious traditions, is a tradition of critical reasoning, and it has a peculiarly intimate and deeply engaged relationship with this other tradition of critical reasoning called Western philosophy. It goes a long way back. What do Christians make of Western philosophy, of Greek philosophy especially? What do they make of the Jewish scriptures? What do they make of the large variety of early Christianity, which includes quite a number or variety of positions? How does the very idea of doctrine, of sound doctrine, teaching the right thing, emerge in Christianity? These are all topics that we'll address in the second part of the course where we're talking about theology in the early church. That will be Lectures Six, Seven, Eight and Nine.

Then, at the end of Part I of this course, Lectures Ten, Eleven, and Twelve, we'll deal with the crucial doctrines of the early church, the doctrines formed by the people called the church fathers. The church fathers being to the early church somewhat like the rabbis of the Talmud are to the Jewish tradition. They're the ones who give Christianity its classic shape as an intellectual phenomenon, just like the rabbis of the Talmud give the classic shape to Judaism, as we know it. These church fathers, they ended up crafting three key doctrines, which we will talk about. One is the doctrine of the Trinity. Then there's the doctrine of the Incarnation. Then there's the doctrine of grace. That's Lectures Ten, Eleven, and Twelve.

The Trinity is the doctrine about who God is, Father, Son, and Holy Spirit. It's a doctrine you get to when you start with these Christian practices of worship where you're worshipping Jesus, as if he's God. This man is God; how can you possibly believe that? Can Christians really be serious about talking about Jesus as if he's God? Yes, they are. They're absolutely serious. The doctrine of the Trinity is a result. So is the doctrine of the Incarnation, the doctrine about how God becomes human in Christ and then the doctrine of grace is about how that humanization of God, that God becoming human, is shared with human beings. In a wonderful phrase, the church fathers say "God became humans so that humans may become divine," meaning immortal, sharing in divine life. The doctrine of grace is how the Incarnation spreads it goodness to the whole human race. There's only one incarnate God, but the Incarnation is a way of spreading the goodness of God among the whole human race. How does that work?

Then we'll go on in Part II to talk about medieval developments from these doctrines, especially in the interesting interaction and contrast between the Eastern church and the Western church, the Eastern Orthodox and the Roman Catholics, as it develops in the Middle Ages. Then in the second half of Part II, we'll talk about the Reformation, Protestant theology.

Then, what we're going to do in Part III is we will trace Protestant theology through the history of modernity all the way up to the 20th century and American evangelicalism because it's such a fascinating story and it has its own logic and so we'll try to follow the diversity and the development of Protestant theology, leaving Catholic theology behind until we get to Lecture Thirty-Three and then we'll go back to the 16th century and pick up the story of modern Catholicism.

My intent here is to try to show that despite their largely separate histories in modernity and their often conflicted history, Protestants and Catholics ultimately need each other. At the end of the lectures on Protestantism, I will suggest that we've reached a kind of end of modernity—maybe we're post-Modern in some deep sense—and Protestantism is faced with new challenges because of that, which it will face better if it turns to look at the ancient tradition of the Christian faith, those ancient doctrines which they share with the Catholic tradition. That's why the lectures will conclude by thinking about the new ecumenical situation raised by the culminating event of Catholic life in the 20th century, the Second Vatican Council, which creates a new kind of ecumenical theology, an ecumenical conversation that is deeply interesting to me and shapes my own theological thinking. Protestants and Catholics, I will propose at that final lecture, need each other in a deep way.

But, now, back to the start. What will the next lecture look like? One of the interesting things about Christian theology is it doesn't start with what some scholars call the historical Jesus. It starts with Christ being worshipped. The earliest documents of the Christian faith, the earliest writings in the New Testament, are not about the earthly life of Jesus. They're not the Gospels, those four Gospels that are familiar to us—Matthew, Mark, Luke, and John—but rather letters of Paul and some fragments of hymns and prayers that we get in the New Testament, all of which point toward an early Christian practice of worshipping Jesus as a resurrected man now having eternal life sitting at God's right hand. We get a picture of these early Christian congregations gathering to call upon the name of Jesus, as if his name is the name of God. That practice is where Christian theology starts historically, I will argue.

Then we'll get on to these later New Testament documents called the Gospels, which tell the story of the earthly life of Jesus. The Christian Church is convinced from the word go that the exalted Lord Jesus at God's right hand is the same person as the historical Jesus who walked on Earth and was crucified and then raised from the dead. There's not a distinction in early Christian thought between the Christ of faith and the historical Jesus. But, we do start with the Christ of faith. Later on, we'll find out why the notion of the historical Jesus becomes a very important notion in 19th-century theology. But, it's just the whole notion that there's a difference between the historical Jesus and the Christ of faith is alien to the earliest Christian strands of theology. Indeed, it's alien to all Christian theology until about the 19th century.

We're not going to start with the historical Jesus. We're going to start with the Christ of faith, which the early Church thought as the same thing as the historical Jesus. The early Church really just made no distinction between the Christ of faith and the historical Jesus. But what they did—and the reason why it's accurate to say they start with the Christ of faith—is that early Christians did this strange bizarre thing. They worshipped the man Jesus, as if he was God. That's where that obsession with the person of Christ starts and that's where the historical tradition of Christian theology begins.

Lecture Two
Early Christian Proclamation

Scope:

Christian theology begins with reflection on the practice of Christian worship, and what is distinctive about Christian worship is that it is directed at Jesus Christ. The earliest recorded Christian hymns, prayers, and sermons envision Jesus as raised from the dead and exalted to the throne of God at the right hand of the Father. From this central vantage point, worshipping Christ on high, the early Christians looked back at the meaning of his earthly life and death, and even to his existing with the Father before his birth. And they looked forward to his coming again in glory to restore all things, raising the dead and establishing the Kingdom of God on earth.

Outline

I. The first recorded Christian sermon is found in Acts 2.
  A. The setting is Jerusalem on the Jewish feast of Pentecost.
      1. This is 50 days after the feast of Passover, when Jesus was crucified.
      2. Jesus's followers, who were all Jews, gathered in Jerusalem.
      3. In fact, Jews from all over the world gather for the feast.
      4. The Holy Spirit, which is the Spirit of the prophets of Israel, descends on Jesus's followers.
      5. They speak in other tongues—a whole variety of languages spoken by the people gathered in Jerusalem.
      6. A crowd comes together and asks, "What does this mean?"
      7. The Apostle Peter answers by giving the first recorded Christian sermon.
  B. The sermon is about who Jesus is and what he has done.
      1. It is Jesus who has sent the Holy Spirit.
      2. He does so from his exalted position at the right hand of God.
      3. He has come to this position by being raised from the dead and ascending into heaven.
      4. He has received from the Father the promised Holy Spirit, and now pours it out on his followers.

- **C.** The sermon contains a brief narrative of Jesus's life, focusing on what God has done.
    1. God appoints and approves Jesus by the miracles he does.
    2. God hands him over to be crucified according to his destined plan and foreknowledge.
    3. God raises him from the dead.
- **D.** The sermon ascribes to Jesus some characteristic titles from the scriptures of Israel.
    1. He is Christ, which is to say the Messiah, the anointed Son of David, King of the Jews.
    2. They call upon his name as Lord, which suggests that in some way the name of the God of Israel ("the LORD") has been bestowed on him.
- **E.** The sermon involves quotations from the Old Testament as ancient witness to Jesus Christ.
    1. King David's psalms, praising God for rescuing him from death, are applied to Jesus's resurrection.
    2. A central project of early Christian intellectuals, their reading and teaching, was to show how the prophets of the Bible (that is, what Christians later call the Old Testament) bear witness to Jesus.
- **F.** At the end, Peter urges his hearers to repent and be baptized in the name of Jesus Christ.
    1. Belief in Christ is understood to begin with an inward and outward change.
    2. The inward change is repentance, a change of heart, turning away from one's old life to join the community of those who follow Jesus.
    3. The outward change is baptism, a ritual washing that signifies new life in Jesus and marks the social boundary of the church.

II. The picture of the exalted Lord Jesus Christ is extended by the early church in two directions, back before his birth and onward to his coming again as king.

- **A.** Although elements of the story are familiar, many of the early church's assumptions are not.
    1. The resurrection of Jesus is not a form of life after death; it means that he is no longer dead.

2. The underlying story (told at Easter) is not about an immortal soul but about a resurrected body.
3. Astonishingly, Jesus at God's right hand is a living man.
4. Believers in Jesus expected a resurrection like his—a resurrection of the body which is not so much life after death as the reversal and defeat of death itself.

B. Early Christian theologians, even in the New Testament, suggested that there was something scholars called the "preexistence" of Christ.
1. This means that before Christ was born as a man, he was already seated at God's right hand.
2. Although he was of the very essence of God, he humbled himself and took on the form of a servant. Thus, God has exalted him and given him a name that is above all others—the name of the Lord.
3. The earliest Christian confession consists in this naming of Jesus as Lord.

Suggested Reading:

Book of Acts, chaps. 1–3.

Letter to the Philippians, chap. 2.

Bauckham, *God Crucified*.

Hurtado, *At the Origins of Christian Worship*.

Questions to Consider:

1. Why did the early Christians worship Jesus—what were they hoping for?
2. How is early Christian worship of Jesus compatible with the Jewish commitment to monotheism?

Lecture Two—Transcript
Early Christian Proclamation

We're going to begin our series of lectures on the history of Christian theology by looking at the earliest Christian documents, the earliest theological writings of the Christian tradition, which are the familiar documents of the New Testament, which most of us know about. We're going to begin by looking at the second chapter of the book of Acts, which contains the earliest recorded Christian sermon, but let's set the stage just a little bit.

We need to remember, we're talking about the New Testament. This is a bunch of documents written in Greek, which is the dominant language of the eastern half of the Roman Empire. So here we are, we're in the middle of the Roman Empire right now, it's the 1st century A.D., and we're in the part of the Roman Empire where they use Greek. That's why the New Testament is written in Greek. But we're also in the part of the Roman Empire where everybody's Jewish. We are in Judea, the word from which we get the word "Jew" in English. Judea has its capital in Jerusalem. So we are located now in Jerusalem in the 1st century, somewhere in the 30s of the 1st century A.D. We're among a bunch of people whose native language probably is Aramaic, which is related to Hebrew. They're Jews, they live in Judea, they're gathered in Jerusalem.

It is the day of Pentecost. Now that's a Greek term, because this is the Greek New Testament. It's a Greek term that means 50. It's the festival, Jewish festival, celebrated 50 days after the crucial Jewish festival of Passover, that's the festival during which Jesus was crucified. The Jewish name for this festival in Hebrew is Shavuot, which means the Feast of Weeks. We translate this into the Greek term and it becomes "the 50," because it's 50 days after the festival of Passover. When we're talking about early Christianity, we have to keep remembering these are all Jews. Jesus is a Jew, his apostles are Jews, all the early Christian believers are Jews. Jesus's mother is a Jew. They're Jews gathered for a Jewish festival in Jerusalem. One other note, they're gathered from all around the world. The great Jewish festivals are gatherings of Jewish people in Jerusalem from all over the world. At this point, the Jewish people are scattered pretty much all over the world, at least all over the known world, the Roman world. So you actually got a lot of people speaking a lot of different languages and having a hard time understanding each other, and that's actually part of the point of the story, for here's what happens.

You've got a gathering of these Jewish people who believe in Jesus. We'll talk about what that means in a second. They're gathered together and here goes the story. There's this big sound, like a rushing of a mighty wind. There seems to be something like tongues of fire that descend and, all of a sudden, something strange happens. This gathering of people are speaking in tongues, is the language used, but tongues meaning they're speaking in different languages, so that all these gathered people from around the world, Jews speaking all these different languages, can hear this Gospel, this story about Jesus, proclaimed in their own language. That's what Christians call Pentecost, this gift of languages in which this Jewish gospel is spoken in all these different languages so the whole world can hear. So we've already got this kind of notion of evangelism going on.

A crowd gathers because there's this strange kind of speaking going on. It sounds very strange, all these different languages. The crowd gathers and they ask, what does this mean? What's going on? Up stands the apostle Peter, he's the leader of the twelve apostles of Jesus. This is a familiar thing I hope, right? Jesus, when he was walking around in Galilee and in Jerusalem picked twelve apostles to be the sort of inner circle of his teaching, and Peter is the leader. Peter stands up and tries to explain what's going on, and this is the first recorded Christian sermon. He says, look, we're not drunk. You may think so, but no, it's not. That's not what's happening. What's happened is that the Holy Spirit has descended upon these people, the spirit of the Lord, the spirit of prophecy, the spirit that is familiar to all Jews from the scriptures of Israel, the scriptures which Christians call the Old Testament, the ancient witness to Jesus. Brief note, when Christians call it the Old Testament. That's not saying it's obsolete, quite the contrary. It's very important to these Christians, these Jewish Christians, that the Old Testament is the ancient witness to who Jesus is. So, they're very intent on the contemporary importance, the living importance, of these Jewish scriptures.

The Old Testament, the spirit of the Lord, comes upon the prophets, Peter says, that's what's happening now. The Holy Spirit, the spirit of the Lord God of Israel, has come upon these people, and they are speaking like the prophets do, but in a way that's designed to spread this message, this good news about Jesus to the whole world, beginning with all these Jews gathered in Jerusalem. The message that comes out here has to do with Jesus, and it has to do with what Jesus has to do with what's happening right now. There's this event, this event of the Holy Spirit descending upon all these people. Where did the Holy Spirit come from? Well, of course the Holy Spirit is the spirit of Lord, the Lord God sends the Holy Spirit upon the prophets in the Old Testament. And then Peter says this striking thing. It is Jesus who has sent the Holy Spirit, Jesus, sending the Holy Spirit from heaven. What? Well, this is Pentecost, this is 50 days after Jesus's crucifixion. Where is Jesus? He's sitting at the right hand of God That's what Peter is trying to point out here. Jesus has been crucified 50 days ago, and then the Christian church is teaching he was raised from the dead. The man who was crucified is not dead anymore and, furthermore, here's the center of the sermon, he is now ascended to heaven. He is exalted at God's right hand. Think of the words "exalt," and "exaltation." The "alt" in exaltation comes from the same root as altitude. He's up there with God. He's exalted.

There's this story now behind this. Jesus was crucified 50 days ago. Three days after that he was raised from the dead in the Resurrection. That's a concept we're going to have to talk about at some length. And now he's exalted to God's right hand. From his position sitting at the right hand of God, it's Jesus who sends the Holy Spirit, the spirit of the Lord upon the prophets. It's as if Jesus gets to do what God does. God sends the Holy Spirit, God sends the spirit of the Lord to the prophets. It's Jesus who sends the Holy Spirit to the prophets because Jesus is acting for God somehow. That's that deep connection between Jesus and God which we need to talk about, because that's so important for Christianity.

Here in Pentecost, we need to get a picture, a crucial and central picture for early Christian thought and early Christian worship. There's God in heaven, sitting on his throne, key picture for how you imagine God in the Old Testament. You don't have to imagine him quite so literally, but if you're going to imagine God, get a picture of God, well, then, he's sitting on a throne in heaven. And now, Christians are saying expand the picture. Jesus is sitting at the right hand of God. He's the Son of God sitting at God's right hand, the right hand of God, the Father Almighty. And from that position in heaven, this man Jesus, the very same man who was crucified 50 days ago, is sending the Holy Spirit upon this community of those who believe in Jesus and call on his name. There's the picture. God the Father in heaven, Jesus at his right hand, the Holy Spirit being sent by Jesus down from heaven, falling from heaven like tongues of fire, and dwelling in this Christian community so that they can speak the Gospel. That's the picture.

Peter has to fill in some of the details. He says a very little bit about the life of Jesus, about how Jesus did miracles and healed the lame and made the blind see and all that sort of thing. That's a typical rehearsal of the life of Jesus, but he goes quickly from there to the crucifixion, to the fact that Jesus was crucified, and one of the things that the early Christian preachers emphasized is that when Jesus was crucified, this wasn't some kind of mistake. God intended this, planned this from the very beginning. "It was predestined," Peter will say in a slightly later sermon in the book of Acts. It was predestined. This is really where the Christian notion of predestination comes from. What's predestined, above all, is Jesus Christ, the life of this man born of Mary, healing the lame and the crippled and the sick and the blind, crucified, raised from the dead, exalted at God's right hand, that's all part of God's plan, including even the crucifixion. It wasn't a mistake. It was part of the plan.

And then there's the resurrection. Again, we'll get back to that in just a second, but let's start with this picture of the exalted Jesus at God's right hand. That's the picture that we need to get if we want to understand what makes Christian religion what it is, the picture of Jesus, the man, sitting at God's right hand.

To explain who Jesus is, which is the central burden and thrust of the Gospel, one of the things that the early Christian theologians did, is use titles, labels for who Jesus is. The most familiar label is one that Peter uses in this sermon. He calls him Christ, Jesus Christ. It's not a name actually, it's a title. In Greek it's *Christos*, that translates a Hebrew term, *Moshiach*, or Messiah, and that's Hebrew for, Anointed One. That is, someone who is smeared with oil. Why? Well, because the kings of Israel, going back to King David many hundred years before, are inaugurated as kings not by being crowned, but by being anointed. So to say someone is Messiah, or anointed one, is to say they're the king, the legitimate descendent of David, the legitimate king of Israel, the King of Jews as the pagans will say. And when pagans wanted to translate this term Messiah, they used this phrase, king of the Jews. Another way of saying it is son of David, meaning descendent of David. All this way of thinking of Jesus is part of what Peter is saying. This is the king that is meant as God's ruler on earth in the Kingdom of God which is meant to be God's ruling on earth so that Israel, Judah, might be freed from their oppression. More about that in a minute.

Here's another title, actually more important even than the title Christ, because the Christ, or the Messiah, is a king and, in one sense, you know, all of the descendents of David who became king were Messiahs, they were anointed ones. And they're called anointed ones in the Hebrew scriptures so that they are actually evil Messiahs. They were evil kings in the Old Testament, and they were descendents of David and good riddance. So, the hope for the Messiah is the hope for more than just a descendent of David, more than just a new king coming. That is the hope, but there's more to it than that, especially for Christians.

Here's what the Christians add. When Peter goes and quotes the prophets of Israel in his sermon, here's what he adds. I'm going to tell you a little bit about this quote. He quotes from the prophet Joel, who talks about the spirit of the Lord being poured out on all flesh, sons and daughters of Israel prophesying. That's what the spirit does. When the spirit gets into you, you prophesy. And at the end of this quotation from the book of Joel. (It's a rather long quotation from the Old Testament that begins Peter's sermon.) At the end of it is this phrase, "And all who call upon the name of the Lord will be saved." Very important phrase. "All who call upon the name of the Lord will be saved." Let's think about the original context, and we're going to talk about this name, Lord, because that's something that gets attached to the name of Jesus, and it's more than just Messiah, more than just Christ, it's Lord, and that's really something.

But let's go back to, again, the Hebrew scriptures to understand what's going on. "All who call upon the name of the Lord will be saved," says the prophet Joel. The name of the Lord, well, what's that? The name of the Lord is the name of the God of Israel. The God of Israel is not just the Supreme Being. He is that but, above all, he is the God of Israel, the God of this one particular people who has chosen this people for himself as his bride as it were. And he has a name. He's not just God in general, not just a supreme being, he has a name. His name is Lord, sort of. Actually, his name is a special name that cannot be pronounced. Even in the day way back in the 1st century A.D., Jews no longer pronounced this name. I won't pronounce it either. I have Jewish friends. I don't want to be pronouncing this name in ways that would be offensive. And it is offensive, by the way. Christians should be aware that trying to pronounce the name of the God of Israel is deeply offensive to orthodox Jews. Let me spell it out for you without the vowels and then you might recognize it. When you translate the name of the God of Israel, transliterated into English, you get Y-H-W-H. It doesn't look at all like Lord does it? And I'll explain why. Y-H-W-H. You leave out the vowels, and you don't pronounce it. That's the name of the God of Israel, which used to be pronounced in the time of the Old Testament, but not anymore, not even in the 1st century A.D., in the time of this story. They didn't pronounce it, except for the high priest going into the Holy of Holies on the Day of Atonement. And now there's no temple so no Jew gets to pronounce this name. No one should pronounce this name. I think not even Christians should. But they do, and that's a problem.

This name, what do you do with this name if you're Jewish and you're reading the scriptures? This is important, because if you know how synagogue worship goes among Jews, reading the Torah is the central act of worship in the synagogue. You come to this name, what do you do? You don't say the name, you say instead, *Adonai*, which is Hebrew for Lord. And that's how the word "Lord" gets to stand in for the name of the God of Israel. The Lord God of Israel, that's his name, but I didn't say his name. And that's typical. This is what Jews do with the name of the Lord. The name of the one God who created heaven and earth. He has a name. You don't say the name, instead you say Lord, so the Lord is, in a sense, his name, the name of the Lord.

Everyone who calls upon the name of the Lord shall be saved, says Joel, writing at a time when people could still call upon the name and actually say the name, the name of the Lord. Well, how do you call upon the name of the Lord when you can't even pronounce or utter the name? Here's how Christians do it. They say Lord Jesus. Peter in this sermon is quite explicitly, quite clearly saying, the way to call upon the name of the Lord, the God of Israel, is to call upon the name of the Lord Jesus. He's saying that when you call upon the name of Jesus, you're calling upon the name of the Lord. That, in some deep way, the name of the Lord, God of Israel, the creator of heaven and earth, the supreme being of all things, that name belongs to Jesus. When you call upon the name of Jesus, you are calling upon the name of the God who created heaven and earth. You are calling upon the name of the Lord. That's the astonishing claim of Christianity and the claim where you wonder, how do they think they can get away with this, giving the name of the Lord God of Israel, to this man. Well, he's sitting at God's right hand, but he's still a man. He's not God, is he? But again, Christians will say, yes, he is God. He has the name of the Lord because it belongs to him by right because he is God in the flesh. How Christians can get away with saying that is going to be part of our story.

Let me say a few more things about what's going on in this sermon. One is, notice that the sermon involves quotations from the Old Testament as the ancient witness to Jesus Christ. Another quotation actually comes from the psalms written by, well, some of the psalms were written by King David. The one that Peter quotes is written by King David, or at least ascribed to him. He talks about when he dies, "You will not let your holy ones see corruption," says David, praying to God. "You will not let your holy ones see corruption." You might think that David is talking about himself, that I'm not going to die and rot. But Peter says wait a minute. David is dead and rotten, his body's in the ground and it's rotting. That's what the corruption is, that is, the rotting of the body. Peter says no, that can't be David that David is talking about, he must be talking about the son of David, Jesus, our Lord, who did not see corruption. He died, but was not left for his body to rot because he was raised from the dead.

What's going on here, you see, is that Peter is reading the Old Testament as saying this is about Jesus. You might think it's about King David, but no, it's about Jesus, the son of David. This is fundamental to Christian intellectual life for the rest of the history of Christian theology. Christian theology will always be committed to reading the Old Testament as a witness to Jesus Christ so that what is said about David is most truly fulfilled in Christ, what is said about Moses is fulfilled in Christ, what is said in this ancient Hebrew document is really about Jesus. For Christians, virtually all things are about Jesus in some way or another because of that obsession with Christ that is at the center of Christian faith.

One more thing, the sermon concludes with an exhortation. Peter urges all of his listeners, including this crowd that has gathered around these Christians, to repent and be baptized. He's urging them to engage in an inner and an outer change. Repentance is a change of mind; baptism is an initiation rite. So you're supposed to change your mind, change your heart, give up the life of sin, give up your old life and embrace a new life in Christ. How do you do that? You go and get baptized, which is the initiation rite into the church. We're going to say a lot more about both repentance and baptism, but I just wanted to mark that as the end of the sermon. After telling this story about Jesus, after identifying Jesus's sitting at God's right hand, after giving us this profound picture of the exalted Christ, Peter concludes the sermon by saying here's what you do about it. If you believe this, then repent and be baptized. Join the Christian community by changing your life and mark that by getting washed in water in the name of Jesus. That's what baptism is, and we'll talk more about that ritual of washing in water marking the entrance into the Christian community.

That's the picture I want you to get and let me repeat it. There's God, the Father, he's up there on his throne in heaven. There's Jesus sitting at God's right hand. Jesus sends the Holy Spirit down upon the community of people who believe in him, the people called the Church, and we'll talk more about what the Church means. That's the picture. Believers on earth, Holy Spirit descending from heaven, through Jesus Christ, who's received the promise of the Holy Spirit and pours it out upon his community from on high, from heaven, pouring it out on the community on earth.

With that picture in mind, the picture of the exalted Christ, let's look ahead and behind, which is something that the New Testament does. It's not just, of course, that Jesus is exalted at God's right hand. There's a story that leads up to that, there's a story that goes on from that. Let me say now something about resurrection, which is the immediately preceding event leading to this picture. Jesus is exalted at God's right hand. How did he get there? Last we knew in the most famous part of the story of Jesus's life, which we all know, he was crucified. He was hanging on a cross, a Roman cross, being executed as a criminal. Then, he's buried. Then, in the story about Easter, there's an empty tomb. He's not there anymore. He's not here, he's risen, says the messenger to the people who come to the tomb. Women come to the tomb on Easter Sunday, or the Sunday that is celebrated as Easter in Christian worship. They come to the tomb of Jesus. There is someone there saying, could be an angel, probably is an angel, looks like a young man, maybe two young men, depending on which Gospel you're reading, but he says to them, what are you doing looking for the living among the dead? He's not here. He's risen. That word "risen" can also be translated, "resurrected." Resurrection simply means rising from the dead. It means something very simple, but of course, something very astonishing. The idea of resurrection is the idea that, look, he was dead, he died, and he is not dead anymore. That's it in a nutshell. He died, but he's not dead. He was truly dead for awhile, but not anymore. Now that's a rather unfamiliar notion it turns out. Very familiar actually to Jewish people of the time, especially the Pharisees who had this idea very carefully worked out, and Christians and Pharisees agreed about this notion of resurrection. But we may be more familiar, many of us, with a very different picture.

It's a picture of dying and your soul going to heaven. You die, your soul gets separated from your body, your body goes into the grave, your soul goes up to heaven. That's not the picture that Peter wants you to have about Jesus. It's not like Jesus's soul is up there in heaven. If that were true, then Jesus would still be dead. Because his body would be in the grave, his soul would be up in heaven. That's maybe what happens to good people when they die, but that's not Jesus. That's not what Peter's preaching. The man at God's right hand, according to this sermon, is a living man. He's there with his body as well as his soul. He's a living human being. He is not dead. Immortality of the soul is a different picture. Let me use that as the label for the alternative picture, immortality of the soul. It's a philosophical idea; it's tied to the notion that the soul is a different kind of being from the body. Unlike the body, it doesn't die, it doesn't rot. It can't go into a grave. It belongs in a different place from the body. Ultimately, it belongs in heaven. So when we die, this immortal part of us escapes and goes to heaven and the body goes into the ground. As I say, that's not the picture that you need to have in order to understand where Christianity begins, what this gospel about the story of Jesus is all about. The picture you need to have is of a man who died, but he isn't dead anymore. His soul and his body are not separated. He's a living human being with a body just like every other living human being, and he's at God's right hand in heaven, exalted on high. That's a strange picture. It's an unfamiliar picture even today, and that's the picture that Peter wants you to get in this sermon. The living man, Jesus Christ, this crucified Jew is now sitting at God's right hand as the King, as the Lord of all. The name of the Lord God belongs to this living man sitting at God's right hand on the throne of God in heaven.

So we need to think more about this notion of resurrection. We will revisit it several times in this course because the Christian hope and gospel is aimed at resurrection. You can combine it with the story of the immortality of the soul. It turns out most Christian theologians do, and we'll talk about why. You can combine the two pictures, immortality of the soul, resurrection of the dead, but you need to understand that the two pictures are different, and even though you can combine them, you need to understand which one comes first in Christian theology. The one that's central to Christian theology is not immortality of the soul, but resurrection of the dead, people who were dead once, and they're not dead anymore. Resurrection is not about part of us surviving after death. That's the immortality of the soul. Resurrection is about the undoing of death. Death is no longer the case. A resurrected person was dead once, but isn't dead anymore, and the Christian hope that Peter wants to preach in this sermon is aimed at that resurrection. Christian hope, the future that this picture is aiming at, is a future of resurrection. So, in other words, here's this community, and we need to have that picture again, God the Father, Jesus sitting at his right hand, the Holy Spirit descends on the community, and they are excited. They are happy. This is good news. Why? What are they hoping for? What are they longing for? What are they looking forward to? They're looking forward to the undoing of death, because Jesus is the first fruits. Jesus is where the resurrection begins, but the resurrection is going to spread. Death itself is going to be defeated. There will be, as Peter says in another sermon a little bit later in Acts, "A restoration of all things. All things will be set right." How? This Jesus, who's exalted at God's right hand, is coming again in glory. He's going to return to earth where he came from. He is going to have a *parousia*, a coming or arrival. *Parousia* is a Greek term used for when a king comes, like when the Roman emperor is marching eastward to fight the battle on the eastern frontier of the Roman Empire, and he comes to your town, that's his *parousia*; his presence or arrival in your town. Jesus's *parousia* is his coming back to earth where he came from, where he will dwell again. He will establish the Kingdom of God. He will be the king, the Messiah, the king of the whole universe now. And he will set all things to right, and he will defeat death. Death itself will be undone by the resurrection of all flesh.

Let's now go back again because I just said Jesus came from the earth, but that's not quite right. That's not quite right. We've got to go all the way back. Where does Jesus come from? If he is seated at God's right hand, if that's where his destination is, where did he come from? Early Christian theologians, already in the New Testament, suggested that there was something scholars called the "preexistence" of Christ. He existed before he was born, before he walked on earth. Before he was born, he was already at God's right hand. There's an ancient Christian hymn in the letter to the Philippians, the second chapter, an ancient Christian hymn used in worship, which starts at that part of the story, at the very beginning, in the preexistence of Christ. He was, says the hymn, "In the form of God." And the word *form* is a Greek word that can mean essence. He was of the very essence of God. But he didn't think that equality with God was something to hang onto or grab as the hymn says. But rather he humbled himself. He emptied himself. He took on, not the form of God, but the form of a servant, and that's a label for his humanity. The form of a servant, the form of someone who is mortal, whose body is going to go into the grave, someone who can die. He took on this form of a servant, became obedient to death, even death on a cross and, therefore, now we get to the part that we've already learned about. Therefore God has highly exalted him and given him a name that is above every name. That at the name of Jesus Christ every knee shall bow, every tongue confess that Jesus Christ is Lord. That's how the hymn concludes, that Jesus Christ is Lord. Once again, the name of the Lord belongs to Jesus. All flesh, every human being, resurrected with death defeated, is going to worship this man, bowing the knee and calling him Lord.

It's actually rather striking because the hymn concludes with language that is once again taken from the prophet, the prophet Isaiah this time. Let me read you what Isaiah says, which this hymn is echoing. The Lord, God of Israel, says, "I am the Lord; that is my name." Remember, Lord is not a title here, it's his name. It's the name that's not pronounced. "I am the Lord; that is my name," Isaiah says speaking for the Lord. "I am the Lord; that is my name; / my glory I give to no other." Nobody else gets the glory of the Lord. Christians are saying, wait a minute, the glory of the Lord belongs to Jesus, when you call Jesus, Lord, that's for the glory of God the Father. Quite striking, that's what they're saying. Here's another quotation from Isaiah echoed in this hymn. "To me every knee shall bow, every tongue shall swear allegiance," says the prophet Isaiah speaking for God again. "Every knee shall bow, every tongue shall swear allegiance" to the Lord, the Lord God of Israel, the Lord, Jesus Christ. Christians are saying yes, the same thing. When you acknowledge Jesus as Lord, bend the knee to him in worship and praise and adoration. It is to the glory of God, the Father, who is the Lord, God of Israel, because Jesus is Lord. That's the earliest Christian confession. Jesus is Lord. It's two words in Greek. You call it Lord Jesus. That confession, Jesus is Lord, he is the Lord, God of Israel. The name of the Lord belongs to him, when you honor him and worship him, then you're honoring and worshiping the Lord, the God of Israel, this man.

That's the startling, stunning confession of early Christian belief. That's the picture. He's right there at the throne of God, and when you worship him, you're worshipping the Lord God of Israel. How can Christians get away with saying that? That's going to be something that will take several centuries to work out and will result ultimately in the doctrine of the Trinity.

Lecture Three
Pauline Eschatology

Scope:

The Apostle Paul, author of the earliest texts in the New Testament, is representative of early Christians' eschatology, that is, their view of the end times. Eschatology is the fundamental framework of their theology because of the way it is tied to their expectation of the coming of Christ. Christians already live a new life by the power of his Spirit in between his resurrection and the final coming of his kingdom. This new life is possible even though the fullness of their eternal life in him has not yet been revealed but is hidden with him in heaven, whence they await the spiritual bodies that will clothe them in immortality. Paul's most distinctive doctrine is his insistence that Gentiles may join in this expectation and new life without being converted to Judaism and circumcised—by simply believing in Christ—being justified by faith in him.

Outline

I. The early Christians lived in a kind of expectation that is called "eschatological."
   A. "Eschatology" means doctrine of the end (Greek *eschaton*).
   B. New Testament eschatology is about life in the time between the already and the not yet, between what Christ has already done (cross and resurrection) and what he is yet to do (*parousia* and establishing his kingdom on earth).
   C. Eschatology is the fundamental framework of early Christian theology, as can be seen in the earliest New Testament writer, the Apostle Paul.

II. Paul is the first Christian theologian whose writings we have.
   A. He is a missionary and founder of churches in the northeastern part of the Mediterranean.
   B. He is author of most of the letters in the New Testament, which were written earlier than the Gospels.

- **C.** There is some disagreement among scholars about whether he wrote all of the letters ascribed to him by the New Testament, but all of them can be taken to illustrate Pauline theology, in the sense of the theology derived from Paul.
- **III.** Pauline eschatology is about life in Christ between his exaltation and his return.
  - **A.** The key expectation (that is, what is yet to be) is the resurrection of all the dead in Christ.
    1. When Christ returns, the dead are raised, for Christ's own resurrection makes him "the first fruits" of the resurrection (1 Cor. 15).
    2. The picture is not of us going to heaven after we die, but of Christ coming from heaven to earth, bringing life for the dead.
    3. Likewise, the picture is not of our souls leaving our bodies behind, but of our mortal bodies "putting on" immortality.
    4. Paul calls this a "spiritual body" and speaks of a heavenly dwelling which will clothe us.
    5. "Heaven" in Pauline eschatology does not mean the place to which we go but the place where Christ is, hidden from our sight but having the power of eternal life, with which we long to be clothed.
  - **B.** The life of believers (that is, what is already) is in Christ, which is to say in his Body, the Church, by the power of the Holy Spirit.
    1. As at Pentecost, the Holy Spirit is the source of prophecy, teaching, and all sacred speech, including "psalms and hymns and spiritual songs" (Eph. 5:19).
    2. It is also the source of holy or righteous living, "walking by the Spirit" and "the fruit of the Spirit" (Gal. 5:16, 22).
    3. Paul writes that the Spirit of God dwells in the plural you, be you all, meaning first of all the community of believers, which he calls the Church (Rom. 8:9).
    4. Paul describes the Church as the Body of Christ, one body made up of many members.
    5. As head of the Body, Christ is "the beginning, firstborn from the dead" (Col. 1:18) and "head of all things for the Church" (Eph. 1:22).

    6. Baptism marks the inauguration of this new life, as well as the death of the old self.

IV. For Paul, both Gentiles and Jews are justified by faith in Christ.
    A. The early Christian movement was Jewish. They did not immediately know what to do when Gentiles started believing in Jesus. Who was the Messiah after all? King of the Jews!
    B. The crucial question was do Gentiles need to be circumcised and become Jews to join the Body of Christ.
    C. Paul's answer, which came to be accepted by the whole church, was no: Gentiles were justified, set right with God, simply by believing in Jesus, without converting to Judaism.
    D. Paul thus conceived of the Body of Christ as a place of reconciliation between Jews and Gentiles.
    E. Paul's famous doctrine of justification by faith was thus about how both Jews and Gentiles were set right with God by believing in Jesus and thus becoming members of his Body by baptism, not circumcision.
    F. Paul contrasted faith with works, because he disagreed with Christians who thought Gentiles, too, must observe the Law of Moses, including circumcision, to join the Body of Christ.

Suggested Reading:

Colossians.

Corinthians 1 and 2.

Ephesians.

Galatians.

Philippians.

Romans.

Sanders, *Paul, the Law and the Jewish People*.

Wright, *Surprised by Hope*.

Questions to Consider:

1. Is this account of early Christian eschatology different from what you expected—and if so, how?
2. Is it possible to conceive of Christianity today as both Jewish and Gentile?

Lecture Three—Transcript
Pauline Eschatology

In our last lecture we left the Christian community in a state of expectation. Jesus Christ is raised from the dead and exalted at God's right hand, they believe, and he has to be received there in heaven until he comes again to restore all things, as Peter puts it in one of the sermons in the book of Acts. So the early Christian church clearly understood themselves to be in this time of expectation, awaiting his coming again, his *parousia*, like a king coming to visit his dominions, when all things will reach a kind of consummation, a restoration, a redemption, the final redemption in the resurrection of all flesh. The theological term for this expectation is "eschatology," E-S-C-H-A-T-ology. *Eschaton* is the Greek term, *eschaton*; it means the end, the last. So, eschatology is the theology that concerns the last things or the last days or the last judgment, or heaven and hell. All those things fall under eschatology. The New Testament has a distinctive eschatology. It's a rather different eschatology from what we might have expected, so we need to get into the guts of this distinctively New Testament eschatology. To do that we're going to turn to the earliest written documents in the New Testament, the earliest writings of the New Testament, which are the letters of the Apostle Paul, Saint Paul, to you Catholics or Eastern Orthodox, Saint Paul's letters. They're the earliest writings in the New Testament and therefore they're important as a witness to what early Christians thought. We'll look at Paul as a representative of this early Christian eschatology or expectation, and then at the end of the lecture we'll turn and look at some of what is distinctive about Paul's theology. But first we'll start with what's representative, how Paul's theology represents a great deal of what early Christians were thinking about eschatology, about the expectation of Christ coming.

First of all, let's say a little bit about Paul. Paul is a missionary, a founder of churches. He travels around the Mediterranean world, especially the northeast quadrant of the Mediterranean from Israel over to Rome, and he founds churches, he preaches the gospel, and he writes letters to churches that he had founded before. He wrote most of the letters in the New Testament. That is to say that we have quite a number of letters in the New Testament, a majority of them are written by Paul. He's the most prolific author of the Bible. In that sense he wrote more books of the Bible than anyone else, although they're smaller books, of course. He writes these letters. There's some dispute amongst scholars about which letters are actually Paul's. Most scholars think that the first letter to Timothy, the second letter to Timothy, and the letter to Titus, are not actually by Paul, but by a second generation disciple of Paul. Some scholars—there's a great deal of disagreement about this—think that the letter to the Ephesians and that the letter to the Colossians might not be by Paul, and then there's a number of letters that everyone agrees are by Paul: Romans, Galatians, 1 and 2 Corinthians. I'm going to be looking at the eschatology in the letter to the Ephesians and the letter to Colossians, as well as the undoubted letters of Paul, because, for my purposes, in this lecture, what I'm looking at is what's representative of early Christianity and not what's distinctive about Paul when it comes to eschatology.

Now, when you have eschatology, you have expectation and you have a kind of tension. You're expecting what is not yet to come. You are expecting what has not yet happened. Jesus has not yet come. That's the expectation, but something has already happened, Jesus has already raised from the dead. So eschatology is a theology that situates the Christian community in the tension between already and not yet. Already Christ is raised from the dead, "the first fruits" of them that sleep, but he has not yet come again.

To look at Paul's eschatology, we're going to start with probably one of the most famous passages he ever wrote, the first letter to the Corinthians, chapter 15. It's famous because most of you have heard it set to music. Handel set it to music in the *Messiah*, and you may hear his music as I give you some of this. For instance, "For now is Christ risen from the dead, the first fruit's of them that sleep." This is in 1 Corinthians 15. Again, that's the "already." Now, there's a whole sort of eschatological story that Paul is telling, and it goes all the way back to the beginning. Paul says, "For as in Adam, all die. Even so in Christ, shall all be made alive." This is very important for Paul's theology. It's very important for all the Christians of the time. There's this relationship between Adam and Christ, from Adam comes death, from Christ comes life. Already, Christ has reversed the reign of death that began with Adam's sin. That's part of the already. He's going to be received into heaven. Already he's sitting at God's right hand, and he will reign from heaven and then come to earth in the *parousia*, coming back to earth, and then, but not yet. Then at his *parousia*, which has not yet happened, comes a consummation. This is not the word *eschaton*. It's the word *telos*. There comes the end, but not *eschaton*, *telos*. This wonderful Greek word from which we get theology. It's a word for goal, consummation, perfection. Then comes the perfection of all things. What happens then, at his *parousia*, when he is king on earth again and visibly glorified king, not on a cross, then we have this consummation when he hands over the kingdom to God, the Father, after destroying every rule and authority and power, for he must reign. Here is now the Kingdom of God on earth, "He must reign until he has put all his enemies under his feet, and the last enemy to be destroyed is death." And that's the final redemption, so that's what is not yet, that's the expectation.

When he hands over the kingdom to God the Father, then we have the fullness of the Kingdom of God, which is the foundational eschatological expectation. The Kingdom of God is coming. Christ will reign, and he will subject all things under the feet of Christ. And then Christ himself will be subjected to God the Father, and God will be all in all. Notice what the expectation is; notice what the hope is. We mentioned this a little bit in the last lecture. We're going to have to dwell on it again in this lecture as we work through the eschatology in Paul's letters.

Paul is not saying you have to hope to get to heaven when you die. Heaven is where Christ is, but that's where he's coming from, in the consummation. The consummation is Christ coming from heaven, not us going to heaven. And that's a reversal of what you might expect, a reversal of what many people think that they're going to find in the Bible. For New Testament eschatology, the expectation is of something coming from heaven. There's a picture in the book of Revelation of the heavenly city descending from heaven like a bride adorned for her bridegroom. The heavenly Jerusalem descends from heaven. It's as if heaven comes to earth. That's the movement of Christian eschatology. The picture is not us going to heaven after we die, but Christ coming from heaven to earth, bringing life for the dead. Likewise, the picture is not of souls leaving bodies behind, but of our mortal bodies being clothed with immortality and everlasting life. This is really a very unfamiliar image, although it shouldn't be so unfamiliar because it's there in Handel again. This is still from 1 Corinthians 15. The way Handel's lyrics put it is like this, "For this corruptible must put on incorruption," and this isn't just Handel, it's also a quotation from Paul, "This corruptible must put on incorruption." Quick interpretation, this corruptible, means this corruptible body. Corruptible means it rots. It will decay. Corruption is for decay and rot. A tree that's rotting on the inside is corrupted. Your body, when it rots in the grave is corrupted. Your body is corruptible. It will put on incorruption. So instead of the image of something immortal escaping from the mortal body, we have the image of something immortal clothing the mortal body.

So, in the next line from Paul, "This mortal must put on immortality," he means that this mortal body is clothed in immortality. So when this corruptible shall have put on incorruption, and this mortal shall have put on immortality, then shall it be brought to pass the saying that is written in the scriptures, "Death is swallowed up in victory." So, reverse the usual picture. Instead of an immortal part of ourselves called the soul escaping the body, we've got this mortal self called the body that is clothed from the outside with immortality. Paul will call this clothing the "spiritual body"— quite a striking phrase—a body that is not a bodily body, but a spiritual body, an immortal body. Elsewhere he will suggest it is a heavenly body.

Now I'm going to switch to a different passage in Paul, the second letter to the Corinthians, chapter 5. We want to talk about this metaphor of being clothed by immortality, or a spiritual body, which is a heavenly body. Again, what we're getting at here is what heaven means in New Testament eschatology. So here we have 2 Corinthians, chapter 5, beginning at verse 1, "For we know," says Paul, "that if this tent that is our earthly house," and that's the mortal body, "this tent that is our earthly house." He uses the image of tents because tents are a temporary domicile. Our mortal body is temporary. So we know that if this tent that is our mortal body is dissolved, we have a building from God, a house not made with hands, that's the spiritual body, everlasting in the heavens. Now notice, if you were thinking of the soul going to heaven when you die, you might read this passage as about our heavenly home, we're going to our heavenly home, that's not what Paul was thinking. He's talking about a heavenly dwelling which is not a tent, not temporary. It's a house, not built with hands, it's heavenly, immortal, incorruptible, and we will put it on, and that's what the resurrection of the dead is, is this putting on of immortality.

So Paul goes on to say, "For in this tent we groan, longing to put on our heavenly dwelling," not meaning going up to heaven, our heavenly home, as the old hymns put it, but rather our heavenly dwelling descending like the heavenly city to clothe us, for "While we are still in this tent we groan, being burdened." Not that we want to be unclothed. He's saying, I don't want for my soul to escape my body, that's not what I'm looking forward to, but that we would be further clothed so that what is mortal may be swallowed up by life, again, that image of death being swallowed up by victory, the mortal being swallowed up by life. The immortal is not some little part of us called the soul, but this thing that comes to us from outside and indeed from above, from heaven. It's as if heaven, which has received Jesus, is where our own everlasting life is stored up, waiting for us, and it will come down to clothe us.

So heaven, in New Testament eschatology, means the future that we're expecting. It's not just up there, and I think many of the early Christians including Paul, who was a very sophisticated man, did not have a naïve picture of heaven as up there as if you took a rocket ship you would find God up there. Heaven is this hidden dimension where Christ dwells now, where we cannot see him, a hidden dimension from which will come our eschatological future, the immortal spiritual body, the heavenly home that will clothe us, because that's where Christ is, that's where everlasting life is. That's where all the good things that Christians are expecting will come from, this heavenly future, this Christ who is hidden from us now, but is coming in the future, that is not yet, but he's coming.

So, to shift now to the letter to the Colossians, here's a picture of what heaven means for the New Testament. Paul starts, in Colossians chapter 3, by saying "if you have been raised with Christ." Now he's saying you've already in some sense been raised from death with Christ through your baptism. We'll get to that in a minute. "If you've been raised with Christ, seek what is above where Christ is." Again, is he saying expect to go to heaven? No, that's not what he's saying. Let's read on. "Seek what is above where Christ is, seated at the right hand of God," there's that key picture that we had from the last lecture. Set your mind on what is above, not on what is at earth, that is set your mind on Christ. He goes on to say, "for you died." He's saying this to living people who've been baptized. They died in baptism, and we'll get to that in a minute. "For you died," says Paul, "and your life is hidden with Christ in God." So already, where you really live, Paul is saying, if this is Paul, it might be a follower of Paul, already where you really live is with Christ, exalted in heaven. That's where your true life is. That's where your spiritual body is. It's stored up for you, this heavenly building which is coming with the coming of Christ. That's what you need to be expecting. That's what you need to set your heart on, this eschatological expectation of what is not yet, what is presently hidden in heaven. Because, he concludes, "when Christ, who is our life, appears, then you also shall appear with him in glory, clothed in that heavenly home."

That's what heaven means in the New Testament. Heaven is where eternal life is already and we wait for it because it's not yet on earth. The life of believers in Christ is a life in expectation, but there's first fruits. Christ, the first fruits, is now in heaven, but something else has been given in his place. We need to talk now about a crucial eschatological concept, which is a concept of God, and that's the concept of the Holy Spirit. It is a crucial concept for a Christian's concept of God because the spirit, remember, is what Jesus pours out on Pentecost on his community. He's in heaven, invisible, hidden, but the spirit is poured out on what is called the body of Christ, the Christian community. The spirit is the spirit of prophesy. Because of the spirit, there is sacred speech, authorized speech, Christian teaching, behind all sound Christian teaching, according to Christian theology, is the Holy Spirit.

There's a nice passage in the letter to Ephesians where the author says, "Be ye filled with the spirit." "Be ye," that means you plural, be you all, filled with the spirit, he says to the Christian community. "Don't get drunk," but be filled with the spirit. And what you do is you speak to one another in psalms and hymns and spiritual songs. That's, I think, what Paul means by being filled with the spirit. Speak to one another in psalms and hymns and spiritual songs. When the church speaks of Christ and preaches the gospel and sings and calls upon his name, it does so by the Holy Spirit, which is the inspiring spirit of the prophets, the inspiring spirit of the Christian community. In a parallel passage in Colossians (the letter to the Colossians and the letter to the Ephesians have a lot of parallels), there's a parallel passage where the way he puts it is, "Let the word of Christ dwell in you all richly, in all wisdom, teaching and admonishing one another, singing psalms and hymns and spiritual songs," the same phrase that you get in Ephesians. The point is that being filled with the spirit is the same thing as letting the word of Christ dwell in you richly.

When the Christian community has the word of Christ dwelling in them richly, that is the Christian community being filled with the spirit, and that's one of the fundamental functions of the spirit. He spoke to the prophets (says the creed). He is the one who authorizes Christian speech and inspires Christian teaching.

Another function of the Holy Spirit is to guide the Christian life and to create holiness. He is the Holy Spirit. He sanctifies or makes holy. By the way, sanctify is just a Latin way of saying to make holy. So, the Holy Spirit makes holy. There's a number of Paul's phrases about this. He talks about "walking by the spirit." He talks about "fruits of the spirit." And when he tries to spell those out, what he gives you essentially is a list of Christian virtues. So, for instance, the fruits of the spirit he lists are "love, joy, peace, patience, kindness, goodness, faith, meekness, and self control." That's what grows in us. That's the outgrowth, the fruit of the spirit, dwelling in the hearts of Christians. He dwells in the Christian community. He dwells in Christian hearts, but primarily it turns out in the community. When Paul talks about being filled with the spirit, as I mentioned before, he uses the plural you, be you all, you might say. Be you all, or be you guys, filled with the spirit. We need a you plural for this. The fundamental locust, the fundamental place, to find the spirit is the Christian community. That's why it's the Christian community that receives the spirit poured out on them on the day of Pentecost. This Christian community is described in a famous and important metaphor, as the body of Christ. And Paul will correlate the body of Christ with the spirit. For instance, he says now in 1 Corinthians 12, "For just as the body is one thing and has many members, and all the members of the body though there are many of them are one body, well, that's how it is with Christ. For, in one spirit, we are all baptized into one body." In one spirit we are all baptized into one body. Again, baptism is the way you enter this body and we'll talk about that in a minute. One spirit, one body. It's as if the Christian community is a body whose living spirit is the Holy Spirit. That's why when it speaks it speaks by the spirit. That's why the virtues cultivated in this community are the fruits of the spirit, when one walks by the spirit with the spirit dwelling in you.

But there's another crucial connection. Christ is the head of this body, and when the ancient writers think about head and body they're thinking of the head really as the source of the body. He governs the body, but he also is the source of its life. So, here's Paul again, or perhaps a follower of Paul in the letter to the Colossians, "He is the head of the Body, the Church. He is the beginning." That's what head means. "He is the beginning, the firstborn from the dead," that is, the first one to be resurrected, "so that in all things he might have primacy." Paul goes on to speak in the letter to the Ephesians, or again, perhaps another follower of Paul, of the "power of God which God exercised in Christ by raising him from the dead, seating him at his right hand in the heavens far above all rule and authority and power and lordship." We've heard this theme so many times now already, "above every name that is named not only in this age, but in the age to come," the eschatological age, "he has put all things under his feet and gave him to be head over all things for the Church which is his Body, the fullness of him who fills all and all." So, by being the head of the body, Christ is the fullness of the whole universe. The whole universe is somehow summed up or heading into this body of which Christ is the head. He's the head in heaven. The body is on earth. But this body is the source of life for the world. Through this body, the spirit is aiming to bring redemption to all flesh.

You enter this body by baptism. We've mentioned this a couple of times. Baptism is an initiation rite. It's a dunking in water. And later Christians would splash water or sometimes sprinkle, but originally it was a dunking. In fact, to baptize, in Greek, means to dunk. There's a scene in one of the Last Supper narratives where one of the disciples dips bread in a dish and the word is to "baptize," because, literally, baptize means to dip or to dunk. You're baptized in water. You're dunked in the water, in the name of the Father, and the Son, and the Holy Spirit, the Son being Jesus. So Paul speaks of being baptized into Christ. You're always baptized into something, dunked into something. It's as if you're dunked in Jesus, drowned in him, and you die. It's a symbolic death. You drown and then you're brought up out of the water in newness of life. And that's why Paul associates this with dying and rising again. That's why in Colossians you hear, you died and your life is hidden with Christ. If you have been raised with Christ in baptism, after dying with Christ in baptism, then set your heart on Christ above in heaven. Baptism is this sort of symbolic entrance, like a doorway into the body of Christ, into a new life. The old self is drowned, the new self rises again.

Paul goes on to say (this is now the letter to the Romans, chapter 6):

> All of us who have been baptized in Christ Jesus, have been baptized into his death. We were buried therefore with him, by baptism, into death, in order that just as Christ was raised from the dead by the glory of the father, so we too might walk in newness of life.

Notice, Christ's resurrection becomes the pattern for our resurrection. The hope, the eschatological future, is based on Christ's resurrection, because our resurrection is going to be based on his.

"So, we know that our old self was crucified with him," Paul says, "so that we no longer should be enslaved to sin." Right, the old self, the sinful self, is dead. For one who has died has been set free from sin. Now, if we have died with Christ, that is, in baptism, we believe we shall also live with him in the resurrection. One of the reasons why some scholars think that Ephesians and Colossians were not by Paul is because they already have us living with Christ in heaven. That's not how Paul talks here where we talk about living with him in the resurrection in the future. So there's some disagreement about where the already and where the not yet goes. For Ephesians and Colossians, we are already with Christ in heaven. And in the undoubted letters of Paul, Paul doesn't speak about that in that way.

Very briefly, we need to say a little bit about what's distinctive about Paul's theology. I've been talking about what's representative about it, about Christian eschatology as mirrored in Paul, who's the earliest of the Christian writers. And these other letters may or may not be by Paul. In the undoubted letters of Paul, Paul engages in a bunch of disputes, in fact, one central dispute is where Paul is fighting with other Christians. In his eschatology, he seems to be agreeing with everybody else. He's not saying anything new, anything that they haven't heard before. In his writings about Jews and Gentiles, he's saying something distinctive. And it's important to see what his problem is. He's got an interesting problem. The early Christian movement was all Jewish. Jesus is a Jew. His mother is a Jew. His apostles are Jews. The early Christian community is a Jewish community, and they're arguing with other Jews about what true Judaism is. Then this striking thing happens. Gentiles start believing in Jesus. What is a Jewish community to do with Gentiles who want to believe in a Jewish Messiah? Well, the natural thing to do would be to convert them to Judaism, which means take the men and circumcise them. And actually they get baptized. They get washed, cleaned off, because Gentiles are dirty, until they become part of the holy community. And there's a circumcision, which is the sign of the covenant. By the way, when Christian baptism gets picked up, that means everybody's dirty. Everybody has to get washed off. All right, so the natural thing to do if you're an early Christian, and you're dealing with these Gentiles that come to believe in Jesus, is to wash them off, circumcise them, make them Jews, and then they can believe in the Jewish Messiah. Paul takes a different view. Paul takes the view that in order to become part of the body of Christ, to be justified in God's sight and set right, all you need is faith, faith in Christ. That's enough. This is Paul's famous doctrine of justification by faith, and we could even add the little word that Martin Luther adds 15 centuries later, "justified by faith alone." Because the issue here is not simply how do you stand before God as a righteous person. That turns out to be Luther's question. It's not really Paul's question. Paul's question is do you have to be Jewish in order to be a Christian? Once again, when we read the New Testament, we're going to have to readjust our glasses or our goggles and say, wait a minute, this is the exact opposite question from the one we're used to asking.

Nowadays, if someone who's Jewish wants to become Christian, the question is, well, they're converting to a new religion. Right? You can't be a Jew and be a Christian at the same time. You can't be a Jewish Christian; there's no such thing. Many people, both Jews and Christians, would just assume that you can't be a Jew and a Christian at the same time, but, of course, all the early Christians were Jews and Christians: all of Jesus's disciples and the earliest Christian church. So, the question was whether a non-Jew could be a Christian. Now, doesn't someone have to convert to Judaism to become a Christian and be a believer in Christ? Paul says no. Paul says these Gentiles don't have to become Jews to be part of the Christian community. They don't have to be circumcised. That's the crucial issue. What they have to do is be baptized and believe in Jesus Christ. Believe. Faith is what matters.

This gets back to the point I made way back in the first lecture that Christianity is fundamentally a faith because what matters is not what law you observe. Jewish Christians will observe the Jewish law, and Jewish Christians did for several centuries observe Jewish law. Gentile Christians won't be bound by Jewish law. They won't be circumcised. But they are believers, and by faith they are justified, says Paul. To be justified, this is a Latin term meaning, to be set right. The word "justification," of course, is related to the word justice. It's related also to the word righteousness. We'll talk about this when we get to Luther and so on. Crucial thing to mark, I suppose, as we get to the end of this lecture is that Paul is responding in his doctrine of justification by faith to a problem that's distinctive of the early church. It's not the problem that later Protestants have when they talk about justification by faith alone.

In one sense, when later Protestants read Paul and get a doctrine of justification by faith alone, which we will talk about in a later lecture, their doctrine is not simply Paul's doctrine. These later Protestants thought their doctrine simply was Paul's doctrine, and that's historically a mistake. On the other hand, I'll suggest that if you're someone like Martin Luther or John Calvin, or indeed like Augustine, the great Catholic theologian of the 4th century, and you bring questions about how we become righteous in God's sight, questions that were 16th-century questions or 5th-century questions rather than 1st-century questions, and you bring them to Paul's texts, then the right answer to these questions that people like Luther and Calvin and Augustine were asking is indeed that we are justified by faith alone. You can get a Pauline answer to a 16th-century Protestant question. That may bother the historians, but that's just how Christians read the Bible. It's always how Christians have read the Bible. They don't ask what did this mean back 2,000 years ago. They ask what is God saying through this text today? This is how Christians read the Bible. We'll talk about that feature of Christian reading a bit later, but the conclusion is there's a new perspective on reading Paul that has to do with focusing on the fact that Paul has this distinctive 1st-century question in mind, not the question that Luther had. And yet, I think it's true that if you're asking Luther's questions or Augustine's questions or, for that matter, Thomas Aquinas's questions in the Middle Ages, then the answer, justification by faith, is the right answer to get from Paul's texts. And that's essentially how Christians read the Bible. They come to this ancient text and ask it questions that get answered for today by this ancient text.

Lecture Four
The Synoptic Gospels

Scope:

The Gospels are the four books of the New Testament, which narrate the life, death, and resurrection of Jesus. Three of them, called the Synoptic Gospels, tell his story in roughly the same order. They have a high point in the middle where Jesus asks his leading disciple, Peter, "Who do you say I am?" Peter answers that he is the Christ, the Messiah, but does not understand why Jesus must be a suffering Messiah. Jesus's identity as Messiah leads to his death when he comes to Jerusalem, where his judges want him to say who he is (either to renounce being Messiah or not), and he makes them responsible for saying who he is, and this gets him crucified. The Gospels implicitly put us in the place of Peter and of Jesus's judges, trying to make us say who he is.

Outline

I. The Four Gospels of the New Testament are our main sources for the life of Jesus.
   A. "Gospel" translates a Greek word meaning good news.
   B. Hence it can mean simply the content of Christian proclamation, as it does in Paul.
   C. The four written Gospels are more than proclamations, but they are also more than historical or biographical documents; they have a literary agenda that attempts to make you answer the question, "Who is Jesus?"
   D. Three of the Gospels tell the story of Jesus's life in roughly the same order (so that it's relatively easy to make a synopsis of them all together) and are therefore called the Synoptic Gospels.
   E. The Synoptic Gospels are the first three books of the New Testament: Matthew, Mark, and Luke.
   F. The order in which they were written is different: Probably Mark was written first, and then Matthew and Mark used it as a source.

II. All the Synoptic Gospels reach a high point in the middle of the narrative when the leading disciple is confronted with Jesus's question, "Who do you say I am?"
   A. Peters answers, "You are the Messiah," that is, the Christ.
   B. Peter is not so happy when Jesus goes on to say he must suffer and die and rise again.
      1. Peter is evidently thinking: The Messiah is the long-awaited King of Israel, who is to restore the Kingdom of God in Israel—not to get killed.
      2. There is something very important about Jesus that Peter doesn't understand: This is a Messiah who must suffer.
      3. Peter takes Jesus aside and tries to rebuke him.
      4. But Jesus rebukes Peter, saying "Get behind me, Satan!"
      5. Jesus follows up with the famous saying about taking up the cross and following him.
      6. But he also mentions that the Son of Man will come in the glory of his Father, using a favorite New Testament image taken from the book of Daniel, 7:13.
   C. Then Jesus is revealed in glory in an episode called the Transfiguration.
      1. He takes Peter, James, and John up on a mountain and appears to them in radiant glory.
      2. Moses and Elijah, representing the Law and the prophets, appear with him.
      3. A voice from heaven says, "This is my beloved Son. Listen to him!"
      4. This repeats what a voice from heaven had said at Jesus's baptism, confirming his identity to the disciples: He is not just Christ, the Messiah, but the Son of God.
III. Jesus's identity is the central issue in the narrative of his suffering and death, or the Passion narrative.
   A. When he comes to Jerusalem just before his death he is greeted as the son of David, that is, the Messiah.
      1. He rides into Jerusalem on a donkey, just like a king of Judea after winning a battle.
      2. He is hailed as the son of David, that is, the legitimate successor of David, King of Judea.

3. He generates the kind of Messianic buzz that makes Roman governors very nervous, especially on festival days when a great many Jews are gathered in Jerusalem—a perfect setting for a riot or the beginning of a rebellion.

B. Jesus's identity as Son of God is the reason for his death.
1. "Son of God" is another Messianic title, since the King of Judea was regarded in the Old Testament as the adopted Son of God, ruling on God's behalf.
2. He is tried before both Jews and Gentiles—the Jewish priests and the Roman governor, Pilate.
3. In both trials, it appears that he could have escaped condemnation if he had clearly renounced any claim to be the Messiah.

C. The scenes in which Jesus confronts his judges constitute the high point of the Passion narrative, because once again the issue is who you say Jesus is.
1. His enigmatic answer to the priests demanding that he say whether he is the Son of God is: "You're saying it!"
2. He is turning the tables on them: They want to know who he says he is, whereas he is pointing out who they say he is.
3. It turns out the judges are being judged by whether they understand what they're saying and by who they say Jesus is—like Peter!
4. Pilate, the Roman governor, asks him if he is the King of the Jews, which is another way of saying Messiah. Again Jesus turns the tables by replying: "You're saying it!"

D. After turning the tables on his judges in this way, Jesus refers to himself as the "Son of Man," who will come on the clouds of heaven.
1. Once again, he is alluding to Daniel's vision of "one like a Son of Man" coming on the clouds of heaven to be presented before the throne of God.
2. The title "Son of Man" is thus a reference to his exaltation at God's right hand.
3. It also points to his return in glory, coming on the clouds of heaven.

E. Because of their narrative strategy, the Gospels are not helpful in finding a historical Jesus apart from the Christ of faith.

F. Ironically, Pilate had the charge against Jesus tacked up on his cross: "King of the Jews." Without understanding at all, Pilate got it right.

Suggested Reading:

Gospel of Luke.

Gospel of Mark.

Gospel of Matthew.

Brown, *An Introduction to New Testament Christology*.

Questions to Consider:

1. What is it about the Gospel that is supposed to be good news?
2. Who is Jesus, really?

Lecture Four—Transcript
The Synoptic Gospels

So far we've been talking about Christ in heaven, that eschatological picture of the early church. But, of course, the early church knew that Jesus walked on earth, and they did want to tell that story. Originally, this was told orally, of course. This was a Christian community and, for probably several decades afterward, most of these stories circulated orally. Some of them were written down. Eventually, probably in the 70s and 80s A.D., as the people who knew Jesus originally start to die out, we get these things written down in connected narratives. And these get into the New Testament. They are called the Four Gospels. There are four books of the New Testament called Gospels which tell the story of the life of Jesus, also his death, and then very briefly, his resurrection. It's important to know, these were written down quite a long time after the letters of Paul. So Paul's letters are written in the 50s and 60s. The Gospels are written maybe in the earliest in the 60s, probably the 70s, the 80s, the Gospel of John, maybe as late as the 90s. So, although the Gospels tell the story of the life of Jesus which takes place before the life of the early church, they're written later than the letters of Paul, which are about the life of the early church, and that's something to be aware of. The Gospels do not represent the earliest strand of Christian thinking about Jesus. At least the Gospels in the form that we have them as connected narratives were written down quite a bit later than the letters of Paul, which is why we started with Paul, and now we're going to the Gospel. And again notice, we're not starting with the historical Jesus sort of thing. We're starting with what Christians believed and this possible contrast between what Christians believe and the historical Jesus will come up in a minute.

Let's look at these Gospels. Gospels they're called. "Gospel" means good news. It's actually a word for proclamation and, in fact, the word "Gospel," when Paul uses it, means the content of Christian proclamation. And the content of Christian proclamation or preaching, this *kerygma* that I mentioned in an earlier lecture, this content is called Gospel. You could also call it the story of who Jesus is. What the Four Gospels in the New Testament are about is the story about who Jesus is; his life, his death, his resurrection, and then eventually his ascension. The content of the Gospel actually goes beyond the content of the Four Gospels, because the Four Gospels end at the resurrection. But the Four Gospels are playing a very important role, telling us, what did Jesus do when he was walking around Galilee and Judea with his disciples. What was the earthly Jesus like?

You might think that with a name like Gospel, a proclamation, good news, that the Gospels would tell you what to believe about Jesus. But it turns out the Gospels are more subtle than that. The Four Gospels of the New Testament are extraordinary, subtle literary narratives. They don't just tell you who Jesus is. They've got a different agenda, a more subtle literary agenda. They're trying to get you to ask the question, who is Jesus? They want to sort of get under your skin and get you asking that question, who is this man? And, they want you to realize that you're already giving an answer. Who do you say Jesus is? It's as if the Gospels are asking you that question. That's their theology, really. The theology of the Gospels is built into this narrative or literary strategy, which is designed to get you to realize you're answering the question, who do you say Jesus is? It's a subtle and indirect strategy, and that's why they're not actually proclamations, the way the Gospel is in Paul.

So let's look at them in a bit more detail. We're going to look at three of the Gospels together in this lecture, and then the fourth Gospel, the Gospel of John, in the next lecture. This is a standard procedure among scholars because three of these Gospels, the Gospels of Matthew, Mark, and Luke, tell the story in roughly the same way. They're called Synoptic Gospels because it's rather easy to make a synopsis in which you fit these three Gospels together. You summarize them in a synopsis that pretty much goes pretty well for all three of these Gospels. The Gospel of John, the fourth Gospel, really tells the whole story in a very different order and a very different way, so that's why we'll deal with it differently and in another lecture.

The Synoptic Gospels as I mentioned are Matthew, Mark, and Luke. They were probably written in a different order than that. They appear in the New Testament in this order, Matthew, Mark, and Luke. They're the first three books of the New Testament. They were probably written in a different order. Mark was probably written first, and then Matthew and Luke seem to be indebted to Mark. They seem to have read Mark and used a lot of material from Mark. Mark is the shortest and probably the earliest of the Gospels. It might be as early as the 60s A.D. There's a big issue about whether it was written before or after the fall of Jerusalem and the destruction of the temple, which is a huge date in Jewish and Christian history. But that's historical New Testament scholarship, which is not our issue. Let's get into the theology.

The theology of the Gospels is our focus. Because the theology of the Gospels is our focus, I won't say a whole lot about the overarching structure of the story. I'm going to assume that that much of the Gospel is familiar to you, and focus on key episodes that illuminate what the Gospels are aiming at and what their theology is. But I'm assuming you know that Jesus heals people. He casts out demons. He gives sight to the blind. He preaches. He preaches a Sermon on the Mount. He gathers a following. He goes to Jerusalem. He gets crucified.

All right, those should be familiar to us. Most of us have heard of these things if we haven't read them. I want to talk about the structure of the Gospels as literary documents because the structure has a whole lot to do with the theology. I want to land us right in the middle of these three Synoptic Gospels, all of which have a high point in the middle of the Gospel. It's a three-stage narrative in this high point. The labels for it are Peter's confession, and then we could say Jesus's rebuke, and then the Transfiguration. Peter's confession, Jesus's rebuke, the Transfiguration, together these are the high points at the center of the Gospel. And then there's another high point at the end.

The high point at the center of the Gospel begins with Peter's confession. "Confession" is an old word which can mean confession of faith, as well as confession of sin. So when you hear confession, it's not necessarily that he's confessing his sin and, in fact, Peter is not confessing his sin. He's confessing his faith. He's confessing what he believes. Because, what happens is, Jesus takes the disciples aside, and he asks them who do people say I am? There's the question of the Gospel, who is Jesus? Who do people say I am? And they suggest, well, some people are saying you're Elijah. Some people are saying you're one of the other prophets come back from the dead, maybe Jeremiah. Some people say you're John the Baptist come back from the dead because John the Baptist had been preaching and had been executed earlier. And then Jesus asked, but who do you say I am? So here begins the high point of all the

Synoptic Gospels. Who do you say I am? That's really what the Gospels are about. And to understand the literary strategy of the Gospel, imagine the Gospel sort of turning its face toward you and saying, dear reader, that's the question, who do you say Jesus is? So we're supposed to sort of put ourselves in Peter's place.

Peter gets the answer right at the beginning. He confesses faith in Jesus as Messiah. He says, you are the Christ, the Son of God, the son of the living God. The exact wording differs from synoptic to synoptic, but in each one of the Gospels, he confesses that Jesus is the Christ, the Messiah. The fundamental reaction to this, fascinatingly, is that Jesus tells Peter to be quiet, not to tell anybody. Once again, Christ's Messiah-ship, Jesus being the Christ, Jesus being the Messiah, is not being proclaimed here. Keep it a secret, says Jesus. The question is how well Peter understands this secret that he has just confessed. You are the Christ. What does that really mean? Well, Jesus tells Peter to be quiet about it, and then he goes on and makes a prediction. He predicts that he will suffer and die and rise again. The Son of Man he says—he refers to himself as the Son of Man a lot—and we'll talk about that in a minute. The Son of Man has to suffer many things at the hands of the scribes and the Pharisees and the chief priest, and he is going to get killed. He is going to rise again on the third day. That's the prediction.

Peter doesn't like it. He really doesn't like that. I think he wasn't quite listening when he got to the resurrection part. He really was hearing this part about suffering and dying, and that didn't fit his picture of who the Messiah was. After all, the Messiah is the king, the successor to David. He's going to restore the kingdom to Israel. Implicitly, the idea is he's going to kick those Romans out of there. The Jews are no longer going to be under Roman subjection. We're going to have a king who's a Jewish king, and we're going to be free from oppression. That's the kind of Messiah we want, someone who will free us from oppression. This is not a trivial thing by the way. There's Christian polemics against Jews about this, which is just wrong. You want to be free. You want your children not to be oppressed and enslaved. It's a good thing to wish for a good thing to come. So Peter's desire to have a Messiah who really will be king and free Israel from their enemies is a good biblical desire. It's throughout the whole Hebrew scriptures. It's a good thing to wish for, but he doesn't understand what's actually happening. It's a good desire, but it doesn't determine how Jesus is going to do things.

What Peter can't really wrap his mind around is that this is a Messiah who's going to suffer. He's not ready for that, and he tries to tell Jesus, don't do this. He rebukes Jesus says the Gospels. He basically tries to persuade Jesus not to be that kind of Messiah, a Messiah who suffers. That's not the kind of Messiah that anybody wants. In a sense, it's not even what Jesus wanted. At one point in the Gospels, he asks for God to change his mind about this. If it be your will, take this cup away from me, he says, he prays. But no, it's God's will that Jesus go on. Nobody wants a suffering Messiah. Even the suffering Messiah would prefer not to be a suffering Messiah. It's very tempting to be the Messiah who kicks out the Romans and rules. Jesus is aware of this temptation, and so when he replies to Peter, what he says is shocking. "Get behind me, Satan," he says to his leading disciple, his friend Peter. "Get behind me, Satan." He identifies Peter as someone who speaks for the tempter.

Now, "to tempt" is an old Greek word. It comes from the Greek word meaning "to test." Earlier in the Gospels, you may know, Satan came, the devil came, and tempted Jesus, that is, tested him, and tested to see whether he really was willing to be a Messiah who suffered. Because the temptation, the test was, wow, you can have rule over all the kingdoms of the world. Why go through this suffering Messiah stuff is the essence of the temptation of the devil that Jesus had already rejected way back at the beginning of the Synoptic Gospels. So once again this temptation comes to Jesus, now through the mouth of his own leading disciple, and Jesus recognizes it as the temptation of the devil, the devil who wants him not to be a suffering Messiah. And he says, "Get behind me, Satan." You're thinking about the things of men, not the things of God, and he says that to Peter. It must have been a shock. Peter gets it right, and then he really, really gets it wrong. Jesus goes on, it gets worse, he sort of piles it on. He goes on to this famous saying which you've probably heard, "If anyone wants to follow me, he must deny himself," says Jesus. "He must take up his cross and follow me, for whoever would save his life will lose it, whoever will lose his life for my sake will find it." Quick note, the word for life can also be translated soul. It's the Greek word *psuche*, from which we get psychology. So whoever would save his *psuche*, his soul or life, will lose it; whoever will lose his *psuche*, his soul or life, will also save it, if he's following me. It's important to realize that the word soul is not quite working the way we might expect from our current use of the word. Soul means life.

You want to save your life, then you have to lose it by following Jesus and taking up the cross. It's not what Peter had in mind.

But, it's not all bad news. Jesus did mention the resurrection. Now he goes on in this follow up to Peter's bad confession, he goes on to mention the eschatological future, the *eschaton*. He says, "You're going to behold the Son of Man coming in the glory of his father." So he leaps ahead to when the Son of Man, when Jesus, comes in glory from heaven. He is alluding to, referring to, a passage in Daniel, chapter 7, where there's the Ancient of Days sitting on the throne. And that's a word for God, so Ancient of Days, God the Father, sitting on the throne of heaven, and one like a Son of Man says the text, Daniel 7. "One who looks like a Son of Man comes and is presented to the Ancient of Days." He comes on a cloud, says the text. It's visually pictured that way, and that coming on a cloud becomes a theme when Jesus describes himself as the Son of Man coming again. We'll see that again in a minute. So Jesus concludes his rebuke of Peter by referring to his glory. It will be glory in the end. First, there's suffering and death, then there's resurrection. In the end there's glory. And just to show that, the concluding episode of this three episode high point in the Gospels is the Transfiguration. It's a glimpse of heavenly glory.

So we've had Peter's confession, then Peter gets it wrong and we get Jesus's rebuke. Now we're going to get a glimpse of heavenly glory, the eschatological glory that we're looking for, that we're waiting for as Christians, expecting Jesus to come again. We get to see a glimpse of it, or at least Peter and James and John do, because Jesus takes them up on a mountain so they can see his glory. He takes them up on a mountain because that's what Moses did. He went on a mountain in Mount Sinai. He saw the glory of God up there. So Jesus is deliberately mimicking Moses in this point. When he gets up in the mountain he is transfigured, and what that means is he shines with a blinding radiance, a radiance of light that represents the glory of God, this eschatological glory. This is what it must look like when Jesus is sitting at God's right hand. This is what it must look like when he comes in the glory of the father on the clouds of heaven as the Son of Man like Daniel 7 says.

And in this shining glory he's accompanied by Moses and Elijah. Elijah you may recall never died, he got taken up into heaven. There's some legends about Moses. Well, there's fascinating legends about Moses we can't get into. The point is, Moses and Elijah are present bodily as living men, anticipating the resurrection, and also representing the Law and the prophets. Moses represents the Law, Elijah represents the prophets. It's the Old Testament witnessing to Jesus yet again. And then a voice from heaven comes and says this is my beloved son. Listen to him. The word "listen" can also be translated "obey." This is my beloved son. Listen to him. Obey him.

We've heard this voice before, it turns out, earlier in the Gospels if we've read through the Gospels, when Jesus is baptized by John the Baptist. He comes up out of the water of the River Jordan, and a voice from heaven says, this is my beloved son in whom I am well pleased. Listen to him. So it's repeated now, except he's not coming out of a river, he's up on a mountain like Moses, and he's up there with the glory of God. We're catching a glimpse of what is to come, just to reassure Peter and James and John that it is heading toward glory, but first it's got to go through a cross.

So let's get to the cross. Let's get to the last part of the Gospels, called the Passion narrative, or it's also called the Passion of Jesus Christ, the Passion. Funny word, it's an old word from Latin *passiō*, it means "suffering." Interesting that the word "passion" originally meant suffering. So the Passion of Christ is his suffering. We'll have to come back to that interesting connection between passion and suffering in a later lecture. But for now, just think of it as the label, the Passion narrative, the suffering narrative.

Jesus goes down to Judea, which is where Jerusalem is. As you know, Jesus comes from Galilee from the north. He spends a lot of time in the north, but then he comes down to Judea. He comes down to Jerusalem at the time of the Passover festival. And he rides into Jerusalem on a donkey, celebrated in Christian churches on Palm Sunday. He rides in on a donkey, and he is greeted as the son of David. That's a Messianic title. He's a descendent of David. He's the true king. He's the Messiah. In the Gospel of Matthew, they say "Hosanna to the son of David!" *Hosanna* being a form of a Hebrew phrase, meaning save us. So they're saying, you're the king. You're the son of David. Save us. The Romans are there. They've occupied Jerusalem. Come on. You're walking as a king. You're riding in as king. Save us. You might not think that someone riding in on a donkey looks like a king, but in fact, that's a very royal thing to do in the Jewish setting. It goes back to a passage in the book of

Zachariah, which is being alluded to by the Gospel writers. When King David, or David's descendent, the son of David, wins a battle and frees his people from their enemies and comes back to Jerusalem, he rides back on a donkey, because horses, in those days, didn't have stirrups. So horses were not really good to ride on. If you were riding for normal peaceful purposes you rode on a donkey. Horses were for pulling chariots. So if you're in the middle of a battle and you're a king, you're going to ride in your chariot pulled by a warhorse. But when you've won the battle, when you've defeated the enemy, when you've freed your people from oppression, you ride back to Jerusalem on a donkey, an animal that signals peace, and, therefore, triumph. You've defeated the enemies of your people. You've defeated the enemies of God's people. And you're the king, under God, riding in triumph to Jerusalem. That's what's symbolized by Jesus riding into Jerusalem on a donkey being greeted by people saying "Hosanna to the son of David, save us now!"

Well, that's going to get him into trouble. What ends up happening is as Jesus enters into Jerusalem, there seems to be something like a Messianic buzz going around. People are saying, look, it's the Messiah, or maybe he's the Messiah, or maybe he thinks he's the Messiah, or he's claiming to be the Messiah. You can imagine all sorts of rumors circulating. This is going to make the Roman governor, Pilate is his name, very, very nervous. It makes all the Romans nervous. They're always nervous at this time because it's festival time. This is Passover and, remember, in these Jewish festivals, Jews from all around the world gathered. There are hundreds of thousands of Jews gathering in Jerusalem, and there aren't that many Romans to keep order, to keep them under their thumb. If you want to start a rebellion against Rome and free the Jewish people from Roman dominion, the time to do it is at a festival like Passover. All these people are gathered here. And now, here comes someone riding in like he's King David.

Well, Pilate is not happy. Also, the chief priests, the Jewish priests in Jerusalem are not happy because they're collaborating with Pilate. Typical conquest and typical occupation tactic, the Romans were smart about this. You've got to have collaborators in order to rule these people. So the chief priests who get their living by running the temple, they basically owe their job to Pilate, so they also don't like having Jesus come in acting like a Messiah. It turns out Jesus gets crucified because of this Messianic buzz. It's his identity as the Son of God which gets him in trouble. And let me say a little bit about that title, the Son of God. It's a Messianic title because King David and David's descendants, the sons of David, are regarded as adopted sons of God, ruling in God's place. So Son of God is a Messianic title. And when Jesus is arrested and brought before the judges, both Jewish judges, the high priests, and then the Roman judge Pilate, he's judged by both Jews and Gentiles. When he's brought before his judges, they basically ask him, are you the Messiah? Are you the Son of God? And Jesus gives this strange answer. Except for the Gospel of Mark, which has him just simply answer the high priest, "I am." But most of the time, in most of the synoptics, when Jesus answers either Pilate or the priests in these two trials he has before Jews and Gentiles, his answer is, "You said it." Or maybe the translation should be, "You are saying it." So imagine this. He's on trial before either the Jewish high priest or the Roman governor. The Jewish high priest's question is, are you the Son of God? "I abjure you by the living God," says one of those Synoptic Gospels, that you tell me whether you're the Son of God, the son of the blessed one. And Jesus says, you are saying it.

It's very, very strange. He seems to be evasive. But I don't think this character, whoever he is in this Gospel, Jesus, he's not an evasive character. So I think that what's going on here is something very important and part of this subtle narrative strategy that I mentioned at the beginning of the lecture. Remember, the point is not to proclaim who Jesus is. The Gospels are not telling you who Jesus is. The Gospels are trying to get you to say who Jesus is, just like Jesus asking Peter, who do you say I am? So Jesus's response to his judges is, you're saying it. Now, the judges want to say, are you saying you're the Messiah? Right, there's this Messianic buzz. Are you saying you're the Messiah, because if you're saying you're the Messiah, we're going to crucify you. If you're renouncing being Messiah, if you're not the Messiah, and you're willing to admit that, then we can let you go. The Messianic buzz will disappear and dissipate. So as long as you admit that you're not Messiah. If you're willing to renounce any claim to be Messiah, we can let you go. But if you're going to claim to be Messiah, you're going to get strung up on a cross, nailed on a cross.

Jesus does not renounce the title Son of God or Messiah, but his point is, you judges, you have to make up your mind. You want me to say I'm Messiah, says Jesus, in effect? No. You're saying it. What do you say? So that's the fundamental aim of the Gospel as a literary narrative. The Gospel wants to say, what do you say Jesus is? The judges of Jesus, both Jew and Gentile, are being judged by the judgment they make about Jesus. Judgment is being reversed. The judges are being judged by the judgment they make upon Jesus. And Jesus says, you're saying it, as if to say, take responsibility for who you say I am. I'm not going to make it easy for you by telling you who I am. You have to decide. You make the judgment, who am I? Who do you say I am? That, I think, is what the Gospels are all about. And that's why, interestingly enough, in the Passion narrative, so much more time is actually devoted to the trials of Jesus than to the crucifixion. The crucifixion is almost an anticlimax because everybody knows it's coming. The early Christian readers would all know about the crucifixion. The crucial thing is this trial scene, or the two trial scenes, because that's when the tables get turned. That's when the judge is judged by how he judges Jesus. And again, imagine the Gospel turning its face to you, the reader, and saying, you be the judge. You're the reader. Judge this text. You're a scholar maybe, a New Testament scholar. Make your judgment. Who do you think he is? Who do you say? You're saying it. Don't ask who Jesus is. Who do you say he is? I think the text says this to every scholar and every ordinary person who reads the text. Who are you saying he is? That's the point of that strange, apparently evasive answer. You are saying it.

That I think is the second and maybe the deepest high point of the narrative. We get something similar with Pilate. Pilate's question is not are you the Son of God, but are you the King of the Jews. But the King of the Jews is just a Roman way of saying Messiah and, again, Jesus answers, you're saying it. Pilate, you own up to what you're saying. Who do you say I am? And just to make sure that he's not being evasive, the Gospel writers do have Jesus saying to the high priest, "You will see the Son of Man seated at the right hand of power and coming with the clouds of heaven." That's Daniel 7 again, that picture of the Son of Man coming on the clouds of heaven. He does, in fact, identify himself as the Son of God coming from heaven and glory. Although the phrase, the Son of Man, interestingly enough, the title Son of Man, is really a more heavenly designation than Son of God, because Son of God is something that you can call any of David's descendants because they rule as adopted sons of God. The Son of Man title identifies Jesus as coming from heaven.

Jesus isn't really being evasive here. He does identify himself as the one who comes in glory from heaven, or who will come in glory from heaven. First, he has to get crucified. He knows that he can escape crucifixion by renouncing his Messiah-ship. That's that same temptation. Maybe he doesn't have to be a suffering Messiah. But no, he's going to be a suffering Messiah. And so he offers himself up like a lamb to the slaughter. Here, I think, is the literary strategy of the Gospel. It's almost like a trap. It's aiming at trapping you into being in the position of the judge. Who do you say Jesus is? Because of that literary strategy, which puts you, the reader, in this uncomfortable position of saying who Jesus is and being judged by what you say, do you want to be like Pilate? Do you want to be like the chief priests? Do you want to be like Peter? Even Peter doesn't really get it, but better to be like Peter is the implication. Because of this literary strategy, the Gospels are not going to give you much help if you want to look for a picture of the historical Jesus that is different from the Christ of faith. This is what a great many biblical scholars want and, as a theologian, I look at the biblical scholars and say well, good luck to you. But you're going to have a hard time finding the historical Jesus in the Gospels, unless you think that the historical Jesus is the same thing as the Christ of faith, which of course, is what the Gospel writers thought. There's the Christ of faith. There's the historical Jesus. They're really just one guy.

The earthly Jesus who walked on earth and healed the lame and gave sight to the blind and got crucified, rose from the dead, is sitting at God's right hand, are all the same guy. If you want to find a historical Jesus who's different from that, say, a historical Jesus who didn't know that he was going to get crucified and, therefore, couldn't have predicted it and, therefore, never predicted it to Peter and never said take up the cross and follow me and didn't think of himself as the Son of Man who comes in the clouds of heaven, but who somehow had an earthly career apart from what the Christian faith says he is, you're going to have a hard time finding that Jesus in the Gospels. You might be able to find some evidence for it, but these Gospels are designed to give you Jesus, the human man, the human Jesus, only by giving you the Christ of faith, and only through your own judgment about who Jesus is.

So once again, imagine you're a biblical scholar and you're confronted with this really ornery text, which keeps on saying to you, Scholar, who do you say Jesus is? Do you think he's different from what the church says, what Christian theology says, what Christian faith says? Do you think there's a historical Jesus who isn't the one who is raised from the dead and sits at God's right hand? Well then, you must be agreeing with Pilate and with the chief priests.

Last irony, Pilate asks Jesus, are you the King of the Jews. Jesus says you are saying it. Well, that's what gets him crucified. He doesn't renounce being King of the Jews. And when he's crucified, Pilate puts a superscription on the cross, and guess what it says? King of the Jews. That's what he's being crucified for. In the Gospel of John, people come along and say, but Pilate, you should say he is being crucified because he said he was king of the Jews. And Pilate says, this is not in the synoptics, but the Gospel of John, but I think it's the point in the synoptics as well, "I've written what I've written." It's as if, you know, in your face guys. Here's your king. I'm the Roman governor. Here's your Jewish king, the King of Jews. Here he is on a Roman cross. So it is. He's the King of the Jews, the only king you got. Pilate meant it as an abrasive and nasty sort of thing. But, of course, all the Gospel writers think, ironically, that Pilate got it right.

Lecture Five
The Gospel of John

Scope:

The Gospel of John tells the story of Jesus differently from the Synoptic Gospels. It dwells at length on Jesus's divine identity, presenting a high Christology from the start. It begins with a brief prologue identifying Jesus as the preexistent word of God made flesh, a very important text for the doctrine of the Trinity and Christology. It proceeds through the "book of signs," in which Jesus performs miracles with a message, punctuated by "I am" statements, in which Jesus describes himself in divine terms. The second half of the Gospel, which can be called the "book of the passion," includes a long Last Supper discourse in which Jesus describes his relation to God his Father, to the Holy Spirit and to his followers.

Outline

I. The Gospel of John, probably the last of the Gospels to be written, is structured very differently from the others.

A. It omits important episodes in the Synoptic Gospels, includes many episodes they do not, and reports some episodes in a strikingly different order.
   1. It omits the institution of the Eucharist, but includes a long discourse in which Jesus describes himself as the bread of life (chapter 6).
   2. It omits the baptism of Jesus, but includes Jesus offering to give believers "living water" (4:14).
   3. It reports Jesus's driving the money changers out of the temple in chapter 2, but not immediately before the Passion narrative.

B. After a prologue, it includes a "book of signs" organized around Jesus's seven miracles and then the "book of the passion" or, more accurately, the "book of glorification."

C. Throughout the Gospel is a series of "I am" statements, in which Jesus declares his identity.
   1. "I am the bread of life" (6:35).
   2. "I am the light of the world" (8:12).
   3. "I am the Good Shepherd" (10:11).

4. "I am the Way, the Truth and the Life" (14:6).
5. All the "I am" statements recall the name of the God of Israel, which means, "I am."

II. The Prologue contains a famous description of Jesus as the Word made flesh.
  A. As the Word (*Logos* or Reason), Jesus existed before the creation and hence before his own humanity.
  B. In a crucial passage for the doctrine of the Trinity, John says, "The Word was God."
  C. In a crucial passage for the doctrine of the Incarnation, John says, "And the Word became flesh."
  D. In a crucial passage for Christian soteriology (the doctrine of salvation), John says, "To all who received him, who believed in his name, he gave the authority to become children of God."
  E. The Prologue is an example of John's high Christology, his insistence on the exalted nature of Jesus from the beginning.
  F. To receive Jesus, in the Gospel of John, is to believe that he came from heaven and was sent by the Father into the world as Light and Life.

III. The miraculous signs Jesus performs have a meaning pointing to who he is.
  A. He feeds a huge crowd with a few loaves of bread and fish, and then describes himself as the bread of life.
  B. He gives sight to a man born blind, then condemns the Pharisees for their blindness.

IV. The "book of signs" culminates with Jesus raising Lazarus from the dead.
  A. When Jesus gets news of Lazarus's illness, he delays coming, knowing he will die.
  B. Lazarus's sister Martha goes out to meet him, and he tells her "I am the Resurrection and the Life."
  C. Instead of Peter, it is Martha who confesses, "You are the Christ, the Son of God."

- **D.** Jesus weeps—probably not for Lazarus's death, which he knows he will undo, but for the unbelief of people like Mary, Martha's sister.
- **E.** As John tells it, it is this miracle, rather than the cleansing of the temple, that precipitates the plot to kill Jesus.

V. Jesus's controversies with his opponents are especially intense in the Gospel of John.
- **A.** His opponents are often called "the Jews," but this is more accurately translated "the Judeans."
- **B.** "He came to his own, but his own received him not," John says, which seems to be a warning not just to Jews who did not receive Jesus but to Christians who are tempted to deny him.

Suggested Reading:

Gospel of John.

Bauckham, *The Testimony of the Beloved Disciple*.

Watt, *An Introduction to the Johannine Gospel and Letters*.

Questions to Consider:

1. How different does the portrait of Jesus in this Gospel seem from the portraits in the Synoptic Gospels—and how similar?
2. What does this Gospel tell us about the hopes of those who believe it?

Lecture Five—Transcript
The Gospel of John

In this lecture we'll conclude our survey of the New Testament, the theology of the New Testament, which really is the first set of theological documents in the history of Christian theology. We'll go to one of the later documents of the New Testament, written perhaps in the 90s of the 1st century A.D., called in your New Testament, the Gospel of John. Scholars sometimes call it the Fourth Gospel. For reasons I should mention, none of the Gospels identifies the name of its author and so the names of the author come from later Christian documents, and some scholars are skeptical about whether those attributions of authorship are correct. The Gospel of John is particularly puzzling because it claims to be an eyewitness document. And the tradition is that this is written by the Elder John (probably not the Apostle John), who lived in Ephesus into the 90s, and who was an eyewitness and a disciple of Jesus. And yet, boy, does he tell the story differently from the other Gospels. Perhaps that's because he's not drawing on the stories and documents that the other Gospels drew on. He's drawing on eyewitness knowledge. But perhaps he's doing something differently. He certainly is doing something differently as a literary document because the Gospel of John is really just a lot different from the other three Gospels in the New Testament. The other three, as you recall, are called synoptics because it's relatively easy to make a synopsis that fits all three of those stories into the same framework. The Gospel of John doesn't fit into that framework. It really doesn't fit into the same synopsis as the Synoptic Gospels.

John does just about everything differently from the Synoptic Gospels, not everything, but a whole lot. For instance, he doesn't have a story of the institution of the Eucharist, an enormously important Christian ritual, a Christian ceremony that the other Gospels talk about at the Last Supper, the last time Jesus eats with his disciples, and he takes bread and says this is my body. He takes wine and says this is my blood. John doesn't have that episode. He has a long—five chapters long—discussion of the Last Supper, but doesn't have the Eucharist. He has Jesus washing his disciples' feet instead. He has in place of the Eucharist narrative, he has a long discourse of Jesus where he describes himself as the bread of life, and if you eat this bread you have eternal life. John seems to be aware of the eucharistic narrative and of the notion that Jesus is bread for the soul, but he doesn't narrate the Eucharist, so he seems to be covering some of the same bases as the Synoptic Gospels, but in a very, very different way, and that difference is the reason why we have to discuss the theology of the Gospel of John in a separate lecture.

Another thing he leaves out is the baptism of Jesus, which is close to the beginning of all the other Gospels. This very important event ties Jesus to John the Baptist who baptizes him. Instead of it, John has a discourse where Jesus describes himself as the water of life, which seems to be related to the notion of baptism. Once again, he's covering the same bases of the synoptics, but in a different way. Maybe most striking in terms of John's not having the synopsis that the Synoptic Gospels have is the episode where Jesus, after riding in on a donkey to Jerusalem, goes into the temple in Jerusalem and drives out the money changers. In the Synoptic Gospels this is what precipitates his crucifixion. He's going into the temple as if he owns the place. He calls it my father's house, as if this belongs to him. That's an act of daring and of authority that the authorities cannot put up with. And that's what precipitates the events leading to his crucifixion. In the Gospel of John, that event is narrated, it's narrated in chapter 2, long before the events of the crucifixion, so that's an illustration of how you really can't get a similar synopsis for the two Gospels, unless maybe it happened twice. Historians go through conniptions trying to figure out how to fit the Synoptic Gospels' narratives with John's narrative. As a theologian, we'll talk about it as a theologian as to what happens when you put these two sets of Gospels side by side, the synoptics and John.

But let's get back to the structure of the Gospel of John. It works differently from the synoptics. You don't have that high point with the Transfiguration and so on. You can really divide it into two main parts. The first 11 chapters, the scholars call it a "book of signs." John doesn't use this title, but scholars call it the "book of signs" because it's organized around seven signs, that is, miraculous signs, that Jesus performs in order to point out who Jesus is. Like the synoptics, the key issue in John is who is Jesus? The signs are a way of identifying who Jesus is. And then, the second half of the Gospel of John, starting with chapter 12 is, we can say, the "book of the passion," if we want to use the synoptic term. But if we wanted to be a bit more faithful to John's own terminology, we could call it the "book of glorification," because this is one of the features of John's Gospel. When Jesus refers to his passion, he calls it his glorification. At the beginning of this "book of the passion" or "book of glorification" in chapter 12, Jesus says, "The hour has come for the Son of Man to be glorified," and he's referring to his crucifixion. Jesus's crucifixion is his glorification, or at least it's the beginning of it, so that's a very strange way of putting it. There's a lot of strange things in the Gospel of John. Jesus seems to be in charge throughout the Passion narrative. He's an authority. He explicitly passes judgment on Pilate and says your guilt is not as bad as the guilt of those who betrayed me. Jesus is explicitly the judge of his judge in John. I think that's implicit in the synoptics as I suggested, but it's explicit in John.

So Jesus is a more commanding figure in the Gospel of John. He knows that he is divine. He knows that he came from heaven. He knows that he came from the Father. And the point of his miracles and his signs is to get other people to recognize that he came from heaven, that he came from God the Father, and that's what the gospel is about. So let's say a little bit about the "book of signs," and then we're going to go to the very first part of the Gospel, the first 18 verses which is a prologue, very, very important, but first let me say a little bit about the "book of signs."

The "book of signs" is organized in an interesting way. There's these seven signs, which we won't go through all. There is a set of festivals in Jerusalem, where Jesus visits Jerusalem and does different things in different festivals which have a symbolic meaning. And then there's a set of "I am" statements which are also important to look at. And they're perhaps the most familiar part of the Gospel of John. Jesus says things like, "I am the bread of life." Let me read how he follows that up. "I am the living bread that came down from heaven." There's that key notion in John's Gospel. He came from heaven. Now that's the preexistence of Christ which we'll get to.

> I am the living bread that came down from heaven. If anyone eats of this bread, he will live forever, and the bread I will give for the life of the world is my flesh. Whoever eats my flesh and drinks my blood has everlasting life, and I will raise him up on the last day.

Astonishing statement. Notice how very much it's like the Eucharist, whoever eats my flesh and drinks my blood has everlasting life, but there's no eucharistic narrative in John. Yet clearly this is eucharistic language, and John knows about the Eucharist. And then this stunning statement, "I will raise him up on the last day." Only God can give life to the dead, and Jesus is saying I'm going to give life to the dead on the last day, on the *eschaton*. "The eschatological life from the dead comes from me," says Jesus in the Gospel of John. He also says "I am the light of the world. Whoever follows me will not walk in darkness, but have the light of life." The symbolism there is pretty clear. He says, "I am the Good Shepherd." By the way, shepherd in any ancient Near Eastern culture is a metaphor for king. The Lord is my shepherd means the Lord is my king. Agamemnon of the Greeks is called the shepherd of the people. David is called a shepherd. So in saying I am the Good Shepherd, he's saying I am the king. It's a Messianic claim.

He goes on to say, "My sheep," that is my people, "hear my voice. I know them. They follow me. I give them everlasting life." Once again, who can give eternal life but God? "I give them everlasting life. They will never perish, and no one can snatch them out of my hands." My people, the people who believe in me, they belong to me. No one can take them away from me because I'm going to keep them in life forever. Why? How can Jesus say this? He goes on to say, "My Father, who has given them to me, is greater than everyone, and no one can snatch them out of the Father's hand." So, it sounds like being in the Father's hand is the same as being in Christ's hand. And then he goes on to say indeed, "I and the Father are one." Jesus is saying he's one with God the Father. Whoa. That's something that will require some thinking about. And again, this is part of the trajectory that leads over the centuries to the Christian doctrine of the Trinity. Jesus, in some sense, is the same as the Father. I and the Father are one. In another sense he's different because he is a human being, and God's not a human being, right? So he's both one with God the Father and different from God the Father.

How do you express that properly? Well, that's what the doctrine of the Trinity will turn out to be about. And the Gospel of John gives Trinitarian theology a whole lot to think about. Here's another "I am" statement—famous one—"I am the Way and the Truth and the Life." And finally, let me talk about one of the most stunning ones, Jesus says, "Unless you believe that I am you will die in your sins."

A little later in the same discourse he says, "Before Abraham was, I am." At that point, the crowd, a bunch of Judeans where Jesus is speaking in Jerusalem pick up some stones and get ready to kill him, to stone him to death, because he's just claimed to be God. Everyone recognizes it. Why? Because "I am" is the root of that unpronounceable name of God, the God of Israel, who's called the Lord. But in fact the Lord is not his name, but a way of not saying the name. The name that you can't say, if you're a good Jew, is based on a verb in the first person which basically means I am who I am. So when Jesus says I am, he doesn't say I am he or I am this or I am that, he just says, in this verse, I am. That's the name of God. Everyone recognizes that he's claiming to be the God of Israel. It's another way of saying I and the Father are one. And so people who don't believe that this man is God pick up stones to execute him. And after all, if he's not God, he certainly deserves it by any Old Testament reckoning. Claiming to be God is deeply, deeply offensive, unless it happens to be true, and of course, that's the issue.

How can he say this kind of thing? Well, this all goes back to the prologue, the opening 18 verses of the Gospel of John, which is one of the most important passages in all of the New Testament for Christian theology. And again, this will be very important for the Trinity, indeed also for the doctrine of the Incarnation, and for soteriology, the theology of salvation. Let's start at John 1, verse 1, famous words, "In the beginning," the Gospel begins. Now remember, this should echo Genesis. "In the beginning, God created the heaven and the earth." So how do you continue when you start off "In the beginning?" What John continues with is, "In the beginning was the Word." Famous, "In the beginning was the Word," the *Logos* in the Greek. *Logos* is a word that means "word." But it's also the word from which we get our English word "logic." It can mean reason as well as word. It can mean discourse, speech, reasoning, logic, all those sort of things. It seems like John is suggesting on one hand that Jesus should be identified. By the way, this is going to be identified with Jesus in just a minute. Trust me on that. "In the beginning was the Word." On the one hand, John is saying that the word is something like the word of the Lord. Remember again in Genesis, God says let there be light. He speaks his word, and there's light. This is before there is any air around, so it's not a spoken word echoing in the air. It's God's Reason, God's Wisdom, which brings the world into being. So this is the word of the Lord, the word of the prophets. We hear about this all the time in the Old Testament, the word of the Lord. But it also seems to be the reason of God, the plan, the Wisdom of God, the wisdom by which he made the world. There are Old Testament passages about wisdom being with God in the beginning, the wisdom by which he made the world, especially a passage in the eighth chapter of the book of Proverbs. So early Christian theologians will talk about Christ as the Word and Wisdom of God.

He is the Word who is with God in the beginning. So, "In the beginning was the Word, the Word was with God," and then the kicker, "the Word was God." Once again, we have this interesting issue of identity and difference. The Word was God, and yet the Word was with God. In some sense the Word is God, the same as God. In another sense, the Word is not exactly the same thing as God. What's going on here? Well, there's more to come. By the time you get to verse 14 in this prologue, again, still John chapter 1, verse 14, John says, "And the Word became flesh and dwelt among us full of grace and truth." The Word became flesh. That's the Incarnation. That is the Word, the divine word of God that's there in the beginning, before the creation, before there is heaven and earth, before there is light and life and air and any of those things. Back in the time when there is nothing but God, there's the Word. That Word, the Reason or Word or Wisdom of God became flesh and dwelt among us, and that's Jesus. So Jesus, the man born of Mary under Augustus Caesar, crucified under Pontius Pilate. That man is the same as the *Logos* by which God created the world.

An astonishing claim, of course. In order to make sense of it, you have to have astonishing doctrines like the doctrine of the Trinity and the Incarnation. But this also explains why Jesus keeps identifying himself in the Gospel of John as the one who came into the world. He was there before the world, there in the beginning, there in the very beginning of all things. And yet he came into the world as its redeemer, as Light shining in the darkness. Another thing that the prologue says is "The Light shined in the darkness." The darkness didn't get it. That's the best way I know of translating the Greek at that point. The Light shined in the darkness. The darkness didn't get it, meaning both. And the Greek is like the English here, meaning both that the darkness didn't understand and the darkness couldn't overcome or overpower or grab onto it. The darkness just didn't get it. But the Light shines in the darkness and defeats the darkness.

That's almost the whole story of the Gospel of John in a nutshell, Jesus speaking in the midst of darkness. People who don't understand, don't see, are blinded spiritually, but the Light triumphs.

Finally, there's one other element in the prologue of the Gospel of John [to discuss]. We've had a bit of the Trinity, the wordless God. We had the Incarnation, the Word became flesh. Then there's also soteriology, the doctrine of salvation. Those who received Jesus and believed in him are born not of blood nor the will of the flesh or the will of man, but rather born of God. To all who received him, who believed in his name, he gave authority to become children of God. The word of God gives to others the ability to become sons and daughters of God. That's salvation in a nutshell. Later, there's the famous passage in the third chapter of the Gospel of John where Jesus says you have to be born again. Same basic idea. You need a new identity as children of God. You have to be born into a new life.

This prologue of the Gospel of John is an example of John's high Christology as opposed to a low Christology. A low Christology is a theory of who Christ is, which doesn't emphasize his divinity, which maybe leaves it unsaid or maybe even denies that he's fully divine. John clearly thinks that Jesus is, in some very deep sense, divine. That's a very high Christology. It's right there up front in the Gospel, and then the rest of the Gospel illustrates it. Because what you need to know about Jesus is that he's the one who comes into the world from God the Father. Very briefly, theologically what's going on here is you've got the high Christology of the Gospel of John, then you've got what looks like a lower Christology in the Synoptic Gospels. And scholars are very interested in this. If you put them together as the church did, the early Christian community, reading both the Gospel of John and the synoptics, what happens? What happens when you put together a high Christology and a low Christology? Well, you affirm them both. You affirm both that Jesus is fully human, and you've got a very human Jesus in the synoptics. In the Gospel of John, he looks a little super human. He certainly looks divine. He seems to be in charge of everything. All of the events of the Gospel of John flow the way Jesus wants them to, even his crucifixion, which is his glorification. So if you put them together, you get someone who is fully human and fully divine. Theologically, putting the Gospel of John and the synoptics together results in what the church and its theological tradition regards as a well-rounded picture of who Jesus is. The historians go nuts because they can't make it fit a synopsis. But the theologians like it.

So we have this high Christology. Let me point out a couple of the signs in the "book of signs" that point to that high Christology. One is the feeding of the crowd. In all four of the Gospels there's a miraculous feeding of a crowd where Jesus takes a couple of fish and a few loaves of bread and feeds a whole multitude. And that's the basis then in the Gospel of John of Jesus saying, "I am the bread of life. Whoever believes in me will not die, but will have everlasting life." So the sign of feeding points to Jesus as the bread of life who feeds us with eternal life. Jesus points out, your fathers died in the deserts. Israelites who had manna, bread from heaven, in the desert as they were wandering through the desert on their way to the Promised Land. They had manna, bread from heaven, but they died. You eat this bread, my flesh, and you will never die. You will have life everlasting. So both the manna in the desert and the feeding of the crowd points forward to Jesus as the bread of life. The sign is pointing toward Jesus. Likewise, he gives sight to a man who is born blind. And really this is all about whether you have the vision to see who Jesus is, the light shining in the darkness. The rulers in Judea, they question the man born blind. And they say what happened here? And the man says I don't know. I once was blind, but now I see. They say, oh, don't believe this man. He's a sinner. Well, I once was blind, but now I see, that's all I know. When he does meet Jesus later and sees him for the first time, he recognizes him. How? Jesus says, do you believe the Son of Man? He says yes, who is he? I am says Jesus. OK, I believe you. That's true vision to believe Jesus. That's a crucial equation throughout the Gospel of John. To believe Jesus is the one who comes from heaven is to see rightly. And Jesus condemns the Pharisees, the Jewish leaders in Jerusalem, for not seeing. You think that you see, but you're still blind. If you were blind you would have no sin. But now that you say we see, your sin remains, says Jesus. You are darkness. But this man, the man born blind, has light because he knows who Jesus is, because he believes. Believing who Jesus is is what it's all about.

Let me say something about the culminating sign in the "book of signs," the miracle of the raising of Lazarus from the dead. This is what actually precipitates the crucifixion in the narrative of the Gospel of John, not the cleansing of the temple where he throws out the money changers, but this raising of Lazarus from the dead. That's the last straw. That's what gets him crucified. Jesus is living at some remove from a place called Bethany where a man named Lazarus and his two sisters, Mary and Martha, live. And he gets word from the two sisters that Lazarus is sick. Actually, the word is, your "friend" is sick. Jesus says, "Well, this isn't a sickness unto death." It's not a mortal sickness. That famous phrase, the sickness unto death, comes from this passage. Although interestingly enough, he knows that Lazarus is going to die. This is not a sickness unto death. He's just fallen asleep. And I'm going to go wake him, he says to his disciples. His disciples don't get it. They say, well, if he's just fallen asleep, then he's going to be fine. And Jesus says, all right, let me be plain with you. Lazarus is dead. And for your sake, Jesus adds, I'm glad that I wasn't there, so that you might believe. I'm glad that I wasn't there.

That's a very important remark, because when Jesus does come to Bethany where Lazarus has been dead for four days by the time he arrives, he is greeted by Martha, one of the two sisters. She runs out to meet him. Basically, this is what you do with an honored guest, like a king, coming to a town. The dignitaries of the town come out to meet him. Martha comes out of the town to meet Jesus as he comes in, and she says, "Lord, if you'd been here, my brother wouldn't have died." Now remember, Jesus has said earlier, for your sake I'm glad that I wasn't there so that you might believe. Because it is true. Everyone's assuming if Jesus was there, he would have healed Lazarus and Lazarus wouldn't have died. So Mary, I keep on reversing this because people tend to think that Mary is the faithful one but, in fact, it's Martha who gets it in this story. So I have to remind myself of this. It's Martha who gets it because she comes to Jesus and says, "Lord, if you'd been here my brother wouldn't have died." And Jesus asks her, let me get this right now, "If you were here, my brother wouldn't have died," says Martha. And before Jesus responds to her she adds this. This is what Martha says and Mary doesn't, "But even now I know," says Martha, "that whatever you ask God, God will give you." Now, Jesus then mentions, well, your brother's going to rise on the last day, right? And Martha believes in the resurrection. Her brother's going to rise on the last day. Jesus says, in essence, your brother will rise again. Martha's response is, I know he's going to rise in the last day, in the *eschaton*. Then Jesus takes that notion of resurrection, which is a common Jewish belief of the time, and he applies it to himself in one of these "I am" statements. He says, "I am the Resurrection and the Life. Everyone who believes in me, though they die, they shall live."

This is what's going to happen to Lazarus. Lazarus is dead, but he's going to live. And then he adds something even more astonishing, "And everyone who lives and believes in me shall never die." That's pointing forward because what's going to happen is Jesus will raise Lazarus from the dead. But it's really kind of a resuscitation. I mean, Lazarus is really dead. But when he comes to life again, he just gets ordinary human life And Lazarus is going to die again. The sign, and this is a miraculous sign pointing forward to Jesus, the sign of Lazarus rising from the dead is pointing forward to a resurrection to everlasting life, a life in which people never die. So the sign points forward to the resurrection in Christ, because when Christ is raised from the dead, he's never going to die again. And those who are raised in Christ will never die again, unlike Lazarus. So, when Jesus says, "I am the resurrection and the life," he points forward to that deeper resurrection of which the resuscitation of Lazarus is just a sign.

Now, what's fascinating is Martha gets it. I keep on trying to say Mary. Martha is the one who gets it. Jesus says do you believe this, and Martha says "I believe that you are the Christ, the Son of God, who's coming into the world." The confession that Peter makes in the synoptics, you are the Christ, Martha makes in the Gospel of John. It's very striking. She's the one who recognizes who Jesus really is. Before he makes the miracle, she hasn't seen the sign yet. Lazarus is still dead. And she recognizes that Jesus is the Christ, the Son of God who comes into the world. Mary comes later when Martha goes back and gets her and brings her to Jesus. And Mary says the same thing that Martha began with, "Lord, if you'd been here my brother wouldn't have died!" Seems to be a kind of accusation. She was probably staying back in the house because she was sulking. Well, Martha gets her and Mary is essentially accusing Jesus. And she doesn't say, oh, whatever you ask God, God will give you. She doesn't say you're the Christ, the Son of God, who comes into the world. She just weeps over her brother Lazarus. She believes in Lazarus's death, but she doesn't believe that Christ is the Resurrection and the Life. And that's when Jesus weeps. Famous little verse, the shortest verse in the Bible, "Jesus wept." Why did he weep? Probably not because of the death of Lazarus. He knew that Lazarus was dead days ago. He was glad that he wasn't there, so that people could believe. What he's weeping over is the unbelief of these folks who can't believe that Jesus is the Resurrection and the Life. They can only believe in Lazarus's death.

Defeating death is easy for Jesus. He knows how to do that. Dealing with people's unbelief, that's a problem, that's what he weeps over. And so in the Gospel of John there's in fact a whole lot of confrontations with unbelief.

Let me say briefly a little bit about those confrontations because they're famous and they're abrasive. Jesus's dealing with his opponents are very intense in this Gospel, and what's shocking is that his opponents are often called "the Jews." I want to say just a little bit about that so we can clarify this. The word for Jews in Greek is *Ioudaios*. A literal translation would simply be Judeans. So for instance, there's a passage in the Gospel of John where Jesus is not going to go to Judea because the Judeans want to kill him. But in most English translations it comes out he doesn't go to Judea because the Jews want to kill him. Sounds quite different, doesn't it? In the Greek, it's very clear. He doesn't go to Judea, which is where Jerusalem is, because the Judeans are planning to kill him. One of the reasons why Jesus speaks so harshly of the Jews, rather, I would say the Judeans, in the Gospel, is because in one sense, Jesus is not a Judean. He's from Galilee up in the north. He's not a Judean. He's not from Judea. It's the Judeans who are going to kill him, especially the Judean leaders, the chief priests in Jerusalem. So he's opposed by these Judeans who want to kill him, and, therefore, he labels them the Jews, the Judeans, as his enemies, the ones who want to kill him. But you have to be clear. If we use the word Jews in the modern sense of the term where it applies to every one of the children of Israel, then Jesus is a Jew. So Jesus is a Jew in this broad sense. But in the New Testament sense, especially in the sense of the Gospel of John, he is not a Judean and, therefore, his enemies are these Judeans who want to kill him. I think that's important to get in focus.

Light shining in darkness, but there's plenty of Judeans who believe in him, including those who are gathered around him, and probably the beloved disciple who is the one who writes the Gospel. The light shines in the darkness. And the crucial question the Gospel wants to pose is do you recognize the light or are you part of the darkness that doesn't get it? You don't have to be a Judean not to get this light. "He comes into his own," says the prologue. He comes to his own and his own don't receive him. That can be true of both Christians and Jews. Once again, this is a document which is asking you the question, who do you say this man is? That's a question for both Jews and Gentiles. And the Judeans don't have an exclusive right to reject him, and certainly the Christians don't have an exclusive right to believe in him. There's a whole lot of Christian rejection of Jesus which we see in all the Gospels, beginning with Peter who wants to confess him as Christ and doesn't get it. Well, that's a story that we'll continue as we head through the rest of *The History of Christian Theology*.

Lecture Six
Varieties of Early Christianity

Scope:

Although Jewish Christian groups remained in existence, the Christian church was largely Gentile by the 2nd century. Among Gentile Christians a large variety of offshoots arose, most of which rejected the Jewish roots of Christianity in favor of a more spiritual view of the universe. Called Gnostics, they typically regarded the physical world as a prison to be escaped after death by souls making use of special or hidden knowledge (*gnosis*) so as to rejoin a divine world of spiritual beings or aeons beyond the visible heavens. Christ is a savior-aeon who enters this evil world without ever taking a real body, because matter is evil. And he is far above the Jewish God, who is so proud of creating this foul material world. The "lost gospels" recovered in recent times are Gnostic documents, one of which may contain hitherto unknown sayings of Jesus.

Outline

I. In the sometimes bewilderingly large variety of early Christian theologies, a central issue was always the relation of Christian belief to its Jewish roots.

II. Jewish Christians soon became a marginal group, leaving no extant writings after the New Testament.
   A. Jewish Christians continued to live as Jews observing the Law of Moses until the 4th century.
      1. They were called Nazarenes and were originally based in Jerusalem. They were rejected by mainstream Judaism and increasingly disapproved of by Gentile Christians.
      2. They believed in Jesus as Son of God and did not accept the emerging rabbinic interpretation of Judaism. They also refused to live like Gentiles.
      3. They accepted Paul and hence the validity of Gentile Christianity—for Gentiles.
      4. They were labeled heretics in the 5th century, when they were dying out, but not before.

- B. The Ebionites believed Jesus was a righteous man, but not divine and not the Son of God.
    1. They evidently arose by splitting from the Nazarenes.
    2. They are the classic example of a low Christology, denying the divine origin of Jesus as Son of God.
    3. They also rejected the writings of Paul, whom they regarded as a renegade against the Law of Moses.
- III. Among Gentile Christians, the most important alternatives to what later became orthodoxy is a large variety of teachings usually brought under the broad label of Gnosticism.
    - A. The word "Gnosticism" comes from the Greek term *gnosis*, meaning knowledge.
        1. For Gnostics, salvation means knowledge of who you are and where you come from.
        2. The physical world, including earth and heaven, planets and stars, is an evil prison for our spirits, which come from outside this world, beyond space and time.
        3. The angels in the heavens are often called rulers or archons. They are evil and try to block the soul's escape from this world after death.
        4. The soul or spirit is divine, belonging to the other world, which is why it wants to escape this world and all bodily things, where it is not really at home.
    - B. Gnosticism's disdain for the physical world is linked to a profound rejection of Judaism.
        1. The God of the Jews is the creator God, maker and ruler of this physical world, which means he is at best ignorant, and probably evil.
        2. He forbids humans to eat from the Tree of Knowledge (*gnosis*) because he wants them to stay ignorant and under his power.
        3. He is described as an arrogant archon who boasts of being the only God, ignorant of the divine realm above him.
    - C. The Gnostics' view of Christ fits with their other-worldly view of divinity.
        1. The divine world or Pleroma consists of spiritual principles called "aeons."

2. According to some Gnostics, the physical world originates from a disruption in the Pleroma when the lowest of the aeons, Sophia or Wisdom, gets in a passion.
3. Christ is an aeon sent into this world to bring saving knowledge of the world above, the Pleroma.
4. Because matter is evil, he is never really embodied: Either he dwells in the man Jesus only for a time or his body is an illusion, a mere appearance (which is the view now called Docetism).
5. The God of the Jews is not Jesus's Father but his enemy.

IV. The "lost Gospels" in the news lately are mainly Gnostic.
   A. The most important were found in a cache of buried books in Nag Hammadi, Egypt.
   B. The Nag Hammadi library is very important for our understanding of ancient Gnosticism but, with one possible exception, is not an important source for the life of the historical Jesus.
   C. The possible exception, the Gospel of Thomas, is a "sayings Gospel."
      1. The sayings are all attributed to Jesus, though many are actually much later.
      2. The later sayings are in a broad sense Gnostic, in that salvation consists of the soul's awakening to the knowledge that it does not belong to this world.
      3. Among the earlier sayings, most are similar to those found in the New Testament, and some may be closer to what Jesus actually said—though scholars are divided on this point.
      4. Some may be *agrapha*, that is, sayings of Jesus not found in the New Testament.

V. One of the most important opponents of mainstream Christianity was Marcion.
   A. For Marcion, an avid reader of Paul, the key to salvation is not knowledge but faith.
   B. Marcion taught there are two Gods, the Jewish God who creates the world and the alien and unknown God, the good God, who out of sheer grace redeems people from it.

- **C.** In a version of Docetism, Marcion says Christ is the Son of the good God, sent into the world fully grown with an angelic body.
- **D.** The good God was utterly unknown before Christ, which means the Jewish prophets did not serve him, nor did they prophesy Christ's coming.
- **E.** To support his views, Marcion accepts as scripture only an abridged version of the Gospel of Luke and the letters of Paul.

VI. Early orthodoxy was characterized by belief in the goodness of the Creator, the God of the Jews.
- **A.** The God of the Jews is "the God and Father of our Lord Jesus Christ," as a recurrent New Testament phrase puts it.
- **B.** The God of the Jews is good, and therefore the physical world he created is good.
- **C.** The Jewish scriptures are accepted as the ancient witness to this good Creator and his Son Jesus.

Suggested Reading:

"The Gospel of Thomas" in Layton, *The Gnostic scriptures*.

Jonas, *The Gnostic Religion*.

Pagels, *The Gnostic Gospels*.

Pritz, *Nazarene Jewish Christianity*.

Questions to Consider:

1. Do you find Gnostic spirituality attractive? Why or why not?
2. How insistently—or not—should Christianity hang on to its Jewish roots?

Lecture Six—Transcript
Varieties of Early Christianity

In this lecture we're going to move beyond the theology of the New Testament and get into the theology of the early church in the first few centuries of the history of Christian theology. Think about the period from say A.D. 100 to about A.D. 500. That's what we'll be dwelling on for the next few lectures. As we move beyond the New Testament, we end up taking a step out of a Jewish world into an almost entirely Gentile world. All of the New Testament writings that we know of, anything we know about the authors of the New Testament, indicate that they're all Jewish, just like nearly all of the main characters are Jewish. But all of the early Christian writings beyond the New Testament that we have are Gentile writings, pretty much without exception. We do not have writings of Jewish Christians outside the New Testament. So there's a big gulf here as Christianity spreads among Gentiles, that is non-Jews, and the Christian church ends up becoming largely Gentile. Certainly already by A.D. 200, Gentile Christians are in a large majority. By the time you get to say A.D. 400, the idea that Christians could be Jews started looking weird, as it does today. And indeed, Jewish Christians started to be regarded as heretics. Let's talk about that. That, in fact, is one of the key issues as we think about the diversity of early Christianity as it goes beyond the New Testament. The issue is, what should Gentile Christians make of the Jewish roots of Christianity? That will be one of our themes throughout this lecture as we think about the diversity of early Christianity beyond the New Testament.

Let's start by thinking about those Jewish Christians. That's where they all started. All the early Christians were Jews. They were called Nazarenes, after Jesus of Nazareth. In the book of Acts in the New Testament, they're called the Sect of the Nazarenes. Actually, in the Greek it's literally the heresy of the Nazarenes. A heresy was originally a party, a sect, so the Sect of the Nazarenes. But the Pharisees were called a sect. The Sadducees were called a sect. The Nazarenes, the believers in Jesus, were called a sect. They're called Nazarenes for the next four centuries, Jewish Christians. These Nazarenes, well, we don't know much about them beyond the New Testament. We do have a few documents from late church fathers like Jerome and Epiphanius in the 4th century. What we learn from them about the Nazarenes is roughly this: They're Jewish Christians. They tend to be based in Palestine, originally in Jerusalem. They believe that Jesus is the Son of God, has some kind of divine identity. They do not live like Gentiles. They follow the Jewish law. They circumcise their male children. But on the other hand, they don't follow the rabbinic interpretation of Jewish law. They're not following the early rabbinic interpretation that eventually becomes the Jewish Talmud. They still disagree with the scribes and the Pharisees the way Jesus did. The scribes and the Pharisees are pretty much the proto-rabbinic Judaism. So here they are, Jews, obeying the Law of Moses, but not rabbinic Jews. They're an alternative form of Judaism, and they still conceive of themselves that way, just as the early Jewish Christians did in the New Testament. They're not a new religion. They're a competing form of Judaism.

Interestingly, they accept the writings of Paul. That is, they accept the fact that Gentiles can be Christians, that Gentiles don't have to keep the Jewish law in order to believe in Jesus. Gentile Christianity is legitimate for Gentiles. So here are these Jewish Christians in Palestine and, around the Roman world, in Alexandria and Antioch and Rome and Greece. There's all these Gentile Christians. And these Jewish Christians evidently are looking at all these Gentile Christians and saying that's fine. It's OK to be Gentile and Christian. Evidently they have something like Paul's vision of the Body of Christ as a community which unites Jew and Gentile in one body, where Jews remain Jews and Gentiles remain Gentiles. Jews keep the law. Gentiles don't have to be circumcised. It's a generous vision, and it dies out. By about the 5th century, by about A.D. 500, they seem to have disappeared. Within the period of the 4th century or the 5th century, Gentile Christians are looking at them and saying they're heretics. Look, they're Christians who try to be Jews. You can't be Christian and keep the Law of Moses, despite the fact that that's what Jesus did. That's what Paul himself did. You can't be Christian and be Jewish. That modern notion that you can't be Christian and be Jewish had pretty much set in and become standard fair for theology in the church by about A.D. 400 And somewhere around A.D. 500, there weren't any more of these Jewish Christians. There was another group of Jewish Christians we need to mention, which seems to have broken off from the Nazarenes. They were called Ebionites. They are a classic example of Christians with a low Christology, Christology meaning again, the doctrine about who Jesus is. A low

Christology is one that says he's not really divine. When early Christian writers wanted to get an example of people with a low Christology, the first example they would come up with is these Ebionites, Jewish Christians located again in Palestine, probably broke off from the Nazarenes. They rejected Paul. They rejected the divinity of Christ. They regarded Paul himself as a renegade from the Law of Moses. They rejected Gentile Christianity. And they were labeled as heretics very early on.

The Nazarenes got labeled as heretics in the 5th century, in the 400s. The Nazarenes evidently were not treated as heretics in the 2nd and 3rd centuries. They were marginalized because there were so few Jewish Christians already by that time. But they weren't labeled as heretics until maybe around A.D. 400. The label heresy we're going to have to talk about in this lecture and especially in the next lecture. It's important because much of the information we have about these groups that I'm going to be talking about in this lecture comes from heresiologists, that is, orthodox Christian writers who are describing non-orthodox forms of Christianity And, of course, these are the orthodox who regard themselves as orthodox, and the other folks as heretics. They're heresiologists because they're writing books about those non-orthodox people, the heretics. We could call them non-mainstream Christianity. There's a lot of non-mainstream Christianity about, lots of different groups that the orthodox labeled as heretics. And it's about time we launch into some of those groups. Not just the Jewish Christians now, but the Gentile non-mainstream groups, because Gentile Christianity ended up having a lot of non-mainstream groups.

A fair number of these non-mainstream Gentile Christian groups, non-orthodox, maybe heretical depending on whether you're orthodox or not or how you would label these things. A fair number of these groups got the label Gnostic. It's really a pretty good label for many of them. Gnostic comes from a Greek word, *gnosis*. It's like agnostic, but without the "A." An agnostic, as you may know, is someone who doesn't know whether God exists, can't be sure whether God exists or not. Agnostic means not knowing. A Gnostic, take away the A, is someone who thinks that he or she does know. So Gnostics are named after this Greek word for "knowledge." They're named that because Gnostics believe that salvation consists in a certain kind of special, maybe secret, knowledge. To describe these Gnostics, and there's quite a number of different Gnostic groups, but they have a lot in common. To describe these Gnostics, really what we need to get a hold of is what knowledge do they think they have that other people don't. It's a special knowledge. The Gnostics are the ones who are in the know.

What the Gnostics know and the rest of us don't, the Gnostics think, is that the physical world, the cosmos, is evil. It's a prison. The material world is a bad place. And this means not just the earth, but the visible heavens, the stars up above. In ancient astronomy, which the Gnostics were taking for granted, the world is round. Ancient astronomers knew this in the Greek tradition. The world is round. The earth is at the center of the solar system. And there's these crystal spheres. Imagine a bunch of hollow crystal spheres nested inside each other. That's the heavens. And in one of these crystal spheres is a dot of light called Mercury. The larger crystal sphere has the dot of light called Venus. Another one, Mars, Jupiter. So there's these concentric crystal spheres nested inside each other. The planets ride around these crystal spheres as they revolve around the earth. The outermost sphere is the fixed stars which all move together. So the cosmos, the physical world, looks like this set of crystal balls nested inside each other with the earth at the center. And all of it is a prison. All of it is evil. All of it is nasty. We need to escape. Because what the Gnostics think they know is that they don't belong in this wicked, evil, filthy, disgusting physical world. Even the heavens are evil. We want to get out of there. The Gnostics have the knowledge that they came from outside this evil physical world. They don't really belong here. They want to go back outside the physical world. That's their secret knowledge, their special knowledge. They have to get through the heavens, beyond the physical heavens, beyond the stars and the planets, to get outside the physical world altogether. So if you're outside the outermost physical sphere then you're no longer in space or time. You're in the eternal realm, the realm that they call the Pleroma, which means the fullness, which we'll get back to.

But before you can get to the Pleroma, before you can get outside the physical world, you got to go through the heavens. Now the Gnostics, unlike New Testament Christians, they really do have this notion of the soul going to heaven. That's a big deal for them. The body, after all, is physical. That means it's evil. It's disgusting. Think what's inside your body, blood and guts and filth of all kinds. What's inside your bowels? Ew. Disgusting. Ew. Get away from that physical stuff. Your soul is pure like a shard of light, but it's not even physical light. The soul wants to get away from all that physical stuff, which means it needs to get through all those spheres of heaven. But there's a problem. There are these heavenly guardians, rulers or archons in Greek, and they're guarding the heaven. They don't want to let any souls to get through, because the physical world is a prison. Our souls are imprisoned here, first in our bodies, but then under the heavens where these archons, these heavenly beings who are nasty, are trying to prevent us from escaping. It turns out, in classical thought, the demons live in the air, not under the earth. And they're trying to block our access to heaven, to the heaven that is beyond heaven.

Notice what this says about us. Our bodies are filthy and disgusting and we want to escape them. But the true self, the soul, or more often the Gnostics will call it the spirit, is pure and divine. It's nonphysical. It comes from outside the whole physical world. What they know, their *gnosis*, their knowledge, is that we don't belong here because we came from outside. So it's like the Gnostics were reading the Gospel of John. And they did certainly read the Gospel of John. And they say, not only did Christ come into the world from outside of it, we did too. We came into the world. Unfortunately, we don't belong here. We don't like to be here. We'd want to escape, but we, too, came into the world, this evil physical world.

Now, notice the implications for Judaism. The God of the Jews created the physical world. The Lord God of Israel created the world. And in Genesis 1, he looks at the world he created and says it's good! The Gnostics read that narrative and say, boy, the God of the Jews, is he ever ignorant! He thinks the physical world is good. He thinks it's a big deal to make this disgusting, filthy, dirty place called the physical world. What an ignoramus the God of the Jews is. He must be an evil God. He's one of the archons. He's one of these heavenly rulers who's trying to prevent us from escaping. In fact, in a sense, he's the worst of the archons. He's called the arrogant archon. Now again, this is the Lord God of Israel, the God of the Jews, who is called the arrogant archon. Because what does he do? Well, in the book of Isaiah, the Lord God says, "I am God alone. There is none besides me." And the Gnostics say, what an ignoramus. He thinks he's the only God. Heaven's sake, there are lots of gods above the God of Israel, the Jewish God, who made the physical world. After all, the fact that he made the physical world shows that he's pretty low down on the scale of divinity.

Before we get to the really higher divinities, let me say one more thing about the God of the Jews according to the Gnostics. Part of his commitment to ignorance is that in Genesis 3 he takes the Tree of Knowledge, which in the Greek translation is the Tree of Gnosis, the Tree of the Knowledge of Good and Evil, the Tree of Gnosis, and he forbids human beings to eat from this tree. So the God of the Jews wants us to remain ignorant. He's committed to ignorance. Ignorance is his modus operandi. It's how he made the world. It's how he tries to keep us. He keeps us from knowledge so that we don't know that we actually come from outside of the wicked, evil world that he created. Well, what is there that's beyond this world then that the God of the Jews doesn't know about? That's the realm that I called earlier the Pleroma. This is a Greek term meaning fullness. Think of it as the divine fullness. So again, think of these nested crystal spheres, and then outside all the crystal spheres, beyond anything physical, beyond anything that moves. Because the crystal spheres are moving. And the movement of the heavens create time, months and days and years, the movement of the heavens and sun and the moon. Beyond those crystal spheres, there's no time. There's no space really. It's purely nonphysical. There's nothing but spiritual principles in this divine fullness. These spiritual principles are called "aeons," the Greek word for an age, which is also really the word for a "world." They are aeons, can mean eternal principles, spiritual principles. The Gnostics had a whole genealogy of how the aeons sort of generate each other. There's eight of them to begin with, and then there's 32 at the end. Well, it depends on which Gnostic teacher you're listening to. And they have names usually of something like abstractions. There's the beginning, there's silence, there's mind, there's truth. These are aeons. There's another aeon named man or human being, Anthropos, which is not, of course, an incarnate or embodied human being. There's no flesh out there in the Pleroma, but the spiritual principle that's the basis of humanity down here. There's another aeon called church. So you can imagine, talking about these aeons will end up being a way of interpreting or giving sort of a secret esoteric interpretation of the New Testament and even of the Hebrew scriptures.

There's two other aeons to know about. Christ, we'll get to him in a second, but first, Sophia. *Sophia* is Greek for wisdom. She's the lowest of the aeons. And she has a problem. She wants to know the first of the aeons, the *archē* or "beginning," also called "father," sometimes called "abyss." Because the father or beginning or abyss is incomprehensible. No one can know the depths of the very first of the aeons, and Sophia is the very last of the aeons, and she wants to know! And so she's in a passion. She has this passionate desire to know. It's frustrated. And there's a kind of fall of Sophia, the sort of super heavenly fall, this passion of Sophia, because passion is a bad thing, it turns out. It's emotion. It moves you. It's ignorant. And poor Sophia wants to know what she can't know. What that does is generates what's called a lower Sophia, a second Sophia. Some of the Gnostics called this second Sophia, Achamoth. All sorts of strange names in Gnosticism. This lower Sophia is the first being that isn't an aeon. The first being that kind of cascades downward that eventually results in the creation of the physical world. Eventually there's a story about how the lower Sophia eventually gives birth to the arrogant archon, the God of the Jews, who's so proud of making the physical world that he thinks he's the only God. And he doesn't even know about the Pleroma above him.

The God of the Jews has created this awful prison in which we're stuck. Christ is the one who gets some of us out of it. He's one of the aeons. And he comes into the world, just like the Gospel of John says. But unlike the Gospel of John, the physical world is just plain evil. He comes into the world as a savior, which means he comes into the world to give knowledge. Jesus's job is not to get crucified. I mean the crucifixion is actually not an important part of Gnosticism. The cross is a kind of symbol for the way Jesus gets across from the Pleroma down to the physical world. Jesus's real job is to give us knowledge, special secret *gnosis*. So in fact, he's not really embodied. And this is an important feature of Gnostic views of Christ or Gnostic Christology. The Gnostics said that Jesus's human body was a mere appearance. This view of Jesus, this view of his Incarnation or Christology is called Docetism. The Gnostics had a Docetistic Christology, meaning they thought that Christ's humanity, and, in particular, his body, was a mere appearance. After all, he's an aeon. He wouldn't get stuck in an awful, physical, disgusting body. Aeons don't get embodied. Bodies are evil. He couldn't rescue us if he was stuck in a real body. Bodies are prisons, and Christ was not imprisoned in this world. And also, the God of the Jews is his enemy. That's very different from the New Testament. We'll say a little more about that.

Let me mention, you have probably heard of the "lost gospels." It's an interesting phrase. And there were in fact a bunch of "lost gospels." All of them are gospels that are not in the New Testament. Many of them were missing or lost, not known for hundreds and hundreds of years. We heard about them in early Christian writings, but don't have their texts. But we found the texts in a place called Nag Hammadi in Egypt. A bunch of texts of these "lost gospels" have been buried probably around the 4th century or so and have been buried in jars in the desert for, literally, more than a millennium. And they were dug up and discovered. And there really are these ancient documents from 2nd, 3rd, maybe 4th century. None of them, except for one important exception, which I'll get to, none of them are as early as the canonical Gospels, the Gospels of the New Testament. But they are very important evidence for early Christianity and especially for these early Gnostic Christians. They don't really give us any new information about the historical Jesus. They don't give us any new information about Mary Magdalene, despite what some novels might tell you. We learn nothing about Jesus or Mary Magdalene from these gospels because they are much, much later than the New Testament. Mary Magdalene does appear in them, interestingly, as a teacher of *gnosis* and one of Jesus's favorite disciples. So that may say something about the early Gnostics' view of women teachers. And that's actually very interesting. But it doesn't tell us anything about the actual historical Mary Magdalene.

I said there was an exception. It turns out that one of the "lost gospels" is called the Gospel of Thomas. It is a "sayings Gospel." It's basically a list of sayings of Jesus without any kind of narrative. There's no story tying them together. It's not clear if there's any real ordering principle. They just seem to be a collection of sayings of Jesus. Many of these sayings seem to be probably 2nd century, around A.D. 150. They tend to be Gnostic sayings about how you overcome the duality between male and female. Women can be saved because they become men in the Gospel of Thomas. That's clearly not anything Jesus actually said. Now on the other hand, the Gospel of Thomas also contains sayings that are very close to the sayings of the biblical Gospels, the Gospels of the New Testament. Some of them are slightly different from the sayings in the New Testament. And one of the interesting discussions amongst scholars is are these sayings in the Gospel of Thomas closer to the original sayings of Jesus than the Gospels in the New Testament? There's wide disagreement, sometimes fierce disagreement among scholars about that. Some scholars think the Gospel of Thomas that we dug up in Egypt in Nag Hammadi has the more authentic versions of the original sayings of Jesus. Other scholars say no, no. The New Testament Gospels are more authentic. And not only that, there are few sayings of Jesus in this Gospel of Thomas which are not in the New Testament Gospels. They just might possibly be authentic sayings of Jesus that are not in the Gospels in the New Testament. That would be pretty exciting if it's true. Again, some scholars think, definitely, there are authentic sayings of Jesus in the Gospel of Thomas dug up in Egypt just recently rediscovered, that had been lost to Christianity for thousands of years. Other scholars say no. That doesn't really sound like the authentic Jesus. The scholars are still disagreeing about that. And I don't have a professional opinion about it, so I'll leave it alone.

Just the last note about these "lost Gospels." They are exciting evidence for early Christianity. They're not really any new evidence about Jesus, except for the Gospel of Thomas, which is highly controversial, but very, very interesting. It may give us some information about Jesus that we don't have from the Bible.

Now, let me go on to another teacher, not exactly a Gnostic, probably the most important challenge to the mainstream orthodoxy of the early Christian church, a man named Marcion. Marcion actually started a whole alternative church. The other Gnostic teachers, interestingly, tended to lead Bible studies within the church and sort of started a little splinter group within the church. Marcion started a whole new church. He was the deepest challenge to the early Christian church. He's a lot like the Gnostics in some ways, but different in other ways. He literally did not believe it was knowledge that got us salvation, but faith. For Marcion, it was faith alone that saves us. He loved Paul. Probably the other Gnostics were more fans of the Gospel of John. Marcion is a big fan of Paul. He loves the idea of being saved by faith alone. Why?

Marcion believed there were basically two gods. He doesn't have this Pleroma stuff with all these aeons. There's only two gods. One is that familiar evil, God of the Jews, who created the physical world, ignorant, violent, likes to kill people, sort of likes all the blood and guts of the physical world. How awful. Another is the good God because the Jewish God is at the very best ignorant, and probably lawless and violent. Well, he believed in law, but in the sense of he liked to execute people. The good God, the good God is different from the God of the Jews. He's merciful. The God of the Jews believes in law and the death penalty and mere justice in the most cruel and violent sort of way. The good God is merciful and kind and he has nothing to do with the physical world. The physical world belongs to the evil Jewish God, the violent God of the law. The good God is the god of mercy. And the physical world is not his world. He is an alien God. And the physical world is alien to him. And unlike the Gnostics, Marcion thinks we belong thoroughly to this physical world. It's evil. It's our world. We didn't come from outside of it. We don't have special knowledge of the world outside the physical world. The alien God who's outside the physical world is an unknown God. We do not have knowledge or *gnosis* of him, we can only believe, because we don't belong to him.

In contrast to orthodox Christian theology, where Christ comes into the world to save what belongs to him because he's the Creator. The redeemer is redeeming what is his own because the created world is his. He's redeeming it from corruption and death. To Marcion, by contrast, the redeemer does come into the world. The savior of Christ comes into the world that is utterly alien to him. As an act of sheer love, there's something very poignant about this. Christ the savior enters the world out of sheer love, sheer mercy. He redeems people who don't even belong to him. He has no need for them, no vested interest in them. And yet he's going to help us escape from this awful physical world and bring us to this alien unknown god, by faith alone. We don't know this god, but we can believe in him. We can believe in this alternative god and this alternative world which is not ours, which we don't know anything about. But by believing in Christ we can get there and escape this awful physical world made by the God of the Jews. That's a powerful alternative to Christian orthodoxy.

Let me mention two things. One is, you have a kind of Docetic Christology again in Marcion, Docetism where Christ doesn't have a real human body. Turns out he has an angelic body. He is never born. He sort of enters the world in an angelic body, but then he really gets crucified. He enters the alien world that is not his own, and they kill him for it. But it's an angelic body, not a human body. The other thing is, Marcion wanted to support his views from the scriptures but, of course, not the Jewish scriptures. He wanted to read

Paul and some of the Gospel of Luke. So what he did actually say was that the only truly Christian documents are the letters of Paul and parts of the Gospel of Luke. Some of the parts of the Gospel of Luke are too Jewish, and he got rid of them. This is a very actually important idea. What Marcion was proposing was a canon of scripture, a set of approved documents of Christian scripture. The later Christian church would say yes. We need a canon, a scripture, that is an approved list of Christian documents that belong to the New Testament. But it's going to be a much larger list than Marcion's. So we'll find out more about that in the next lecture.

Let's leave Marcion behind a bit and introduce the next lecture by thinking about the folks who called themselves orthodox, the folks who said, we're not Gnostics. What characterized the mainstream church, the church that was not Gnostic, and the church to which the Jewish Christians for a long while belonged? What's this early orthodoxy look like?

Well, first and foremost, it takes a different attitude toward Judaism. The early orthodox church regards the God of the Jews as the God and Father of our Lord Jesus Christ. When Jesus is the Son of God that means he's the son of the Jewish God, the God of Israel. The Jewish God, the God of Israel is good, in the same way that Christ is good. Christ does not redeem us from the world made by the Jewish God. He reclaims what is lost and broken and corrupted and mortal, what has been spoiled in the world that the Jewish God made good. It was a good world, but it got spoiled by sin and death. The Son of God comes from the Jewish God, the God, the Father, the God and Father of our Lord Jesus Christ. He comes from that God, the God of Israel, to redeem what truly belongs to the God of Israel and give life to what has been corrupted by sin and death. The world is the world of the God of Israel. And it's a good world. And it's a good God who sends a good redeemer to redeem him.

That means also that embodiment is not evil and therefore, Christ, the Son of God, can take on a real human body, be really born from a woman, be really crucified. That's humiliating. It's a humility of God. But being embodied is not in and of itself evil. And therefore God himself, or at least the Son of God, can become embodied. And finally, the early orthodox had a different attitude toward the Jewish scriptures, the Hebrew scriptures. They looked at it, as I mentioned before, as the Old Testament, which is to say the ancient and revered and venerated witness to Jesus Christ. Because the Jewish God is the God and Father of our Lord Jesus Christ, the Jewish scriptures bear witness to Jesus Christ. The prophets speak of him. The psalms are sung about him. And, therefore, it's one crucial characteristic of the early Christian church that it sees itself as rooted in Jewish scriptures, even though, by the time you get to A.D. 200 or so, the early Christian church was a Gentile church. So that's one of the interesting features of Christian theology which we'll be dealing with in the future. It's a Gentile church by and large by the time you get to A.D. 400 and 500. And yet it's rooted in the Jewish scriptures. And it's a Gentile church that has to read Jewish scriptures in order to understand itself. Gentiles, who have to think like Jews in order to understand who they are in Christ. That's going to be an important part of the history of Christian theology as we proceed.

Lecture Seven
The Emergence of Christian Doctrine

Scope:

Because Christianity is based on faith in a particular person, it has a great concern with sound doctrine, which is to say the right teaching of what to believe about this person, Jesus Christ. A mark of orthodoxy in doctrine was catholicity or universality, as opposed to the fresh new ideas proposed by charismatic leaders of subgroups or sects, which the larger church (called the "Great Church") called "heresies." Orthodoxy was preserved and heresy resisted by the social structure of the Great Church, in which bishops kept local congregations in touch with each other, aiming to preserve the apostolic tradition of teaching handed down to them. The earliest Christian writings did not include treatises on theology or doctrine but rather defenses of the faith against pagans, Jews, and heretics. Brief summaries of Christian teaching were found in what were called "rules of faith" and creeds.

Outline

I. The very idea of "doctrine," with its implication that there is a difference between sound doctrine and heresy, is a characteristically Christian notion.
   A. Paganism, with its roots in myth and its tolerance for many alternative forms of ritual, had little need of doctrine at all.
   B. Judaism focused its intellectual energies on questions of how to live more than what to believe.
   C. In the pagan world, the competing schools of philosophy came closest to having an official doctrine, but they were not lifelong communities defining their members' identities.
   D. Christians invented the idea of religious doctrine, because their religion was fundamentally a "faith," which is to say a belief which had to be taught.
      1. For Christianity everything depended on believing the truth about Christ, which therefore had to be rightly taught.
      2. "Doctrine" comes from the Latin word *doctrina*, meaning "teaching."

3. The crucial criterion of sound doctrine was "orthodoxy," which meant both "right belief" and "right worship."
4. Orthodox doctrine became the "official" teaching of the church, meaning that it was the responsibility or "office" (in Latin, *officium*) of the church's leaders to teach it.

E. The concept of heresy follows as the negative side of the concept of orthodox doctrine.
1. "Heresy" originally meant "sect," a subgroup within the larger church (the "Great Church," as it was called), which differed from the church's official teaching.
2. Orthodoxy was closely associated with "catholicity" (meaning "universality"), as the Great Church sought to formulate doctrines Christians everywhere held or should hold in common.
3. Vincent of Lerins, in the famous "Vincentian Canon," articulated a widespread view of the ancient church when he proposed that the criterion for sound doctrine is that it is what is taught "everywhere, always, and by all."
4. It became a fundamental obligation of the bishops, as leaders of the Great Church, to exclude heretics and their teaching.

F. The complex legacy of apostolic teaching accepted by the church, including the startling claims about Jesus made by the Gospel of John, needed to be sorted out and understood, which took centuries.
1. It also resulted in excluding some forms of teaching, such as Gnosticism, as heresy.
2. A key consequence of this need to reason carefully about its doctrines is that, early in its history, Christianity came to have a deep commitment to the harmony of faith and reason.

II. The social structure of the Great Church was particularly well adapted to resist new doctrines.

A. The church in each town remained in communion with churches in other towns, on the understanding that all the churches in the Great Church taught the same things about Christ.
1. To be "in communion" meant to share the sacraments, that is, admitting visitors from other churches to the Eucharist and accepting the validity of their baptism.

2. Thus the fundamental punishment for heretics was excommunication, exclusion from the communion of the church.
   3. The effect of this social organization was fundamentally to conserve old teachings and resist innovations.
B. The local churches understood themselves to be handing down the teaching of the apostles who founded them.
   1. The name for this "handing down" is "tradition."
   2. "Apostolic tradition" thus became the fundamental norm of doctrine.
C. The New Testament was accepted as the written form of apostolic teaching.
   1. For the earliest Christians, "scripture" meant the sacred writings of Israel, what Christians now call the Old Testament.
   2. The list of approved writings is called the "canon," and the decision about which books to include in the canon was one of the most fundamental theological decisions of the Great Church.
   3. The New Testament was the collection of Christian writings approved to be read aloud in church.
   4. All books included in the New Testament canon were understood to have been written by an apostle or to have apostolic authority.
D. The crucial responsibility for Christian doctrine belonged to the office of bishop.
   1. The most important leaders at the very beginning of Christianity were itinerants: Jesus, the apostles, and the prophets.
   2. Local leaders were bishops, presbyters, and deacons, all of whom were about equal in status, essentially meaning that each church had several bishops.
   3. By the 2nd century, only one bishop presided over each church.
   4. Since the bishops were responsible for correspondence with other churches, the network of bishops became a secondary social location for Christian teaching and especially for deciding which teachings were "heresies."

- **E.** The Great Church rejected attempts to establish alternative sources of authoritative teaching in addition to the apostolic teaching handed down by the succession of bishops.
    1. The most important attempt to establish a new source of authority was Montanism, named after Montanus, a Christian leader in Asia Minor.
    2. He advocated a New Prophecy and called himself the Paraclete (that is, the Holy Spirit).
    3. In rejecting Montanism, the Great Church made a crucial decision about the doctrine of the Holy Spirit: The era of prophecy and new revelations of the Spirit was past.
- **III.** The essential early Christian doctrines are found in brief summaries. The boundaries of sound Christian teaching were often expressed in "rules of faith," which later developed into trinitarian creeds.
    - **A.** Statements of the rule of faith found in early Christian writers are typically trinitarian, mentioning God the Father, Jesus the Son of God, and the Holy Spirit.
    - **B.** A basic narrative is given of Jesus's life, including usually birth, crucifixion, resurrection, ascension, and return.
- **IV.** The orthodox theological writers up to about A.D. 500 have come to be called "church fathers."

Suggested Reading:

Chadwick, *The Early Church*, chaps. 2–4.

Martyr, *Apology* in *Ante-Nicene Fathers*, vol. 1.

Pelikan, *The Christian Tradition*, vol. 1, chap. 2.

Questions to Consider:
1. Is it legitimate for the church to have such a notion as "sound doctrine," which excludes heretics?
2. Given the church's purpose of teaching Christ, does its governing structure and its resistance to innovation make sense?

Lecture Seven—Transcript
The Emergence of Christian Doctrine

We saw in our previous lecture that early Christianity broke into a large variety of different groups and sects, you could say, and teachings, but there was also a mainstream, a group that called themselves the "Great Church." We'll talk about what that means, a mainstream that became what later is identified as orthodox Christianity. These orthodox folks wanted to figure out what the right thing to teach about who Jesus is. And they regarded people like the Gnostics as heretics because they taught the wrong thing.

So, this concern about teaching the right thing about Christian "doctrine," as it's called, ends up becoming a central concern of Christian theology, indeed, really the central concern of Christian theology in a way that doesn't really happen with other religions. And that's something I mentioned in our very first lecture when I was defining Christian theology. In the definition I proposed that the focus of Christian theology is on Christian doctrine, which means what's the right thing to teach? What is sound doctrine? How do you teach the right thing about Jesus? What's the "official" teaching of the church as it were? And that ends up, I think, becoming not only something central to Christianity, but something distinctive about Christianity as a religion. I think it's probably true to say that Christians invented the notion of religious doctrine or official teaching because it is so central to Christian religion in a way that's not true of other religions.

An interesting contrast, for instance, would be with pagans. Ancient pagans—there are a lot of them around in the time of the early church. Think about how pagan religion worked. They had all these local cults. Every city had its own set of gods which might be similar to but also different from other cities and their gods, their own rituals, their own stories about the gods, what we call myths.

The cities didn't worry much about what you believed. They didn't have an official doctrine. They just had these practices of civic worship, and you get in trouble if you don't practice civic worship. So, for instance, the city of Athens had its own gods and Socrates, the famous philosopher, got executed because of the crime of impiety, not heresy. The pagans didn't have the notion of heresy. That's just not a notion that they worked with. It's not like he was teaching the wrong thing or had the wrong beliefs. It's that he wasn't participating in public worship in the way that they believed he should. So impiety was a crime. But heresy was something that pagans didn't even know about. They didn't really worry about what you believed so long as you were worshiping the gods the right way.

More interesting or closer at least to Christianity, of course, is Judaism. In Judaism, there's definite beliefs about who God is, but the focus of intellectual activity is the Jewish law, not doctrine. In fact, the very notion of Jewish doctrine doesn't just roll off the tongue like the notion of Christian doctrine. Christian doctrine is something natural to Christianity. Jewish doctrine, well, there is such a thing but it's not so central. The closest you get really to a notion of doctrine about the gods, outside of Christianity, in the ancient world, is among the philosophers because it turns out there were different sects of philosophers, different schools of philosophy. The Platonists, the Stoics, the Epicureans, each of them had different doctrines about the gods. But these philosophical schools were not religious communities. They weren't shaping people's identity. They were not a focus of life-long loyalty, and they didn't shape your heart.

So there was doctrine, but it wasn't a matter of life and death the way that Christian doctrine was for Christians because it shaped Christian faith. As I mentioned in the first lecture, Christianity is essentially a "faith" because it's essentially about believing in this one person, Jesus. And that's why Christianity is doctrinal. Christianity is about doctrine because it's about this one person. And you need to teach the faith right in order to get people believing what is true about this one person. And if you're one of the mainstream orthodox people in the ancient church, you don't want people believing what the Gnostics believe about Christ. That's the wrong faith, the wrong doctrine. And, therefore, they're misleading people about who Jesus is. So precisely because Christianity is so focused on this one person, and in that sense it's very personal, it's also doctrinal. You can't really separate the personal from the doctrinal in Christian religion because Christian religion is doctrinal precisely because it's personal in the sense of being obsessed with this one person, Jesus Christ.

So let's think about how Christians went about, as it were, inventing the very notion of religious doctrine. As I mentioned before in that first lecture, the word "doctrine" comes from the Latin word *doctrina*, meaning "teaching." The criterion of sound teaching was that it was orthodox. That was the key word for it that the mainstream Great Church used for the right kind of teaching. It's orthodox.

"Orthodox" (or orthodoxy) is an interesting word because it means two different things that are closely related for early Christians. It means "right belief" but also "right worship." It means both. And again, this is an interesting contrast with paganism. Among the pagans, you have to worship the right way or you could get executed for impiety. But your beliefs—they don't worry too much about your beliefs. So for instance, lots of pagan philosophers didn't really take those pagan myths very seriously. But they participated in civic worship. So they had the right worship. But who cares about their beliefs? And the pagan philosophers didn't take the mythological beliefs very seriously. Whereas Christians took the combination of belief and worship very seriously, because, as you remember, their worshiping Christ exalted on high, at God's right hand. You need to know about that, about who Jesus is, how he was crucified, resurrected, raised from the dead, exalted at God's right hand. You needed to have the right beliefs in order to worship him the right way. So, right belief and right worship were intimately connected in Christianity. And that's why orthodoxy is such a good label for what the mainstream church regarded as sound doctrine.

Now, this orthodox doctrine becomes, what I will call, the official teaching of the church. That's an interesting term. "Official" comes from a Latin word *officium*, which means "office," "responsibility," or "role," like the office of the president, we might say, when we're not talking about the Oval Office but his responsibility as president. Well, likewise, the teachers of the church, especially the bishops, as we'll point out, had an official responsibility, an office, a responsibility of teaching the faith the right way. Contrast say, the rabbis in Judaism where their responsibility is teaching the law the right way, a slightly different focus.

Christianity has an official teaching, or at least mainstream orthodox Christianity does, and it matters. And Christian theology and its history is a history of how Christians work out this official teaching. The contrast term, of course, is heresy. Heresy is a concept that goes along with the concept of official teaching. Heresy is the lack of official teaching, not teaching what ought to be taught. The word "heresy" originally meant "sect," or "party."

So for instance, the Greek word, *hairesis*, from which this word "heresy" comes, is used in quite a number of writings in 1st century A.D. to refer to the sect of the Pharisees, the sect of the Sadducees, which are different sects or parties within Judaism. When Christianity, or mainstream Christianity, labels some groups heretics, what they're saying is the church should not be divided into parties which have disagreements about doctrine. The church should not have competing doctrines.

Competing doctrines are not quite such a problem in Judaism, where it's the Mosaic Law that unites you. But in Christianity, where it's doctrine is crucial, having competing sects with competing doctrines is a disaster, at least according to the mainstream. So the contrast term for heretics is not only orthodoxy but, an interesting term, "catholic," or "catholicity" you can even say. This comes from another Greek word. "Catholic," *katholikos*, is the word for universal. So the sound doctrine, the orthodox doctrine, is catholic in the sense that it's the universal doctrine of the whole church, not the doctrine of some little sect, not the doctrine of some subgroup. Many of the Gnostic teachers, interestingly, were really leaders of subgroups. They would lead Bible studies. They were often charismatic teachers in a local church who would gather a following around them. And what the mainstream church said is that's not how you do Christian doctrine.

Christian doctrine is what the whole church throughout the whole world shares. It's universal. It's catholic. Orthodox Christian doctrine is catholic doctrine. And the early church theologians pretty much identified orthodoxy with catholicity. The terms are almost equivalent, orthodox and catholic.

This underlying notion of what is catholic is beautifully formulated in a little phrase that is called by the name of the "Vincentian Canon," attributed to a man named Vincent of Lerins in 433. Although the idea, I think, goes back a long ways. It's called a "canon" because *canon* is a Greek word for "rule" or "ruler," like a measuring rod. We'll get back to that word in a minute. The "Vincentian Canon" is that sound doctrine is what is taught "everywhere, always, and by all." That's a way of talking about catholicity, universality.

The mark of heresy, by contrast, is that it's local, some local charismatic leader and his little subgroup. By contrast, sound doctrine is taught everywhere, throughout the Roman world, throughout the whole world wherever the church is spread. It's the same doctrine. At least that's the aim, and that's the criterion of sound doctrine. Likewise, sound doctrine is taught not only everywhere, but always. It's not a new thing. Innovation, or novelty, is a bad thing. It's actually a bad word in early Christian theology. When you call someone an innovator, you're saying they're a bad teacher because they're teaching a new doctrine that the apostles of Jesus didn't teach. And we'll get to that point, too. Likewise, it has to be taught by all. It's not just some charismatic leader's bright new idea. Catholic orthodox doctrine is taught "everywhere, always, and by all"—*ubique, semper, et ab omnibus*—lovely Latin phrase.

This teaching became an official teaching because it became the obligation of the teachers of the church throughout the world to teach it. It was their office. And it was also their office to exclude the wrong kind of teaching. It became the social obligation of the official teachers of the church to exclude heretical teaching, which sometimes meant to exclude heretics. In the early church, what you did with heretics is you kicked them out of the church. You excommunicated them. That's the worst punishment that happened to heretics. The vivid pictures of burning heretics, that's much later. That's the Middle Ages. It doesn't happen in the early church. What you do with a heretic is you kick them out. You say, your teaching is not sound Christian teaching. You're misleading people. You're not leading them to the faith of Christ. You're teaching a different Christ. Get out of here. We want to teach and believe the real Christ, the Christ that was taught by the apostles.

The whole process of getting Christian doctrine right ended up taking centuries. There was a long sort of sorting out process because the orthodox faith goes back to these New Testament documents. And the New Testament documents have a great deal of variety in them already. We mentioned, for instance, the difference between the Gospel of John and the Synoptic Gospels. How do you put together these two pictures? There's a sorting out process that goes on. You think of, well, how can you say that the man on the cross is also the Word, who was there in the beginning, the divine Word who was in the beginning with God as if the man on the cross is the word by which God created the world? Can we really say this? How can we say this? How can we make sense of this? The early church was committed to making sense of this, but it took several centuries to work it all out. It required rejecting certain false versions which were labeled heretical. And sort of, well, orthodox Christian doctrine emerges as the formulations that are used to make sense of these astonishing claims that you get in things like the Gospel of John, to make sense of these astonishing claims and to exclude certain rejected interpretations that ended up being labeled heresy.

In this sorting out process, we get a very interesting thing arising. In order to make sense of Christian teaching, you're going to have to reason about it. Theology involves critical reasoning, as I said back in the first lecture. Christians were very serious about their faith being true, about it really being true that Jesus rose from the dead at God's right hand. So you have to get it right, and you have to be able to show that it's right. You have to be able to show that it's true or, at least, you have to be able to defend its truth. You have to be able to make sense of it. It can't just be mumbo jumbo. It can't just be poetry; although there's a lot of poetry in Christianity. It can't just be poetry. It can't be mythology. It's got to be serious claims to truth and, therefore, it can be reasoned about.

Christian faith has always regarded itself as reasonable. Faith and reason have always been treated in the mainstream Christianity as partners. Faith is primary. But reason is part of the picture because this is doctrine; this is to be taught as true. And you can ask the question, well is it true? Is it really the apostolic doctrine that goes back to the apostles of Jesus? Is it really true that Jesus is like this? Well, let's reason about this. What's fascinating about this is that the Christians, I think, were the first group that were so very, very serious about uniting faith and reason.

Other religious groups [didn't] reason about their beliefs. Again, the rabbis of Judaism are a perfect example. But for Christianity, because doctrine is so central, the unity of faith and reason is an essential part of Christian religion. And they got to this uniting of faith and reason before the philosophers did. And this is a fascinating point. The pagan Greek philosophers, as I suggested, when they went to worship their pagan gods, didn't take that worship very seriously. They didn't take it literally. They certainly didn't believe the myths. So, the pagan philosophers were not trying to unite faith and reason. They were not trying to unite worship and truth, not serious philosophical truth. Serious philosophical truth is for the philosophical schools. Worship is what you do in public. You don't quite take it seriously, as opposed to Christians who took their public worship seriously as a truth claim.

So it's Christians before the philosophers who were working on the union or the harmony of faith and reason. Once the pagan philosophers tried to give a rational defense of paganism—well, that wasn't until A.D. 300, 400, 500—once they started doing that, they were playing catch up. They were trying to catch up to Christians, who'd been doing that for centuries before them. There were pagan Platonist philosophers trying to give a philosophical justification for pagan religion. And they were really behind because Christians had been doing it for several centuries. And that's because of the Christian focus on doctrine.

Let me say a little bit about the social structure of the Christian church in the early centuries because that says a little bit more, again, about how Christian doctrine worked. The church was designed both geographically and historically to preserve the teaching of the apostles. Think about it geographically, first of all. The church is a set of churches in various localities led by bishops. We'll talk about the bishops in a minute. And they're always in communication with each other.

Throughout the Mediterranean world, and then off into Syria and Persia, these churches communicate with each other, and they agree about the doctrine. It's important to have this agreement, this catholicity. So the churches are "in communion" with each other when they agree about doctrine. And you can travel from one church to another in the Mediterranean world, and your baptism in one church is recognized as a valid baptism in another. You take communion in your local church in Ephesus. And you go to Athens and that local church will invite you to their communion. And so these churches are in communion with one another. If one church doesn't recognize another church's doctrine as sound doctrine, then they're not "in communion."

And so the desire to be in communion with all the other churches in the world is a conservative force that preserves older doctrines and avoids that evil thing innovation. Excommunication means you're no longer in communion. If you're a heretic, you'll be kicked out of the church, which means especially you're not invited to the communion service, the Eucharist, the bread and wine that Christians share. And that's the fundamental discipline that's meted out to heretics.

So you can see that this has a conservative effect. Why? Because the teaching that is catholic will be taught not only everywhere but always which means going back to the beginning. It's apostolic teaching, as I've mentioned a couple of times already. Apostolic teaching means the teaching of the apostles who knew Jesus, the ones who followed him, who were his eyewitnesses, beginning with the twelve. But then a few others like Paul are added to the list. "Apostolic tradition" becomes one of the criteria of sound doctrine. "Tradition," again, remember, means what is "handed down." The apostolic tradition is the teaching handed down from the apostles, and it goes all the way back to the eyewitnesses of Jesus.

This is very important for early Christian teachers. Here, for example, is Irenaeus, a 2nd century mainstream Christian theologian, an orthodox theologian, talking about apostolic tradition. He mentions a man named Polycarp who is a bishop in Smyrna who had known John, who is the author of The Gospel of John, according to Irenaeus. And Irenaeus mentions how Polycarp had reported his conversation with John and with others who had seen the Lord, that is, the Lord Jesus, how he remembered their words and what were the things concerning the Lord, which he heard from them. That is what Polycarp heard from John, who heard it from the Lord himself, and about their miracles in their teachings. That's the teachings of the apostles, and how Polycarp had received them from the eyewitnesses of the word of life and reported all things in agreement with the scriptures. Notice this apostolic tradition, which is oral, is not in competition with the scriptures.

The scriptures indeed, the New Testament scriptures are regarded as the written version of apostolic tradition. Originally, of course, for the earliest Christians, the word "scripture" meant the Old Testament. But as the New Testament writings got collected, they got called scripture as well. They were all regarded as having apostolic authority. All of the writings in the New Testament were traced in some way back to the apostles, like the Gospel of Mark, which the early Christians regarded as written down by Mark, who is a friend of Peter and learned this stuff from the Apostle Peter.

So, all of the New Testament documents are regarded as having apostolic authority. That's why, for instance, I mentioned the Gospel of Thomas, which was not accepted as having apostolic authority. So, to this day, if you are Catholic or something, one of these mainstream Christian groups, if the Gospel of Thomas has authentic sayings of Jesus, it doesn't matter to Christian doctrine, not orthodox Christian doctrine because this document is not accepted as having apostolic authority. So even if that is an authentic saying of Jesus, well, who knows? Scholars still disagree about it. It's not going to change Christian doctrine despite this interesting historical discovery.

The key idea here is the idea of the canon of scripture. Canon, again, means "rule," literally a ruler or a measuring rod. It was used to talk about the list of approved writings, the list of writings that became the New Testament. The Canon of The New Testament it was called. This list of writing was literally the list of writings that were allowed to be read in church, read aloud in the context of Christian worship, which is still done in Christian worship today. People get up and read the scriptures aloud just like in the Jewish synagogue, where people get up and read the Torah aloud or chant it. In fact, early Christians often chanted the scripture when they read it.

The point is, you needed to know which books you would read. This is very important because in the ancient world, most Christians are going to be illiterate. They're going to learn their scriptures from hearing it read. They will hear it read when they gather together to worship in the name of Jesus. So the reading of scripture allowed in that worship setting is a very solemn act. And only the most important, authoritative apostolic documents can be read aloud in church in that way, and that's the canon of scripture.

Very much later, this canon of scripture would be bound in one book, Old Testament and New Testament together and called the Bible. They didn't have Bibles in the ancient world For one reason, mainly because bookmaking technology did not allow them to make such a huge book with so many pages. So what they had instead was a canon, a list of approved writings to read in church. They all had apostolic authority. In one way or another, they went back to the eyewitnesses of Jesus, or at least so the church thought.

The people who guarded Christian teaching, the people who had that official office of teaching sound doctrine, were the bishops. They're a very important social feature of the early Christian church and early Christian doctrine. The early Christian doctrine is fundamentally the doctrine of the bishops.

Let me say a little bit about the history of Christian leadership. If you go back to the New Testament itself, you see a lot of people who are traveling. Jesus travels around. He's an itinerate preacher. Paul is a missionary. He travels around. But, of course, churches are established in particular localities, and they have to have a settled leadership, not itinerates like Jesus and Paul.

The settled leadership ends up being divided into three groups: bishops, presbyters, and deacons. Although originally, we can tell from the New Testament that there wasn't a strong distinction between bishops and presbyters. Presbyters are elders, The word "Presbyters" comes from a Greek word meaning "elder." Bishops are supervisors, are overseers. "Bishop" comes from a Greek word meaning "supervisor" or "overseer." Deacons are servants. "Deacon" comes from a Greek word meaning "servant." The deacons would take care of things like distributing the money that is collected for the poor, and making sure the widows of the community are taken care of. The presbyters became the priests. The word "priest" in English is a formation from the Greek word *presbyteros*, presbyter. So priest is literally an elder. And the bishops became the chief leaders of the churches.

Eventually, by the 2nd century, there was a rule established in practice and then also in theory that there was one bishop per church. Originally, probably in the 1st century, priests and bishops were the same thing. Presbyters and bishops were the same thing. There were going to be many, many bishops in one church. But by the 2nd century, there's only one bishop per church. And the bishop is essentially responsible for corresponding with other bishops in other churches, and, thus, for instance, writing letters saying so-and-so from our church would like to visit your church. Please accept them into communion. And of course the bishop, therefore, would be responsible for making sure that this other church is one with his church in communion. And if there was a doubt about that, the bishops would get together in what is called a synod, basically a conference or a meeting of bishops. And they would say, well, this guy, this bishop over here, he's not teaching a sound orthodox apostolic faith. He's going to get excommunicated. He'll get deposed, kicked out of his bishopric.

And so these synods or councils, as they came to be called, were a fundamental locus for deciding on what is sound Christian doctrine. The primary locus for Christian doctrine is the reading of scripture and the exposition of scripture in the context of worship with sermons and homilies. But the secondary locus, social location of Christian doctrine, is these meetings of bishops as they confer with each other about who they're in communion with. Is that bishop over there, this town over ten miles from my town, is his church really in communion with my church? Is he teaching the sound faith? Well the bishops get together, and they make decisions about that.

One of the things that happens is that there had been another form of authority in the early church, prophets. We hear about women who are prophets. We hear about traveling prophets. We hear, for instance, about a prophet in the Church of Antioch. We hear the Church of Antioch had prophets. And we hear that the Holy Spirit spoke to the Antioch Church while they were gathered for worship and said "Set apart for me Barnabus and Saul for the work to which I called them." The Holy Spirit basically appoints Barnabus and Saul to be missionaries. How does he do this? Almost undoubtedly by speaking through one of the prophets. And thus, in the early church's creed, you have the Holy Spirit speaking to the prophets.

So the prophets had a great deal of authority in the early church. But eventually the fundamental authority for the teaching of the church was the official office of bishop. Prophecy ended up fading out and, at one point, was explicitly rejected because, in the 2nd and 3rd centuries, there arose another heretical group called the Montanists. They, of course, didn't think of themselves as heretical. They proposed a new prophecy. So Montanus was a prophet. He claimed to be the Paraclete, the Holy Spirit. The Holy Spirit spoke through him. He had two women followers who were also prophets. And again, there were clearly women prophets in the churches. We have evidence from that in the New Testament.

And they were proposing new rules and regulations for Christian life and asceticism and sort of strict moral guidelines, stricter than the Great Church, stricter than this larger church, the "Great Church" meaning the universal church. And the Great Church, the bishops of the Great Church, essentially rejected this and said, look, no, we're not going to have new doctrines proposed by prophets anymore. We're going to stick to the apostolic teaching. And it's the bishops' job to preserve the apostolic teaching by conferring with each other and being in communion with each other. And that conservative mechanism of teaching ended up excluding new prophecies in the name of the Holy Spirit. That's a very important development in the history of Christian thought. Prophets pop up now and then, but they never have anything like apostolic authority and are never accepted as such in orthodox Christianity.

To preserve the apostolic faith—let me mention we do have some early texts that aim at preserving the apostolic faith, the apostolic tradition. They are called "rules of faith." Again, the notion of a rule is here. Let me give you one of these rules of faith from a Christian writer. He's presenting what he takes to be the common faith of the whole church, the Catholic faith. He calls it the rule of faith. This is Tertullian, an ancient church father.

> The Rule of Faith is completely one and only,
> unchangeable and unimprovable [he says], which is to believe
> In One God, the Almighty, the maker of the world,
> his son Jesus Christ, who was born of the Virgin Mary … crucified under Pontius Pilate
> on the third day he was revived from the dead
> received into heaven
> sitting now at the right hand of the Father
> coming to judge the living and the dead
> through the resurrection of the flesh.

These rules of faith intended to affirm God the Father as the God of the Jews who's the Father of Christ, then a brief narration of Jesus Christ, often then concluding with something about the Holy Spirit, as well. These developed into what were later called creeds. And we'll talk about creeds in a later lecture. The crucial thing to get is we've got this trinitarian structure, Father, Son, and Spirit in these rules of faith. They develop into a trinitarian creed as we'll see. And this becomes the basis of later Christian writing. We don't really have a lot of theological writing in the early centuries of the church. We have writings against pagans, writings against Jews, writings against heretics, but no systematic theology. But the theology develops in response to these other pressures.

The theologians who develop these theologies in response to say pagans, Jews, heretics, are called by the name, "church fathers." So pretty much parallel to the Jewish rabbis of the time, who are developing the rabbinic Judaism of the Talmud, are the church fathers developing the earliest forms of Christian theology as they work through this sorting out process of Christian doctrine, which leads eventually to the crucial official doctrines of Trinity and Incarnation and Grace, which we will head to and get to discuss in a later lecture.

Lecture Eight
Christian Reading

Scope:

Christian reading begins with the New Testament writers reading the scriptures of Israel as bearing witness to Jesus Christ. Characteristic of the Great Church is the determination to continue reading these scriptures (which Christians later came to call the Old Testament) as authoritative even for Gentile Christians, despite the fact it is the history of the Jews and many of its laws do not apply to Gentiles. One key strategy for such reading is typology, in which people and events of the Old Testament prefigure those of the New Testament. Another key strategy is allegory, in which the text has another meaning in addition to its literal sense, one which points beyond historical events to eternal truth.

Outline

I. Convictions about the relation of Christian faith to the scriptures of Israel are fundamental to early Christian reading, its practices, and problems.

  A. Rejecting the Gnostic belief that the God of the Jews was evil or ignorant, the Great Church had committed itself to shaping its worship and teaching in accord with the scriptures of Israel.

  B. The scriptures can be divided into books of law and books of prophets. Gentile Christians were much more at home with the prophetic writings.

  C. But how are Gentile Christians to understand the Law of Moses, which they are committed to read as their own scriptures but not to put fully into practice?

  D. Joined with some philosophical convictions that the church's theologians came to adopt, these problems led them to reading that was often more spiritual than literal. As Paul says, "The letter kills. The Spirit gives life."

II. From the beginning, Christians read the scriptures of Israel as prophetic witness to Jesus Christ.
  A. An example is Psalm 22, which begins, "My God, My God, why have you forsaken me?"
    1. Perhaps the crucial disagreement was the Christian conviction of a Messiah that suffers.
    2. Early Christians argued with Jews about whether Scriptural passages such as these were actually predictions of Jesus's suffering.
  B. More fundamentally, the scriptures were read as explaining Jesus's identity.
    1. Psalm 110 says "the LORD says to my Lord" (that is, Christ) is to sit at his right hand.
    2. Daniel 7:13 describes the Son of Man (that is, Christ) as coming on the clouds of heaven.

III. A central form of Christian understanding of scripture from the beginning is typology.
  A. The term comes from the Greek word *typos* or type, often translated into Latin as *figura* or figure.
  B. Typology means figurative reading, which sees one person or event as prefiguring another.
  C. An Old Testament type was matched with a New Testament "anti-type" or counter-figure as, for instance, when Moses prefigures Jesus as prophet, or David prefigures Jesus as Messiah.
  D. Typology is an inevitable feature of Christian reading of the Old Testament.
    1. If Jesus is the Christ, he is the fulfillment of the Messianic promises made to David. And David and all the good kings of Israel are types of Christ.
    2. If Jesus is the Christ, he is the greatest of the prophets, and all the prophets of Israel are types of Christ.
    3. If Jesus is the Christ, then his Body, the Church, is a renewed Israel.
    4. If Jesus's death has power to save, it is because it was a sacrifice for sin, and his blood made atonement, fulfilling the meaning of the sacrifices of the Law of Moses.

           5. If Jesus's death has power to save, it is because he is the true Lamb of Passover.
   E. Some typologies are less inevitable but are still a deep part of the New Testament.
      1. Christ's body becomes the true temple, the holy place of divine presence (John 2:21).
      2. Christ's flesh is the manna of everlasting life, bread from heaven (John 6:30-58).
      3. When he feeds the multitude, he is the Good Shepherd of Psalm 23.
      4. When Moses gets water from a rock, "that rock was Christ" (1 Cor. 10:4).
   F. Other typologies developed after the New Testament.
      1. The passage through the Red Sea is a type or figure of baptism.
      2. Noah's ark prefigures the wood of the cross.
   G. Typology has a complex relation to the literal sense of scripture.
      1. In typology it is not words so much as persons and events that have a figurative meaning.
      2. Typology is a form of reading used not only by the New Testament writers, but also within the Old Testament itself, as when Jacob prefigures the people of Israel.
IV. Scholars often make a distinction between allegory and typology.
   A. Allegorical reading originates among pagan philosophers.
      1. Making Apollo an allegory symbolic of the sun was one way to do away with embarrassing anthropomorphisms in pagan myths.
      2. Allegory was practiced on a vast scale by Philo of Alexandria, a Jewish philosopher who used it to interpret the scriptures in philosophical terms.
      3. A mark of pure allegory is that it is "vertical," concerned with the relation of the soul to higher things, as opposed to the "horizontal" or historical connections with which typology is concerned.
      4. Early Christian use of allegory was sometimes extravagant, but seldom pure: The figure of Christ keeps intruding.

5. This "impure" allegory often mixes with typology, as can be seen in Origen's writings.
 B. Allegory was useful as a way of interpreting difficult passages or laws which Christians did not observe.
  1. For instance, why do animals fit for food need to be cloven-footed and chew the cud?
  2. The wars and massacres of ancient Israel were taken to be spiritual warfare against demons or one's own sins and vices.
  3. The wrath of God did not mean that he got upset but that he punished sin.
 C. Most notoriously, Origen developed the "criterion of absurdity": Where the literal sense of the scriptures is impossible, immoral, or absurd, a spiritual reading is required.

Suggested Reading:

Martyr, "Dialog with Trypho" in *Ante-Nicene Fathers*, vol. 1.

O'Keefe and Reno, *Sanctified Vision*.

Origen, "On First Principles: Book 4" in *Origen*, edited by Greer.

———, "Prologue to the Commentary on Song of Songs" in *Origen*, edited by Greer.

Questions to Consider:

1. Why did early Christians not regard a purely literal reading of scripture as adequate?
2. Why did early Christians think that allegory was a legitimate form of reading?

Lecture Eight—Transcript
Christian Reading

In this lecture, we continue our series of treatments of early Christian theology after the New Testament. We're going to look now at Christian reading. Christian reading is an interesting topic because there's an interesting problem that the early Christian church has. The Great Church, that catholic or universal church, was spread throughout the world. This bunch of churches "in communion" with each other rejected these Gnostic sects or "heresies" that are anti-Jewish. They think that the Jewish God is evil. The Great Church is now largely Gentile. They affirm the goodness of the God of the Jews, that he's the God and Father of our Lord Jesus Christ. Therefore, as Gentile believers, they are worshiping the Jewish God. And they are worshiping a Jewish Messiah. They read the Jewish scriptures, now called the Old Testament as their own scriptures—Jewish scriptures for Gentile believers.

That's a problem. It's also, I think, we have to be aware, that this is really pretty astonishing. We take it for granted that most Christians are Gentiles nowadays. But that's an astonishing development. You see, that's what creates these problems. Here are these Gentiles looking back at the Jewish scriptures where God makes promises to his people of Israel and warns them and threatens them and punishes them and comforts them, all these. This is a deep relationship between the God of Israel and his people. And Gentiles insert themselves into this story as if they're God's people, too, because of their faith in Christ, which is, again, that was Paul's key point. Gentiles by having faith in Christ become believers incorporated into the story of Israel and Israel's God.

So, the promises that the God of Israel makes to his people become promises to Christians, even if they're Gentiles through faith in Christ. But that means that these Gentile Christians have got to figure out how to read these Jewish scriptures. And that includes, by the way, the New Testament, which in one sense are Jewish scriptures because they're scriptures written all by Jews. So the whole Bible, through and through, the Old Testament and New Testament, is a Jewish production. And here are these Gentile Christians reading it as their own scriptures. How can they do this? Well, there's a lot of problems to face and a lot of interesting issues to raise.

Biblical scholars love to talk about what's called hermeneutics, which is a theory of interpretation. And that's one of the issues we'll sort of be circumnavigating around in this lecture. But I want to focus primarily on the practice rather than the theory of reading. We'll say a little bit about the theory, but the practice is really what matters. Christians had to practice reading. That's why I'm going to focus on the notion of reading rather than the notion of interpretation.

How do Gentile Christians read the Jewish scriptures? Well, let's start with a typical way of dividing up the Jewish scriptures. You can speak of law and prophets. Now, the law is the Law of Moses. The prophets include people like Isaiah, Jeremiah, much of the bulk of the Old Testament. Christians felt more on sort of firm ground with the prophets than with the law. The prophets they read as predicting the coming of Christ, predicting the Messiah. The psalms also they read as prophecies of Christ. So prophecy the Christians really liked. They thought they knew what to do with that part of the Hebrew scriptures. The law, law was more difficult.

Typically and fairly early on, the church divided the Mosaic law into two parts, moral law and ceremonial law, the moral law being things like the Ten Commandments. "Thou shalt not kill. Love your neighbor as yourself." By the way, that's part of the Jewish law. "Love the Lord your God with your whole heart, mind, and strength." That's part of the Jewish law. And Jesus repeated it, and Christians believed it. That part was not a problem. But the ceremonial law, that's more difficult, with all these sacrifices, dietary laws, circumcision. Remember Paul had said Gentiles don't have to get circumcised in order to be Christian believers. So the Jewish ceremonial law is not applied literally to Gentiles. And yet it's still part of the scriptures which the Gentile Christians honor as God's word.

They read these scriptures but don't apply them literally. As a result, a whole lot of early Christian reading of scripture pushes in a non-literal direction, pushes away from literalism. The motto for this push away from literalism is a passage in the second letter to Corinthians by Paul that goes, "The letter kills. The Spirit gives life." The letter, the *litera*. All right. literal comes from the Latin word for letter. So the literal, the letter, kills. The Spirit gives life. So the non-literal reading that many Christians practiced and many Christian churches practiced was called a spiritual reading.

Let me say a little bit about literalism, because it seems to me there is two possible crude mistakes to make about literalism. On the one hand, you can talk as if every literalist is some kind of ignoramus, some Fundamentalist ignoramus or something. Well, OK, literalism is not the same thing as ignorance. The church retains a commitment to the literal truth of the narratives of scripture and so on. The early church read the scriptures literally in the sense of saying, well, these things really happened.

On the other hand, one shouldn't make the mistake of thinking that you have to take a text literally in order to take it seriously, as one church father argued. If you take it literally when Genesis says that God walked in the Garden of Eden in the cool of the evening, if you take that literally, you're not taking the text seriously. God doesn't literally walk in gardens in the cool of the evening. That's not a serious way of reading the text and learning what it has to say. So taking the text literally is sometimes a way of not taking it seriously. So don't confuse literal reading with serious reading, especially not for early Christians.

Let's say a little bit about how Christians read the Jewish scriptures in detail. Let's think about some prophecies. And, again, the psalms are often a very crucial form of prophecy for the Christians. Psalm 22, for instance, is a famous one. Psalm 22 in the Jewish scriptures begins like this, "My God, My God, why have you forsaken me." That's a very familiar passage for Christians because in the Gospels, Jesus utters this phrase on the cross. Evidently he was praying the psalm on the cross, or at least he remembered this particular line. "My God, My God, why have you forsaken me?" And the psalm goes on: "Why are you so far from saving me from the words of my groaning? ... For dogs encompass me; a company of evildoers encircle me; They have pierced my hands and my feet." Christians love that bit. "I can count all my bones. ... They divide my garments among them and for my clothing they cast lots."

That's an episode that's narrated in the Gospels. So Christians just love this bit. And then they argued with non-Christian Jews about this, for instance, the line about "they have pierced my hands and my feet." Some Hebrew manuscripts and the Greek and the Syriac versions of the Hebrew scriptures, the Jewish scriptures have that line about piercing hands and feet. Most of the Hebrew manuscripts of the Jewish scriptures have the line reading something like, "like a lion at my hands and feet," picking up the imagery of the dog. So, remember, the dogs surround me. Lions are at my hands and feet. And most Jewish readers say these Christians have got it wrong. The right text doesn't talk about piercing hands and feet. And so Christians and Jews would argue about this. And this argument with the Jews about the meaning of the Jewish scriptures is a typical feature of early Christian reading of the scriptures. They can argue about whether the Jewish scriptures really do predict the coming of Jesus.

Probably the crucial point of argument between Jews and Christians about the prophecies is about the notion of a Messiah that suffers. For, of course, Jewish non-Christian readings of the Jewish scriptures did believe that there were prophecies of a Messiah in the Jewish scriptures. But prophecies of a Messiah whose going to get crucified? That's where most Jewish readers got off the boat. And of course Gentile Christians insist, oh yes, a crucified, suffering Messiah. This form of Christian reading is traced back in the Gospels all the way to Jesus himself in his appearances after his resurrection. There's a story in the Gospel of Luke about how he opened the minds of his disciples, says the text. "He opened the mind of his disciples to understand the scriptures." And he says to them, here's the Gospel of Luke again. "Thus it is written that the Christ, the Messiah, should suffer and on the third day rise from the dead and that repentance and forgiveness of sins should be preached in his name to all nations," that is to the Gentiles, "beginning from Jerusalem."

So Christians traced this reading of the Jewish prophets as prophesying a suffering Messiah. They traced this form of reading back to Jesus himself. It's Jesus himself raised from the dead who teaches Christians how to read the Jewish scriptures properly as prophecies of a suffering Messiah.

We are used to thinking of prophecy as a kind of prediction. And certainly there were early Christians who read the Jewish prophets as predicting Christ. But that's probably not the best way to bring into focus what these prophets are doing for Christian readers. Most fundamentally, what the prophets provide for early Christian readers is something like the back-story of the identity of Jesus. The prophecies help Christian readers understand who Jesus is. Jesus is the man who says, "My God, My God, why have you forsaken me." He's the fulfillment of that psalm, that psalm is about Jesus, whether it's a prediction or not. I mean, after all, is it a prediction Jesus would say this on the cross? Does that make it a prediction? Anyone can say these words. Does that make it a prediction?

The thing to do is to set aside the notion of whether this proves that Jesus is the Messiah and just focus on how it helped Christians understand who Jesus is. That I think was the primary function of Christian readings of ancient Jewish prophecy. It's about the identity of Jesus. So, for instance, you have what is the most important Old Testament text for the Christian church in the early centuries. Psalm 110—here's how it goes: "The LORD," this is the name of the God of Israel, "says to my Lord," this is *Adonai*, not the name of the God of Israel, "sit at my right hand, until I make your enemies your footstool."

There's that picture that's fundamental for early Christian theology, Jesus, as Lord, sitting at the right hand of the Lord God. "Sit at my right hand," says the psalm, "until I, God, make your enemies your footstool." The Lord has sworn and will not take it back saying, you are a priest forever.

Jesus, sitting at God's right hand is the priest, right there in the psalm. And of course, you see Christians read these psalms in church, chanted them in church just like Jewish synagogue worship. And of course when they read and chanted these psalms, they were applying them to Jesus. That liturgical setting is really the important thing to understand, not whether it's proving it or whether it proves that Jesus is the Messiah, but Christians using the Jewish scriptures to portray the identity of Jesus at God's right hand.

Likewise that passage in Daniel 7 where the Son of Man comes on the clouds is very frequently used in the Gospels. Jesus is the Son of Man coming on the clouds of heaven because, again, he's there with the ancient of days says Daniel 7, right here. And the Son of Man Jesus is on the clouds of heaven with the ancient of days in this picture from Daniel 7. So that tells you who he is. That's the primary function of prophecy for these Christian readers.

There's another very interesting feature of Christian reading of the Jewish scriptures, which I need to give a label to and discuss at some length. This label, I'll call "typology." This is a standard label for a way that Christians read the scriptures. Typology comes from the word *typos*, from which we get the word "type." The Latin translation of this Greek word is *figura*, from which we get the word figure. "Type" is originally the same word as "typewriter." Imagine an impression made by a type. So you have the type and then the impression of the type, which is called the "anti-type." You have the figure, and then you have the fulfillment of the figure. You have a type in the Old Testament say, King David, and then you have the fulfillment of that type, the anti-type as it's called, which is Jesus.

So you have the type, the anti-type, the original version of it, and then its impression. But actually the anti-type, it turns out, is the most real thing. So it's as if the impression that the type makes is what it's all about. The type, Kind David, helps you understand who Jesus is. He's important because he helps you understand the identity of Christ. But all these types or figures in the Old Testament prefigure Jesus. So typological reading is a way of looking back in the Old Testament for prefigurations of Jesus, like David, the King of the Jews, like the prophets, like Moses, who also is a type of Jesus as a prophet and a priest.

This typology is, I think, virtually an inevitable feature of Christian readings of the Old Testament. If Christianity is true, if Jesus really is the Christ, then he's going to be the fulfillment of the Messianic promises to David, and things said about King David will be true of Christ. For instance, in Psalm 72, we hear this, "Give the king your justice, O God, and your righteousness to the king's son! May he judge your peoples with righteousness, and your poor with justice!" You can imagine Christians reading this in church, and they're thinking about Jesus, "May he endure as long as the sun and as long as the moon throughout all generations." And Christian readers would come to their Jewish counterparts and say, look, the Messiah lives forever. That's Jesus.

So once again, a psalm which any Jewish reader would say is about King David, Christians say it was about Jesus. It's also about King David, but primarily pointing forward to Jesus. How could Christians possibly read a psalm like this and not think about Jesus? So typology, as I suggest, this prefiguring of Jesus, is something inevitable that Christians will find in the Old Testament scriptures if they believe in Christ at all. If Jesus is the Christ, he's the fulfillment of the Messianic promises to David. He's the greatest of the prophets. And all the prophets of Israel are, in that sense, prefigurations, types of Christ.

Christ's Sermon on the Mount is meant to remind us of Moses on Mount Sinai. Moses gives a law from Sinai. Christ brings the Gospel in his sermon on the Mount. His transfiguration happens on a mountain to remind us of Moses going up to the Mount to see God. His miracles of healing, it turns out, resemble the miracles made by Elijah and Elisha who were Northern prophets in about the same place of where Jesus was working in Galilee. Likewise, if Jesus is the Christ, then the Church, his Body, his community, is going to be the fulfillment of the identity of Israel. Things said about Israel in the Old Testament will be true of the church. Promises made to Israel will be promises made to the church.

This typology reading also ends up becoming the key to interpreting the ceremonial law. Gentile Christians are not going to observe the ceremonial law. What they will do is they'll read the passages about the sacrifices under the Mosaic law and say, ah, these sacrifices which make atonement are about Christ, who offered himself as a sacrifice on the cross. And his blood made atonement for us the way the blood of the sacrifices under Mosaic law made atonement and cleansed the altar of the sin of the people.

Likewise, if Christians seriously believe that Jesus's death has the power to save, then inevitably they're going to think of him as something like the true Passover lamb. And, of course, this imagery of Jesus as the Lamb of God is throughout the New Testament, pretty much inevitable. He's the paschal lamb. He's the Passover lamb. He was slaughtered on Passover. And his blood drives away evil and death just like the blood of the Passover lamb was put on the lintels of the doors of the Jewish people that kept them safe from the plague against the firstborn in Egypt. And like the Passover lamb, his bones are not broken on the cross. This is a passage in the Gospel of John. So, this kind of identifying Jesus with these precursors or prefigurations in the Old Testament is virtually inevitable.

Some of the typologies are less inevitable but are still a deep part of the Christian tradition. For instance, Christ identifies his body with the temple. There's a passage in John where Jesus says, "Destroy this temple and in three days I will raise it up," and people didn't understand. He was talking about his body, "Destroy this temple, my body" and in three days he will be risen from the dead. Jesus's body is like the place of worship, the place where Christians come to find the presence of God, the true temple.

Likewise, we've heard about Jesus's flesh being the bread of life, like the true manna from heaven. That's from the Gospel of John. We hear Jesus being the Good Shepherd. Christians can't read, "The LORD is my shepherd; I shall not want," Psalm 23, without thinking of Jesus as the Good Shepherd. How could they possibly be sitting there worshiping Christ and hearing about the Lord is my shepherd and not think of the Lord Jesus.

And likewise, there's a fascinating passage in the first letter to the Corinthians by Paul where he talks about the rock where Moses got water from. As the Israelites were wandering in the desert, Moses struck a rock with his staff and water came from the rock. And Paul says "that rock was Christ." Now, there's typology for you. The rock prefigures Christ, the rock of our salvation from which flows the water of life; that's typology. What I'm getting at is some of these typologies are rooted already in the New Testament. There are some typologies that come about later, not directly New Testament typology. For instance, the Red Sea is a type or prefiguring of baptism. When the Jews go through the Red Sea and escape from Pharaoh, that's like Christians going through baptism and coming out of the water as a new people, as a new nation. A favorite post-New Testament typology is Noah's ark. The wood of the ark prefigures the wood of the cross. Christian writers love that. That's not in the New Testament itself, but you could see why they would love it.

Now, some of the typologies can get fairly fanciful. It was clear the Old Testament writers writing about Noah's ark were not thinking directly about the cross. But all of them are based in some way on the literal sense of the text. The typologies do not abolish the literal meaning of the text because, in fact, the prefigurations of Christ are typically not words, but persons. The story of David prefigures Christ because David, himself, the person David, King David, prefigures Christ. So, the typology's actually built on the narrative which early Christians typically took quite literally. The story of

David was literally true. It literally happened. David is a real person. And he also is a prefiguring Christ.

So typology is a form of figurative meaning where what has figurative meaning in typology is not so much the words as the persons. David has a figurative meaning. Moses has a figurative meaning, even though they are both literal historical people in early Christian reading. So, typology is consistent with, coherent with, taking the narrative literally as well.

Another thing about typology that's, I think, very important is that typology is deeply woven into the way the Scriptural text works already in the Jewish scriptures. Take the book of Genesis for instance. Genesis has often been called the Old Testament of the Old Testament. It's the Old Testament of the Jewish scriptures because it's the ancient past. Figures in Genesis often prefigure later figures in Israel. Jacob, for instance, who is renamed Israel, becomes a figure of the people of Israel. Abraham prefigures the people of Israel. He goes down into Egypt. He comes back out of Egypt. He prefigures the Exodus. The figure of Judah, one of the sons of Jacob, one of the 12 sons of Israel, who become the ancestors of the 12 tribes of Israel—Judah is the ancestor of King David, and what happens to Judah in the book of Genesis prefigures King David. Typology is already there in the Hebrew scriptures. It's not something that the New Testament imposes on the Hebrew scriptures in an alien or external fashion. I think it's a continuation of the way the Hebrew scriptures already read themselves.

More controversial, I think, is another form of Christian reading called "allegory." As I say, typology's inevitable for Christian readers. No matter how literalist you are, you're going to read some things in the Old Testament scriptures typologically. The most literal Fundamentalist in the world is going to read King David as a type prefiguring Christ. But allegory is a bit different.

Allegory is a form of reading that developed originally with pagan philosophers. For instance, remember, if you think of yourself as a pagan philosopher participating in pagan worship and not taking this stuff literally, what do you do? One thing you can do is interpret these pagan gods as symbols of things like Apollo. Apollo is the symbol of the sun, and Saturn is a symbol of the sky. Poseidon is a symbol of the sea, and so on and so forth. So you can interpret these pagan myths as symbolizing something else. That's what allegory is.

It literally means something like others speaking. You're speaking about the sea when you speak about Poseidon. You're speaking about the sun when you speak about Apollo. You're speaking other than literally.

Allegory is always non-literal. It was developed by pagan philosophers. It gets into the Judeo-Christian tradition through a Jewish Platonist philosopher named Philo of Alexandria, a man born about 20 years before Jesus was born, died about 20 years after Jesus died. So [he lived] roughly the same time as Jesus. But with a longer lifespan, he lived to an old age, unlike Jesus.

Philo of Alexandria is a Jewish Platonist philosopher who reads the Jewish scriptures allegorically. Now, allegory, let me suggest, is different from typology because it's fundamentally "vertical." Let me say typology is "horizontal" in the sense that it's about binding together things in history, past and present. King David in the past, Jesus in the present because Jesus is alive, not dead. Jesus is never in the past for Christians. So with King David in the past and Jesus in the present, typology is this horizontal historical relationship.

Allegory tends to be vertical. Allegory tends to symbolize higher things, the souls relation to higher things. So that allegories of the gods might be symbolizing the soul's relationship to higher truths. Sometimes it symbolizes the soul's relationship to virtue or wisdom or learning. The people who practiced allegory, like Philo of Alexandria, like the pagan philosophers, were very typically learned men who wanted to see reflections of their own learning and education in these difficult, hard-to-understand texts. When you're a learned man reading these ancient Jewish texts and not quite understanding what's going on—for example, God wants Abraham to slay his son. What's going on there? David's involved in all these wars. I want him to be a virtuous man, not a man of blood. How do I interpret this as a learned man, a scholar, of the ancient world? Well, you'll often take, if you're a scholar like Philo of Alexandria, you'll take Abraham as symbolic of certain kinds of virtues. Isaac symbolizes certain virtues. Jacob symbolizes other virtues.

And in Alexandria, a few centuries later, a Christian teacher named Origen picks up the allegorical tradition of interpretation. And what ends up happening is allegory never quite becomes pure allegory in Christianity. There's this vertical element, but then it gets mixed with a horizontal element.

Let me illustrate. Origen reads the Song of Songs, which is in the Hebrew scriptures. It's a love song. It seems to be quite a carnal love song. It seems to be about a bride and a bridegroom who want to get together and get to bed together and are longing and sighing for each other. And Origen says, well, wait a minute. That can't be the proper reading of this text. It's really about the soul's love for God.

Now, if he had stopped there, that would be pure allegory. The man's love for his bride is an allegory for the soul's love for God. Horizontal becomes vertical, the soul loving higher things. But then he proceeds; here's Origen again:

> This book of scripture then, speaks of this love with which the blessed soul burns and is on fire in regard to the Word of God. And she sings this wedding song through the Spirit, by which the Church is joined and united with its heavenly bridegroom, Christ.

What happens in Christian allegory is that Christ keeps getting into the picture, and the allegory becomes mixed up with typology. You get a lot of what we might call "impure" allegory, not purely vertical because for Christians everything ends up being about Christ.

So there's always typology in the area when Christians start doing allegory. Origen is a great example of that. He does a lot of allegory. He's famous for allegorical reading. But you look carefully, and a lot of these allegories turn out to be typologies. Some of this goes back all the way to the New Testament again. Think of allegories as inherently vertical. There's a very famous vertical allegory in the letter to the Hebrews in the New Testament, where there's a heavenly tabernacle, a heavenly temple.

The temple on Earth, the tabernacle on Earth, symbolizes a heavenly tabernacle. That's a very vertical allegory, but then what happens? Jesus, crucified, goes up to heaven, and he sprinkles his blood on the heavenly altar in the heavenly sanctuary. Jesus's literal physical human blood is up there in heaven in this spiritual temple. Instead of this spiritual, nonphysical thing, you've got physical blood in a spiritual heavenly temple. You view impure allegory at its most impure—allegory and typology, physical and spiritual mixed up together—because Christians are obsessed with Jesus.

Allegory was useful because it was a way of dealing with hard texts. Philo, for instance, when he got to the text about the dietary regulations, which he didn't quite know how to make sense of, said, well, there's this rule about what you can eat that has to both chew the cud and have cloven hooves. What does that mean? Chewing the cud means you ruminate over what you've learned. Chewing the cud, sort of chewing over the text because all early ancient readers would chew over the text by murmuring it, because they had to read aloud when they read the text. The cloven hoof means to divide and distinguish good from evil. That's pure allegory. It caught into the Christian tradition. Many Christian readers use it.

Take the wars and massacres in the ancient Jewish scriptures. Here's Israel fighting their enemies, sometimes even massacring their enemies. What does that mean? What does it mean for instance in the psalm which says, "Oh, daughter of Babylon blessed is he who takes your little ones and dashes them against a rock." "That means," says Augustan, one of the church fathers, "you must ruthlessly suppress and destroy your evil impulses while they're young, while they're small, before they grow big and strong."

That's the real meaning of it. It's a way of dealing with this difficult text. Allegory is used to deal with difficult text. Origen suggests that whenever you have a text that is absurd or immoral if read literally, then you should read it allegorically. That's called the "criterion of absurdity." It's often used by early Christian readers, especially by Origen, who's famous for allegorical reading.

The point of allegory—and I'll finish with this—the point of allegory is precisely not to reject the Old Testament, like the Gnostics or the Marcionites. It's to take hold or appropriate these Jewish scriptures, even though you may not be able to understand them on a literal level the way the ancient Jews did. Here's Origen again:

> You should not … blame or reject scripture when it appears too difficult or too obscure to understand or when it contains what either the beginner or the child or the weaker and feebler in his general understanding [that is, the non-scholar, what ordinary people] cannot use [or] does not think will bring him anything useful or saving.

Just because you're an ordinary person who doesn't quite get it, don't reject the Jewish scriptures. The learned people of the Church can give an allegorical reading so that we can still keep reading these Jewish scriptures as scriptures for the Christian Church. And that becomes a fundamental feature of Christian spiritual reading down through the ages, into the Middle Ages, and into much Christian exegeses and reading even today.

Lecture Nine
The Uses of Philosophy

Scope:

Ancient Christian writers' interaction with philosophy was deep and long-lasting. Agreeing with the philosophers' emphasis on reason, wisdom, and happiness, the church fathers adopted many themes of Stoic moralism as well as Platonist metaphysics, though not without critical modifications. When warning about the danger of the passions, they often sounded like Stoics, but did not accept Stoic materialism. And when insisting on the immortality of the soul and the contrast between body and soul, they often sounded like Platonists, though they eventually rejected the Platonist notion of the Fall of the soul into bodies. They thought the Platonists were right in teaching that the divine nature was beyond change and passion, a point which has become increasingly controversial in recent years.

Outline

I. Ancient philosophy was a form of spirituality that was often attractive to early Christian intellectuals.
   A. As the highpoint of ancient education, philosophy offered an understanding of human life and the world that no intellectual could simply reject or ignore—like science today.
   B. The main themes of ancient philosophy were wisdom and happiness.
      1. For ancient philosophers the term "happiness" designated the ultimate goal of human life; it meant something like "true success in life—whatever that is."
      2. The fundamental debate in ancient philosophy was about what happiness really is.
      3. Most ancient philosophers rejected the notion that happiness was a feeling, which is the hedonist position of the Epicureans.
      4. The most widely-accepted view of happiness among ancient philosophers, shared by Stoics, Platonists, and Aristotelians was that it consisted in a life of wisdom.

- **C.** Christians gave biblical answers to philosophical questions.
    1. What is happiness? Everlasting life.
    2. What is wisdom? The Wisdom of God is Jesus Christ, God's Word.
- **II.** The Stoics were the most influential moral philosophers of the ancient world.
    - **A.** They articulated in uncompromising form the ancient moralistic conviction that our passions are what lead us astray from virtue and wisdom.
        1. Ancient moralism saw passion, not selfishness, as the primary obstacle to virtue.
        2. Passion was a form of passivity, even pathology, that made us like beasts.
        3. A wise man is free from passions, and therefore endures suffering "stoically."
    - **B.** However, Stoics were materialists, thinking that both God and the soul were made of heavenly fire.
        1. Materialism means thinking that things are made up of some kind of stuff—the material out of which they are made.
        2. The basic material of the world were the four elements: earth, water, air, and fire—all physical things.
        3. The heavens are made of fire or perhaps a fiery breath, which is the stuff of which God and the soul are made.
        4. A nonmaterialist conception of God and the soul requires us to conceive of God and the soul not made up of stuff, and that's not easy to do.
- **III.** Platonism offered a metaphysics which could conceive of a nonmaterial kind of being for both God and the soul.
    - **A.** In addition to bodily things known by the senses (what we would now call "physical things"), there are intelligible and unchanging things.
        1. Intelligible things are unchanging divine Forms, essences, or truths, including mathematics but also the principles of virtue and ethics.
        2. Bodily or sensible things are formed as imperfect images or reflections of these unchanging Forms.
        3. The Forms are literally unimaginable, because they are not sensible but intelligible, known only by the intellect.

4. What makes the soul different from the body is its intellect, the capacity for an intellectual vision that sees the Forms.
- **B.** The body is not only different from the soul but inferior to it.
    1. Unlike other ancient philosophies, Platonism conceived of the soul as nonphysical, an entirely different kind of being from the body.
    2. The soul is not really at home in the body, but is imprisoned there until it is freed in death.
    3. The soul came into the prison of the body by falling from its heavenly vision of divine things.
    4. Although most souls end up being reincarnated again after death, really pure souls escape the body forever and return to heaven.
    5. Nonetheless, the visible world itself is good, a moving image of divine, eternal beauty.
- **C.** The divine is eternal, beyond passion and change.
    1. The concept of an eternity that is not merely everlasting but unchanging and outside the world of time change is Platonist.
    2. For Platonism, God is an eternal impersonal Mind contemplating eternal truths within itself.
    3. As the timeless source of all being, God does not change and therefore does not have passions or emotions.

IV. Platonist concepts of God and the soul have been deeply influential but also problematic in Christian theology.
- **A.** After some initial hesitation, Christian theology almost unanimously accepted the Platonist concept of the immortality of the soul.
    1. Many early Christian theologians rejected the idea that the soul was by nature immortal, since this suggested the soul did not need to receive everlasting life as a gift from God.
    2. Once immortality of the soul was accepted, the Platonist picture of a disembodied soul going to heaven became widespread in Christianity.

B. The related concept of the Fall of souls into bodies was eventually rejected.
   1. The great 3rd-century theologian Origen proposed, as a speculative hypothesis, that souls fell into bodies because of their sin or imperfection.
   2. These Origenist teachings were eventually condemned by the church, though many current theologians now defend Origen.

C. The concept of God as timelessly eternal and therefore immutable and impassible, though no longer very popular, was universally accepted by orthodox Christian theologians by the 4th century.
   1. Biblical portrayals of God as angry or moved by compassion were read spiritually as describing the just and merciful actions of God.
   2. The deep problem raised by the doctrine of impassibility was how God can be incarnate, suffer, and die.

Suggested Reading:

Augustine, *City of God*, bks. 8, 11, and 12.

Origen, "On First Principles: Book 4" in *Origen*, edited by Greer.

Stead, *Philosophy in Christian Antiquity*.

Questions to Consider:

1. Setting aside modern prejudices, might there be reason to be suspicious of the passions?
2. Setting aside modern prejudices, might there be reason to believe that God is beyond passion and change?

Lecture Nine—Transcript
The Uses of Philosophy

We are continuing in our series of lectures on early Christian theology after the New Testament as part of our course on the whole history of Christian theology, and now I want to turn to the relation of early Christian theology to philosophy, which was both positive and critical.

So understand why ancient philosophy was an important issue for Christians, and also an attractive thing for Christians. You have to think about a kind of fundamental tension that we've already tasted a bit of in earlier lectures that Christian theologians had a tension between, on the one hand, their commitment to their Jewish roots, Gentile Christians with Jewish roots as we've been discussing several times in earlier lectures. That's the one side.

On the other side, there's this attraction to a kind of higher spirituality. In our previous lecture, I associated that with pure allegory, the vertical, the soul's desire for higher things. If you had nothing but pure allegory and higher spirituality in Christianity, you'd be a Gnostic, one of these otherworldly people who want to get away from the physical world and become entirely spiritual. But that means rejecting the Jewish roots of Christianity. So, Gentile Christians in the early Church are hanging on to their Jewish roots. But they're also profoundly attracted to higher spirituality, to a spiritual rather than literal reading of the scriptures.

The thing to think about now is where this spiritual attractiveness or the attractiveness of spirituality comes from. And the fundamental place that this attraction of spirituality comes from, it turns out, is philosophy. Ancient philosophy is a very spiritual business in most of its forms. Ancient philosophy tends to be very religious, not anti-religious. It tends to be skeptical of pagan mythology, but very interested in deeper and higher truths hiding behind the mythology.

So ancient philosophy—even when sometimes the ancient philosophers were sometimes critical of Christianity—was always religious. Ancient philosophers who were critical of Christianity thought that they had a better spirituality than the Christians did. They often blamed the Christians for being too carnal, just like the Jews. So philosophy was not anti-religious, it was spiritually attractive. That was actually part of the danger of the thing. If you get too spiritually attracted to philosophy, you're going to end up being a Gnostic.

On the other hand, the spiritual attractiveness of philosophy isn't really optional for the early Christians. It turns out philosophy in the ancient world, was integral to the education of any learned educated person, sort of like science is today. If you're an educated person in the world today, you may not be a scientist, you may even be intimidated by science, but you can't simply reject science as if it was all nonsense. Well, likewise in the ancient world, if you're an educated person, you can't simply reject philosophy. You have to know something about it. You have to deal with it somehow because it's the intellectually respectable stuff that everyone takes seriously. So Christian intellectuals, the kind of Christians who wrote books, cared about philosophy, and they were attracted to the spirituality of philosophy.

Let me say quite a bit in this lecture about how Christian intellectuals interacted with, used, and also critically dealt with philosophy. The key questions for ancient philosophy were about wisdom and happiness. The overarching question of all ancient philosophy is, "What is happiness?" Now, it's important to realize the word happiness is not quite the right word. It's an English word, of course, and we're talking now about Greek philosophy. The Greek word is *eudaimonia*. It doesn't mean exactly what we mean by "happiness." It means something like true success in life, the true fulfillment or true goal of life, whatever that might be. And the question is, indeed, what is it? What is the true goal of life? What is true success in life? Not just what makes you happy, but what is the true fulfillment and human success which makes a human life into a life well-worth living? What is the true goal at which human life is aimed? Or another way of putting it is what is it that we ought to be desiring for its own sake?

We desire money, but we desire money for the sake of getting something more than money, something better than money. We use money to buy stuff. Anybody who desires money for its own sake is crazy. They're a miser. They're a bad person. We want happiness. We use other things for the sake of getting to this true success in life, whatever it is. So happiness is what you want for its own sake. It's what everything else is for. It's, therefore, a way of talking about what we call nowadays the meaning of life. What is human life for? It's for this fulfillment called happiness.

And so the question, what is happiness, is the crucial question. And it can't be answered just by saying what makes you feel happy. For ancient philosophers, it was parallel to questions like "What is it that makes you healthy?" You might feel like eating lots of candy makes you healthy. You might possibly feel that way. It might even possibly make you feel good, but it's not healthy. The question about what is healthy for you is answered objectively in terms of the nature of your body.

Likewise, the question about what is happiness is an objective question. It's answered by considering the nature of the soul. There's a true fulfillment of the soul. And you can get it wrong. Just like you can be wrong about what's truly healthy, you can be wrong about what truly makes you happy. You can feel like it's making you happy and you can get it wrong, like a miser gathering lots and lots of money. He feels happy about that, but he's wrong about what happiness is. That's the ancient philosophical view.

The question what is happiness is the crucial debate in ancient philosophy. And it's not inevitable that happiness has to be identified with a feeling. We now tend to think of happiness as a feeling. The ancient philosophers didn't—except for some of them. Some of them thought that happiness was feeling good, and they were the hedonists. Hedonism comes from a Greek word meaning "pleasure," *hēdonē*. So hedonism is the view in ancient philosophy held by some ancient philosophers that happiness is a feeling, a good feeling, of course, a feeling of pleasure. So if happiness means feeling good, then pleasure is happiness, and if that's what you think, you're a hedonist. A great many ancient philosophers were not hedonists. The philosophers that Christians were attracted to were not hedonists. The philosophers that Christians were attracted to tended to identify happiness with wisdom. Happiness, true success in life, means a life of wisdom, of knowledge, and understanding. That's the real goal of human life, is to become a person of wisdom.

So Christians came along and they ended up giving biblical answers to philosophical questions. For instance, what is happiness, the crucial philosophical question? The Christian answer was everlasting life. That's a phrase from the Bible. It appears throughout the Gospel, especially the Gospel of John. It appears in the letters of

Paul, everlasting life. It never simply means life after death because people who go to hell do not have everlasting life. In the Bible, everlasting life is never used of people in hell, never used of people being punished. It's used for the word for the goal of human life What you want, ultimately, is everlasting life. And so that is, in fact, a good designation for the Christian answer to the question what is happiness? "For this is eternal life," or everlasting life, says Jesus in the Gospel of John, "that they may know you the only true God and Jesus Christ whom you have sent." Happiness is a kind of wisdom, to know God, to know Christ.

Happiness is everlasting life and it consists of a certain kind of wisdom, which is the Wisdom of God in Jesus Christ. To possess the Wisdom of God in Christ is to possess eternal life and happiness, or everlasting life, I think it would be better to say. I'll say why that is in a minute.

Christ himself is the wisdom which Christians seek. Paul calls him Christ, the power of God, and the Wisdom of God. Just as the Gospel of John identifies him as the Word, which is with God in the beginning, the Proverbs of the Old Testament have a chapter—chapter eight of Proverbs—which speaks of the Wisdom of God, which is there in the beginning. And early Christian writers unanimously identified that Wisdom with Christ. So Christ is the Word and the Wisdom of God. To know Christ is to know the Wisdom of God.

So that's the Christian answer to what happiness is. Happiness is knowing Christ, knowing the Wisdom of God. If philosophy wants wisdom, here's the highest wisdom of all, the Wisdom of God. And if happiness is to live a life of wisdom, then to have this Wisdom, Christ Jesus, is to have everlasting life. There's the Christian answer to the philosophical question.

They also, that is, Christians, also borrowed from philosophical ideas of their time. There's a deep interaction between Christianity and philosophy because Christians have some uses for philosophy. One thing that Christians used in ancient philosophy, it kind of became part of the ordinary thinking of Gentile Christians because it was part of the ordinary thinking of virtually all Gentiles in the ancient Roman world is the philosophy and the moralism of the Stoics.

The Stoics were the most influential moral philosophers of the ancient world. They were non-hedonists. They thought that happiness consists in wisdom, but they also thought that the road to wisdom, and the life of wisdom, especially, is a life of virtue free from passion. The Stoics, like all ancient philosophers, thought that the life of wisdom involved virtue, meaning traits of character-like courage, justice, kindness, honesty, et cetera, et cetera. There are virtues that every good person ought to have, and the wise man is a good person for the Stoics. But the Stoics went a little further. The Stoics said a person of virtue and wisdom will not be driven by passions.

Here's that word "passion" again. Remember, passion comes from a word in Latin, *passiō*, meaning suffering. Passions are what we suffer. That's an interesting phrase, an interesting notion. It's also there in the Greek term for "passion." Passions are what happen to us. The word "passion" comes from a word related to passivity, just as action comes from a word related to activity. Passions are not activities. It's an activity or an action when I raise my arm. It's a passion when I get upset because I don't just choose to get upset. I choose to raise my arm. I raise my arm. I'm responsible for that. That's my action and it's my freewill that raises my arm. Whereas when I get upset, when I get passionate, I am moved. I move my arm, but my emotions are moved in me. I am moved. That's why the very word emotion has the word motion in it. We are moved. We are passionate because we are affected by things outside us that move us, that set us in motion. And therefore, passion is not exactly free. Our free will is in our actions, not in our passions.

The Stoics want us to be responsible for our actions and not to be driven by passion. Ancient moralism focused on the problem of passion, the same way that modern moralism focuses on the problem of selfishness. Modern morality is all about not being selfish. That was not the problem in the ancient world. If somebody in the household steals a cookie from the cookie jar, in the modern world, we would say they're being selfish. In the ancient world they would say they're being passionate. They're being driven by their lusts and passions and desires. They need to discipline those passions.

The Stoics were the radical philosophers dealing with passion in the most radical way by saying, get rid of them. The wise person has no passions. A wise person gets rid of all passions and simply acts according to reason and not according to passion. This may sound awful in a modern context, but it's important to understand the ancient context here. A whole lot of modern morality is worried about the problem of becoming like a machine, whereas in ancient morality, you're worried about the problem of becoming like a beast because, of course, in the ancient world, there aren't a whole lot of machines around.

So the way to become inhuman in the ancient world is to become bestial, driven by your passions and desires without reason, the unreasoning beasts who have no reason, have no wisdom, driven by their passions and desires. So passion was a way of becoming inhuman and bestial, whereas in the modern world, we often want to be passionate because that reminds us that we're not machines. But that just wasn't a worry that ancient people had. They didn't have a lot of machines in their world. They had lots of beasts and they didn't want to be like that.

So the Stoics warned us against passion, and Christians tended to agree. Already in the New Testament you'll have passages which warn you against being driven by your passions. A good person, a virtuous person, is a person who lives according to reason, not according to passion, lives freely, acting, choosing responsibly, not getting upset all the time and driven by emotions.

Now the Stoics and their morality, their moralism, their concern with a life freed from passion, were very influential throughout the ancient world, not just among Christians. But there's a part of stoicism that didn't influence Christians much, or actually influenced them for a little while early on. And then Christians sort of said, we don't want that stuff. The Stoics, you see, were materialists. They thought that everything in the world was made out of stuff. Material means the stuff that things are made out of. We talk about the material of a shirt, that's the stuff the shirt is made out of.

Materialists think everything is made out of something. It makes sense, right? The material world is made out of the elements. There are four of them in ancient physics: earth, water, air, and fire. So think about this, air, fire, those are material things. Something doesn't have to be solid to be a material thing. Light, which is made out of the element of fire, is material. Light is physical. We study light in physics class even today. So light is a physical or material thing. If God is literally light, which the Stoics actually thought, if God is literally light then God is a material being.

Just because it's not solid doesn't mean it's not physical or material. Materialists were people who thought the whole world, including God, including the soul, were made out of material things like light and fire. The Stoics thought the soul was made out of a kind of a fiery breath, kind of a warm air, the breath we breathe, which we stop breathing when we die. So when our soul leaves our body this fiery warm breath leaves our body and goes actually back to God, who is the fire, the heavenly fire and light, which is ruling over the whole world.

The whole Stoic worldview is materialist. The soul is fire or air or fiery breath, depending on which Stoic you ask. God is made out of fire. There were actually some early Christians, like Tertullian, who agreed with Stoic materialists and said, yes, God is made out of heavenly fire, but that really isn't the ultimate direction of Christian thought. Christians did want to conceive of God in a nonmaterial way. But I'd like you to think about how hard that is to do. Try to imagine something that isn't made out of stuff, that has no material. It's not made out of stuff. How do you imagine something that's not made out of stuff? Another challenge related to this, how do you imagine something that doesn't take up space, because every material thing takes up space and indeed anything that takes up space is a material or physical thing. How do we imagine something that has real being and doesn't take up space? Well, you've got to be able to do that if you're going to be a nonmaterialist.

It's actually a fairly tricky thing to think of how you're going to be a nonmaterialist, how you can picture or conceive of a form of being that is not physical, not material, doesn't take up space, is not made up of stuff. Just try it. Try to conceive, seriously, of a nonphysical thing. It's actually very hard. But there was a group of philosophers who did it. They are called the Platonists, the philosophers who go back to the philosophy of Plato, the great Athenian philosopher.

Plato had a nonmaterialist philosophy. That is to say, Plato thought that there was a material world. It was made out of stuff, but there's also a kind of being, a kind of being that is not material. He called that kind of being intelligible being. This is related to the word intellect. And he contrasted it with "sensible being" which he related to the word "senses." The physical world, the material world, is the sensible world. We perceive it with our five senses, like light, which is a physical thing. Remember, you measure light in physics class. Light is perfectly physical, even if it's not solid. Light is perceived by our eyes, so it's physical, it's sensible in Plato's language, but there are intelligible things that are perceived only by the intellect.

Here's how you can imagine this. Or actually it's beyond imagination, but here's the clue to thinking about something that is nonmaterial. Think of yourself in a math class. You are learning, say, the Pythagorean proof, you're writing down the proof, and you're not getting it. You're trying to figure it out. I don't get this, and then all of a sudden as you're listening to the lecture, and you're trying to think it though, you say wait a minute, I get it, ah-ha! Now I see it. I see it. I get it. I see it. What is it you're seeing when you say, ah-ha now I see it? Your seeing is a form of what Plato will call intellectual vision, the seeing of the intellect, not of your senses, not of your bodily eyes, the seeing of your intellect. What you're seeing is an eternal, spiritually, we could say, nonmaterial truth. It's not made up of anything.

If you're thinking about the Pythagorean theorem, for instance, you're thinking about triangles, but not a triangle that you could draw on a chalkboard made up of chalk. You're thinking about a triangle that is eternal. It never came into being, never ceased to be, will always be there. The Pythagorean theorem will always be true. So these triangles that you say ah-ha! Now I see it! is a triangle that is not made up of stuff, not made up of chalk, not made up of anything. It is an eternal, and spiritual, we can even say divine truth. Plato calls this kind of thing intelligible. He speaks of intelligible forms or essences.

We can talk about intelligible Forms or essences that way and that language gets into Christianity. And he thinks of the physical world as made as it were in the image of these intelligible Forms. The intelligible Forms are not just abstractions. They are more real than "physical things," and the way I can prove it is, look, think about that chalk triangle that you have in your math class. How real is it? Well, how long is it going to last? How long will it have being? It's going to get erased tomorrow. It was drawn yesterday. The chalk triangle doesn't last. It doesn't have much being. But the triangle you see when you say ah-ha! Now I see it! in the Pythagorean theorem, well that triangle has always existed, always will exist. It's immortal. It is eternal. It has true being.

And all the triangles in this world that you can see with your senses, the sensible triangles, are made up of stuff They're temporary. They will eventually perish. They are sort of imitations, images, reflections of the true triangle, like a shadow that's a reflection of a real thing. The intelligible world, the world of intelligible form, is the real world. And it's nonmaterial. It's nonmaterial. Plato and the Platonists give Christians a way of thinking about the nonmaterial being of God, also, the nonmaterial being of the soul. Christians, like many other ancient thinkers were very interested in this nonmaterial picture of the soul because, think of this eye you have which is not the eye of your body when you say ah-ha! Now I see it! What vision is this you have? Intellectual vision, says Plato, the vision of the intellect. This is the highest point of the soul. The soul has the power of intellectual vision. The soul's vision shows that it is a different kind of being from the body. The body has material being. It's made up of stuff. It's sensible. You can touch it and feel it and see it. The soul, the intellect, is something you will never see, but it has the power of intellectual vision. It's more real than the body, not physical, but perfectly real, not located in space, doesn't take up space. It's not sensible, but more real than the body.

The Platonists give you a picture of soul and body that's often been called "dualism," which is a little bit misleading, this term because there's so many different kinds of dualism. So I'm not going to use that term. But the Platonists do give you this contrasting picture of two different kinds of being: body and soul. And most Christians were very attracted to this picture. On the other hand, the Platonists also were to call the body a prison for the soul, and that's language that influences Gnosticism. They speak of the soul as originating apart from the body. There's a story that Plato tells. It's a myth that Plato knows, a myth about the soul descending from heaven into bodies, falling even, from heaven into bodies, the Fall of the soul. Embodiment for Plato is a Fall of the soul; the soul sort of falls down from heaven where it originates into the body as a prison. To be in the body on earth is to be imprisoned. Again, that's the sort of thing that Gnostics were thinking about. Because a great deal of Gnosticism is actually derived from the Platonist philosophy.

Now you can see, if the soul originates from heaven and falls into bodies, where it wants to go, eventually, is back to heaven; so the picture of souls going to heaven when they die, good souls that is. A good soul eventually gets back to heaven where it originated from. That's from Plato. You will never see anywhere in the Bible a picture of a soul going to heaven to be rewarded. That's a picture from Plato, and it's rooted in this notion of the soul as a different kind of being from the body having a different origin. On the other hand, unlike the Gnostics, Plato does think that the physical world is good because it's an imitation of, an image of, a resemblance or likeness of, these eternal forms. So Plato and the later Platonist philosophers did say that the physical world is good. Not as good as the intelligible or spiritual world of forms, but nonetheless a good world. And so Plato would actually, in one of his dialogues, Plato talks about a creator God who looks at the forms and then forms the physical world in the image of the forms. So the physical world is a good place.

Some of Platonism influenced Gnosticism. Some of it was adopted by Christianity because Christians liked the idea that the physical world was a good idea. That is, orthodox Christians liked the idea that the physical world was a good place. Gnostics didn't. Gnostics picked up the theme of the body as a prison.

Platonism also did something very important in its picture of nonmaterial being. Platonism gave us the concept of eternity in the strict philosophical sense of the term. Eternity that is outside of time; eternity that is not temporal; eternity that is more than just everlasting. And that's why I kept on using the word everlasting life. Souls, if they have everlasting life or even resurrected bodies, if they have everlasting life, are going to still live in time. They're going to have life forever.

Eternity is a different concept. Eternity is the concept of that which is not influenced by time. In Platonism, think again, say, of the Pythagorean triangle that you study in math class. It never came into being. It never will cease to be. It will never change. It is not temporal in the sense of not part of time. It's eternal. Platonists conceived of God as an eternal mind filled with ideas which were all eternal, unchanging like this Pythagorean triangle. Eternal ideas in an eternal mind, that's God. God, like these intelligible forms that fill his mind, does not change. God also does not have passions.

And here's where Platonists in a sense agreed with Stoics and then took the Stoics one step further. Platonists said, yes, good people don't have passions. God does not have passions. God, unlike good people, can't have passions because he can't change. And if you can't change, then you can't get upset. You can't get passionate. You can't lose it. Platonists would never believe that God could get angry or compassionate. So one of the things that Christians have to do when they adopt Platonist thinking about God and most Christians, in fact, accepted the Platonist notion of divine eternity, God being eternal, changeless, outside of time. Well, what do you say about a God who can get upset as God evidently does in the Jewish scriptures. He gets mad. He loses it.

Most Christian thinkers said well that's not literally true. God doesn't literally lose his temper. That's not admirable to lose your temper, to lose it, to get upset, to say ah! God doesn't do that. God doesn't just lose it and lose his temper. His wrath is an allegorical or symbolic way of talking about his justice which is not passionate, not a way of losing it, but rather, of course, a way of punishing the wicked and rewarding the good. So, Christian church fathers, people like Augustine and Origen, when they read the Jewish scriptures, thinking about, say, the wrath of God, or, for that matter, the compassion of God, would say, well, this isn't really an emotion in God. It's not like God's heart or feelings change, but rather he executes his eternal plan in time by dealing out justice and by having mercy upon the afflicted.

His compassion is a way of talking about his action, not his passion, but his action of having mercy. And his wrath is a way of talking not about his passion, because he doesn't have passions, but rather his action of executing justice. Christians did, in fact, adopt a great deal of Platonism, because they were attracted to this nonmaterialist view. They adopted a nonmaterialist view of the soul including the view of the immortality of the soul, which is not one of the teachings of the New Testament, but as I suggested can be combined with the teaching of the New Testament.

They adopted the immortality of the soul. Although interestingly enough some of the earliest Christian writers explicitly rejected the immortality of the soul because they said look, eternal life, or rather, I should say everlasting life, is a gift. It's a gift of God. It's not natural to us. We're not born immortal. We are not naturally immortal. Immortality or everlasting life is a gift of God to those whom he raises from the dead. But that rejection of the immortality of the soul was an early view of some early Christian teachers. But most Christian teachers ended up changing their minds and saying, no, nope, immortality of the soul is a good idea because the soul is a different kind of being from the body.

The idea of the Fall of the soul ended up being rejected because it was developed, actually, by a Christian Platonist named Origen, Origen of Alexandria, the great allegorical reader that we ran into last time, in our last lecture. Origen taught that souls fell into bodies like the Platonists taught. That view was actually rejected by the church a couple centuries after Origen's death because it made the physical world into a prison, and it really didn't honor the goodness of the Creation enough. Origen himself, by the way, was not teaching this as official Christian doctrine, but as a hypothesis, as a speculation. Origen was loyal to the teaching of the church, and he was simply trying to work out ideas and saying, here's one possible explanation of souls and bodies. He wasn't teaching it as Christian doctrine. I think, actually many Christian theologians of our day say it's unfair to say that Origen's a heretic because of this. He wasn't trying to teach heresy, and a great many Catholic theologians especially will defend Origen on this. He got it wrong about the Fall of the soul, but he wasn't teaching heresy.

No Fall of the soul, but immortality of the soul. And, finally, there is the Christian insistence that you do have an impassable God. Once you get past the Stoic phase and people like Tertullian, who thought that God was a material thing and made up of stuff, out of heavenly fire, once you get past that materialist phase of some early church fathers, when you get into the 3rd, 4th, 5th centuries, all of the church fathers accepted the impassability, eternity, and changelessness of God. Impassability meaning he has no passions. He doesn't change. He doesn't get upset. He doesn't have emotions. He doesn't suffer. No *passiō*, not passions, suffering, emotion, no change in God, and that's an interesting thing for a Christian to adopt because then you have to combine it with the fact that there is such a thing as the passion of Christ, his suffering on the cross.

And that sets up the crucial developments which we're going to be talking about in our next lectures. How can Christians believe an impassable God, eternal, changeless, outside of time, who also suffers, and dies and has the passion of Christ on the cross? Can you believe both of this impassable God, the passion of Christ, who is God in the flesh? How are you going to do that? How are you going to pull that off? That's the challenge of the great Christian doctrines of the Trinity and the Incarnation, which we'll start talking about in our next set of lectures.

Lecture Ten
The Doctrine of the Trinity

Scope:

The Christian doctrine of the Trinity is about how the one true God is Father, Son, and Holy Spirit, even though these three (each of them God) are different from one another. The crucial argument that developed in the 4th century was whether the Son or *Logos*, the second person of the Trinity, was as fully God as God the Father. In answering yes, the Council of Nicaea in 325 laid the foundations of the orthodox trinitarian tradition. This tradition teaches that the oneness of God consists in a single divine essence or *ousia*, belonging equally and fully to all three, while the threeness is not three Gods but three hypostases or persons. Because all divine attributes (such as eternity, omniscience, etc.) belong equally to each, they can only be distinguished from another by their relations of origin (for example, the Father begets the Son, not vice versa).

Outline

I. The doctrine of the Trinity is the distinctively Christian conception of God.
    A. It is not about how God is three and one, but about how the one God is Father, Son, and Holy Spirit.
    B. Trinity and Incarnation are the two fundamental doctrines of Christian theology.
        1. Both arise because of the uniquely Christian insistence on the divine identity of Christ.
        2. Hence the doctrine of the Trinity does not often use the human name "Jesus" but rather speaks of his divine identity using the terms "Word" and "Son of God."
        3. Unlike the doctrine of Incarnation, the doctrine of the Trinity focuses strictly on the divinity of Christ, not his humanity.

C. As Augustine showed, the fundamental logic of the orthodox doctrine of the Trinity can be stated fairly simply, in seven statements.
   1. The first three statements about the Trinity are "the Father is God," "the Son is God," and "the Holy Spirit is God."
   2. Three more statements differentiating the Trinity are "the Father is not the Son," "the Son is not the Holy Spirit," and "the Holy Spirit is not the Father."
   3. Then to cap it off, the seventh statement says, "There is only one God."

II. Gentile Christian theologians found it most congenial to account for Christ's divinity in terms of the Word (*Logos*), the Reason or Wisdom or Mind of God, which caused problems.
   A. Early Christian "*Logos* theologians" could say the *Logos* was "another God."
   B. In pagan neo-Platonism, the *Logos* or divine Mind is a kind of intermediary between the Father, the Source of all being, and the visible world.
   C. As intermediary, the *Logos* is higher than the created world yet lower than the Father.

III. Orthodox, that is, Nicene, trinitarian theology arose in the course of the Arian controversy in the 4th century.
   A. The Arian controversy began with Arius, a presbyter in the church of Alexandria.
      1. Arius taught a radical form of subordinationism, in which the Word or *Logos* is one of God's creations—that is, a creature, not the Creator.
      2. The implication which horrified nearly everyone was that "there was once when he was not."
   B. The first ecumenical (worldwide) council of the church was convened in Nicaea in 325 to condemn the teaching of Arius.
      1. In a new strategy for formulating Christian doctrine, the council adapted a modified baptismal creed as a test of orthodoxy.
      2. To make sure Arius and his followers couldn't subscribe to this creed, they added a phrase saying the Son is *homoousios*, having "the same essence" as the Father.

3. Rather than being created from nothing, the *Logos* comes "from the essence of the Father."
4. Although the exact meaning of this key phrase is often disputed, it clearly has the implication that the Son is God in exactly the same sense that the Father is God.
5. Although Arius was soon widely rejected, many mainstream theologians found it difficult to accept the creed of Nicaea and its *homoousios* clause.

C. Athanasius, bishop of Alexandria, was the most prominent defender of Nicene theology in the first half of the 4th century.
   1. His key point was that the Son is not created but eternally begotten from the Father.
   2. His key argument is that the Father is eternally a Father, never without a Son.

D. As the 4th-century controversy unfolded, the concept of the divine essence or *ousia* was further developed.
   1. Because it is equally shared by Father, Son, and Holy Spirit, it comes to be called the divine essence rather than the Father's essence.
   2. The Father is the Source or First Principle of the Son, to whom he gives being by giving them the whole of the divine essence.
   3. The divine essence is not divided among the three, for it is not a material or stuff out of which they are made.
   4. Rather, it is characterized by its attributes: divinity, eternity, omnipotence, goodness, etc., all of which belong equally and wholly to Father, Son, and Spirit.

E. The controversy concluded with the second ecumenical council in 381 at Constantinople. The council approved an expanded and edited version of the Creed of Nicaea, which is now recited around the world and called the "Nicene Creed."

F. The Doctrine of the Holy Spirit developed on the basis of this Nicene theology.
   1. Later it was made explicit that the Holy Spirit, too, was of the same essence as the Father.
   2. The Holy Spirit, however, is not begotten but proceeds from the Father.

IV. Nicene theology had to face difficult conceptual questions about the threeness of the Trinity.
  A. Why not say there are three Gods?
      1. The short answer, of course, is that Christianity is committed to Jewish monotheism.
      2. It's not quite enough to say they share the same essence and attributes, because three human beings share the same (human) essence.
      3. Gregory of Nyssa's answer is that the three have one and the same will and action.
  B. If they are not three Gods, then they are three what?
      1. They are not three parts of God. The orthodox doctrine of the Trinity emphatically denies that God has parts.
      2. The Greek-speaking church called them three "hypostases," which means complete individual beings.
      3. The West, that is, the western part of the Roman Empire, used the Latin concept of three persons.
      4. The West understood "person" to mean complete individual being (that is, hypostasis) of rational nature.
      5. Thus arose the standard conceptual language for the doctrine of the Trinity: three persons and one essence or, in the Greek, three hypostases and one *ousia*.
  C. What makes the three different from one another?
      1. The Father begets the Son, not vice versa.
      2. In general, their diverse mode of origination differentiates the three persons.
      3. Following Augustine, the West will say that the three are differentiated by their relations.

Suggested Reading:

"The Nicene-Constantinopolitan Creed" in Leith, *Creeds of the Churches*, 28–33; also in Schaff, *The Creeds of Christendom*, vol. 2, 57–61.

Dünzl, *A Brief History of the Doctrine of the Trinity in the Early Church*.

Pelikan, *The Christian Tradition*, vol. 1, chap. 4.

Questions to Consider:
1. Do you agree that the Nicene doctrine of the Trinity was really necessary to make sense of the extraordinary claims Christians made about Christ?
2. The Nicene doctrine of the Trinity was intended as a form of monotheism. Is it successful on that score?

Lecture Ten—Transcript
The Doctrine of the Trinity

In our lecture course on the history of Christian theology, we are about to enter a new phase. We are starting in this lecture on a series of three lectures on great classic Christian doctrines, the doctrine of the Trinity, the doctrine of the Incarnation, the doctrine of Grace.

These doctrines go back to the New Testament but they reach a kind of classic, mature intellectual formulation, theological formulation, in the 4th and 5th centuries in the writings and the work of the church fathers of the 4th and 5th centuries.

They are often called patristic doctrines, patristic named after the Fathers, from Greek *pater*, the Father. So the church fathers, the patristic doctrines of the Trinity, Incarnation, and Grace and this lecture will do the doctrine of the Trinity.

The doctrine of the Trinity is essentially the Christian doctrine about the nature of God. It's the distinctively Christian conception of who God is. It's not about how God is three in one; we can talk about God being three in one if we want, but that's not what the doctrine of the Trinity is fundamentally about.

What the doctrine of the Trinity is fundamentally about is God being Father, Son, and Holy Spirit. And, yes, if you want to count, you get three out of that. But the threeness is not the important part. The name, the three-fold name: Father, Son, Holy Spirit, that's what matters. That's the Christian concept of God. There is one God who is Father, Son, and Holy Spirit. And that's the Trinity in a nutshell.

When we talk about the doctrine of the Trinity, we're talking about something that is so fundamental to Christianity that it's distinctive to Christianity because it arises from something that we've noticed about Christian faith from the beginning of our discussions in this lecture course.

Christians worship Jesus as if he's God. And indeed, orthodox Christians believe quite simply that he is God. How are we going to explain that? That's what we're going to be talking about in the next two lectures.

We have the Trinity, the doctrine of the Trinity about who God is, and then we have the doctrine of the Incarnation about how Christ is God incarnate. Both the doctrine of the Trinity and the doctrine of the Incarnation arise from this fundamental Christian practice of worshipping this man as God. And they are meant to give a satisfying or, at least, an intelligible explanation—well, not exactly explanation. It's a way of trying to make sense of, at least limited sense of, what Christians are doing when they worship this man as God. Make sense of it in the sense of, say things about Jesus that don't end up being silly or wrong or heretical, even though there's a mystery here which Christian doctrine does not try to explain away.

So Trinity is about who God is. Incarnation is specifically about how the second person of the Trinity, Christ, becomes incarnate, and is both divine and human. So we're going to leave off the humanity of Jesus for now and get back to it in the next lecture on the Incarnation.

In the lecture on the Trinity, we'll be talking specifically and strictly about his divinity, his divine nature, and only about his divine nature. And thus, in the doctrine of the Trinity, we tend not to use the name "Jesus," which is the name of a human being, but rather the name of the preexistent Christ, especially names like "Word," *Logos*, and "Son of God." The doctrine of the Trinity is about the identity of this Word or *Logos* or eternal Son of God prior to all creation who later becomes incarnate. But we're going to leave the Incarnation and the humanity of Christ aside for just one lecture and get back to it in the next lecture.

What is the doctrine of the Trinity? What does it really say? The Great Church father Augustine, I think, gave us a wonderful summary of the doctrine of the Trinity. He hits the nail on the head with seven statements which summarize the doctrine of the Trinity, put the seven of them together and you've got the doctrine of the Trinity.

The first three statements are "the Father is God"; "the Son is God"; "the Holy Spirit is God." Three statements.

Three more statements, now: "the Father is not the Son"; "the Son is not the Holy Spirit"; and "the Holy Spirit is not the Father."

Now, statement number seven—here's the clincher—"there is one God and only one God."

So you put all those statements together and you've got the doctrine of the Trinity, says Augustine. And I think he's got it right. Augustine's a very, very smart man, and understands logic very well. That's the essential logic of the doctrine of the Trinity.

Notice you never have to use the word "three" to state the doctrine of the Trinity, if Augustine's right about this. You need to have the words Father, Son, and Holy Spirit, the name of God. You have to have that three-fold name in order to state the doctrine of the Trinity. You do not need to have the word three. You do need to have the word "one," because the doctrine of the Trinity is explicitly a monotheistic doctrine. There's only one true God. The oneness of God is an explicit part of the doctrine of the Trinity; the threeness is implicit. You can count if you want to. Although a lot of church fathers will say something like, well, when we're talking about the doctrine of the Trinity, we forget how to count. They prefer not to talk about the threeness of God, just the oneness.

There's another word we don't have to use in stating the doctrine of the Trinity, and that's the word "trinity" itself. The word "trinity" does not appear in the Bible. It's a good label for this doctrine, but it's dispensable.

What's not dispensable, again, is Father, Son, and Holy Spirit. The word "trinity" is a great label for it. It is a revered label for it, especially in the Eastern Orthodox tradition. They love that label, but it's just a label. Nothing is lost if you don't talk about God's threeness or his tri-unity, all that stuff.

What happens when we develop the doctrine of the Trinity? How do we get to this doctrine? Because Augustine's speaking and writing in the 5th century A.D. How did we get there? Remember, back in the beginning we have Christians worshipping Christ on high. He's at God's right hand. And then we have John in the Gospel of John talking about the Word, the Word who was with God in the beginning. Not only is Christ there with God now, after the Crucifixion and Resurrection, but he was there before the whole Creation. He was the *Logos*, the Word, which any Greek speaker would recognize as meaning "reason."

And all these early church fathers, most of them were reading in Greek, would say, in the beginning was the *Logos*, in the beginning was the Reason of God. A great many early church fathers were called "*Logos* theologians"—theologians of the *Logos*, the Word. They treated the Reason or *Logos* of God as a kind of second God. One early Christian theologian in the 2nd century, Justin Martyr, actually spoke of the *Logos* as "another God." Now that's not quite right, but close. That's going to have to be corrected.

The *Logos*, or Reason of God, was regarded as an intermediary between God and the Creation. There was the most high God who is eternal, never came into being, unchanging. And then the *Logos* is the means, or intermediary, through which God creates the world.

The *Logos* is kind of halfway between God and the Creation. He's an intermediary, a mediator, between God and the Creation. That's a view that ends up getting rejected by the church because it is subordinationist. It's a subordinationist view of the Trinity, where the second person of the Trinity, the *Logos*, is less than God but greater than the rest of the Creation, a kind of in between.

The orthodox doctrine of the Trinity is going to change that. It's going to change that because in the early 4th century, a radical subordinationist came along named Arius. Arius was the arch heretic of the Trinitarian doctrine. He came along and said the *Logos* is not just subordinate to God. The *Logos* is a creature, that is, a creation of God.

Because as Arius recognized more keenly than the earlier *Logos* theologians did, Christianity is pretty much committed to the notion that everything that exists is either the Creator or the Creation. And there's no third kind of being. All being is either God the Creator or the Creation.

And Arius asked the intelligent question, "Well, the *Logos*, is he Creator or creation? Which is he?" and then he gave what the orthodox regarded as the wrong answer. He said, the *Logos* is a creation, a creature. He is not the same kind of being as the Creator, God the Father.

The early Church reacted very strongly against Arius. They didn't like the idea that Christ in his eternal being as the Son of God was a creation. They were horrified by the implication that Arius drew that "there was once when he was not." He was created out of nothing. So there was once when he didn't exist.

They said, no, no, no! The *Logos* is eternal! The early church had to figure out how to formulate a doctrine that didn't get the *Logos* theology wrong the way that Arius and the subordinationists did.

The early Church did this in the Council of Nicaea in A.D. 325, early in the 4th century. It was convened by the emperor Constantine, the very first Christian emperor, who had just recently made Christianity legal, which is why this is the first worldwide, or at least, Roman-wide council.

All of the Roman Empire was invited to send church representatives to this worldwide or ecumenical council, as it's called; "ecumenical" meaning "worldwide." It's the very first ecumenical council. In fact, it actually had mostly Greek-speaking bishops from the eastern half of the empire; only one Latin-speaking bishop as a representative of the bishop of Rome arrived at this council.

They got together; they had to figure out how to formulate a doctrine of the Trinity. They rejected this Arian notion, from Arius, that the *Logos* came into being from nothing, that "there was once when he was not," as if he was just a creation like everybody else. That can't be right.

What they did in order to exclude the heresy of Arianism is they took a baptismal creed, one of these rules of faith that had been formulated into a formula or creed that you recited when you were baptized, to indicate, this is my faith. This is what I believe.

"I believe in God, the Father Almighty. I believe in Jesus Christ, his only Son. I believe in the Holy Spirit." These creeds always have these three-part form representing the doctrine of the Trinity. They took one of these baptismal creeds, these formal confessions of faith that go with baptism, and they added a few clauses to the creed in order to exclude Arianism.

Let me read the part of the creed that's about Jesus, the part that excludes the Arian doctrine of the Trinity. It goes like this, the creed always begins, "I believe," and then about halfway through the creed, you say, "I believe in one Lord, Jesus Christ, the Son of God, begotten from the Father, Only-begotten," that is, from the Father's essence, "God from God, Light from Light, True God from True God, begotten, not made, of the same essence as the Father, through whom all things came to be."

This is the original Creed of Nicaea in 325. In saying that he is begotten, not made, they're excluding the idea that the *Logos* is a creature, a creation. He originates from the Father. He is begotten but he is not a creature. He's not created.

The relation between the Son or *Logos* and the Father is a relation of begetting. You could also call it generation. But it's the relation of a father and a son. The literal meaning of beget goes back to reproduction.

My father begot me, I begot my son. I didn't create my son the way a potter creates a pot. I didn't make him. And that's why the creed goes on to talk about being begotten from the Father's essence.

He was not created out of nothing. He was begotten from the very essence of the Father, from the very being of the Father. He came from the Father, not from nothing.

And finally, they add this crucial phrase, "of the same essence as the Father." The same essence. In Greek, this is *homoousios*. It's a famous phrase, and you'll often see it written in Greek, *homoousios*. It means of the same essence.

Sometimes it's translated "of the same being," or even "of the same substance" as the Father. It means that Christ does not come out of nothing like the creation does. He comes out of the Father, he belongs to the very essence and being of the Father.

And the crucial point that it's making, you see, the word essence is so complex and can mean so many things. At a minimum, the crucial point that it's making, no matter what else you think about essence, which is such a complicated term, at a minimum, the crucial point that it's making is that the Son is God in exactly the same sense as the Father is God.

He's not a different kind of God. It's not like he has a different kind of divine essence from the Father. So the *homoousios* clause you can think of as a commentary on the second of Augustine's seven statements. The first statement is "the Father is God," the second is, "the Son is God."

It's as if the Nicene Creed is adding this remark. The Son is God in exactly the same sense as the Father is God, is exactly the same kind of God as the Father. He's not a different kind of God, not another

God, not a second God, not a lesser God. He's exactly the same kind of God as God the Father.

When we say the Son is God, we mean the same thing as when we say the Father is God. The Father is different from the Son, but they are both God in exactly the same way, exactly the same sense. This excluded Arius's view. But it was controversial because so many of the Christian theologians of the early 4th century were *Logos* theologians who had some form of subordinationism. They hadn't yet gotten clearheaded, as Arius had, and asked the question, is the *Logos* a creature or the Creator?

And they really liked the idea of the *Logos* as intermediary between God and the creation, less than God, but higher than the creation; and the Nicene Creed got rid of that intermediary status. There is no intermediary between God and the creation. There is no third kind of being that is not exactly the creator and not exactly the creature. And that's something that the church had to adjust to. Because what it means is you have this coequal Trinity; Father, the Son, and the Holy Spirit, who are all at the same level. There's none of this hierarchical descent from God to the Son to the Spirit.

That's the way the Platonists of the time, the late neo-Platonists they're called, had conceived of the metaphysics of Divine Being. There's a First Principle and then there's an eternally-generated Second Principle and then there's a world soul and then there's the material world.

And a lot of the early Christian theologians liked that kind of hierarchical cascade, this intermediary stuff, these steps of intermediary levels between God the Father and the creation. And the Nicene Creed got rid of that. There is no third kind of being, intermediary being, between God the Father and the Creation.

The great defender of the Nicene Doctrine of the Trinity is a church father named Athanasius. He's the bishop of Alexandria. He defends this notion of eternal begetting, eternal generation.

Interestingly enough, it is a notion that you find in pagan neo-Platonists. The pagan neo-Platonists did believe that there's a First Principal, and then a Second Principal that is eternally generated from the First Principal, but the Second Principal is lower, less than the First Principal.

And that's what the Creed of Nicaea denied. There is a Second Principal, a second person of the Trinity, but it's not less than the Father. The Son is God in exactly the same way as the Father is. He's not lower or lesser or subordinate to the Father.

Athanasius defended this eternal generation or eternal begetting of the Son from the Father, but also the co-equality of the Son with the Father. And here is a fascinating point. He had to defend the fact that the Son always existed. There was never once when he was not.

That phrase, "there was once when he was not," comes from Arius. The orthodox hated that. That's really what got them to see the point that they had to reject Arius's teaching. The Son is eternal. He's always existed.

On the other hand they did think that the Son owed his existence to the Father. He was begotten by the Father. There's this process of eternal generation which is not a process, because it's eternal.

That's a puzzling concept, right? An eternal process of generating? An eternal process of originating that is not a process in time? In fact, we really shouldn't call it a process at all. There's this origination of the Son from the Father which is eternal. How can that be? How can someone come into being eternally?

That's all the church fathers said. That's incomprehensible. That's where the key mystery is in the doctrine of the Trinity. Not about threeness and oneness but about this eternal generation. So we'll actually come back to that point, the incomprehensibility of eternal generation.

But one thing that does come into the fore, one thing that Athanasius brings forward that is absolutely fascinating, the Son is dependent on the Father for his being. He originates from the Father. But in another way, the Father is also dependent on the Son. Because the Father has to have a Son in order to be Father. And the Father, God the Father, has always been a Father. Therefore, he has always had a Son.

That's one of the arguments that Athanasius makes for the eternity of the Son, the fact that there was not once when he was not. The Father has always been a Father. The Father has always had a Son. And although the Son owes his very being to the essence of the Father, he was begotten from the Father's essence, the Creed says, nonetheless.

Although the Son owes his being to the Father, the Father owes something to the Son. Because the Father owes to the Son the fact that he's Father. So there is this kind of mutual dependence going on, even though the Son owes his very being to the Father.

There's a lot of talk about the divine essence after this phrase "of the same essence as the Father" gets into the creed. And a great deal of Christian theology about God will develop this concept of divine essence. In the original Nicene Creed it was called the Father's essence, but because the Son has the same essence as the Father, and later on the Holy Spirit has the same essence as the Father, it came to be called the divine essence. The essence of God originates with the Father. It starts out as the Father's essence.

But in begetting the Son, giving the Son being, the Father gives the whole of his essence or divine being to the Son. And also the Spirit gets the whole of the divine essence or being. The divine essence is not divided among the three of them as if it were some stuff out of which they were made. That would be materialistic. God is not made out of material or stuff. So the divine essence is not stuff out of which God is made. It is not divided among the three persons. It is something that each one of the three persons has in its fullness. Each one is fully God, having the same essence as God the Father.

The divine essence is characterized, therefore, not by what it's made of, because it's not made of anything, but by certain divine attributes like eternity, omnipotence, omniscience. The Son has the same eternity and omnipotence and omniscience and goodness as the Father. The spirit has the same eternity, omniscience, omnipotence and goodness as the Son and the Father. That's the shared divine essence which each one has fully.

The controversy about the doctrine of the Trinity that arose after the Nicene Creed and the Council of Nicaea in 325, because there was so many of these *Logos* theologians who had to overcome this subordinationism before they could accept Nicaea. That controversy lasted for about 50 years.

It was resolved in 381 at the second ecumenical council, which took place in Constantinople. And which produced a revised version of the Creed of Nicaea which is nowadays called the "Nicene Creed." If you go to church and recite the creed, the Nicene Creed in church, you are actually reciting the creed that was formulated in 381 at

Constantinople, called the Nicene Creed because it was meant as an affirmation of the creed of Nicaea.

As a result of the Council of Constantinople in 381, the Holy Spirit also ended up being regarded as of the same substance with the Father and the Son. The Council of Constantinople didn't explicitly say that, but it's pretty much inevitable at the end of that council that the Holy Spirit would also be regarded as "of the same essence as the Father and the Son."

However, the Holy Spirit is not begotten like the Son, but proceeds from the Father. So once again there's this mode of origination which is eternal, not a process in time, not a form of creation. But it's different because the Spirit originates from the Father in a different way from the Son.

The Son is begotten, the Spirit proceeds. But both of them are not creatures. Both of them are eternal. Both of them have always existed. Father, Son, and Holy Spirit have always existed. God has always been triune, Father, Son, and Holy Spirit.

Well, then, since the Father is God, the Son is God, the Holy Spirit is God, each of them is fully and wholly God and has the divine essence, why don't Christians say there are three Gods? Why not say there are three Gods?

Well, of course, the short answer is that Christians believe in Jewish monotheism. Christians are Jewish enough to believe in only one God. It's never really an option, never was an option for Christians to believe in three Gods. That's why it was a mistake when some of the *Logos* theologians were willing to say that the *Logos* was another God.

No. There's only one God. He's Father, Son, or Holy Spirit. But we need to explain how it is that Father, Son, or Holy Spirit can be different from one another. The Father's not the Son. The Son's not the Holy Spirit. They can be different from one another and yet be only one God.

It's not quite enough to say that they have one essence because after all, three human beings have one essence. They have the human essence. Peter, James, Mary, they are three human beings. They each have the same human essence. They are *homoousios* in that sense.

So that's, the *homoousios*, the phrase "of one essence," does not explain the oneness of God. It explains how the Son is equal to the Father and has the same divinity of the Father. It doesn't explain the unity or oneness of God. What explains the fact that the Father, the Son, and the Holy Spirit are one God even though they are different?

One of the church fathers in the 4th century, a man named Gregory of Nyssa, gave the answer that the three persons of the Trinity have the same will and action. There's only one will in the three persons in the Trinity. Not three persons with three different wills like Peter and James and Mary, but one God with one will and one action.

Every time the Trinity acts, every time the Father acts, the Son and the Spirit act with him. Every decision, every choice the Father makes, is a choice made with the Son and the Holy Spirit. They have one will, they can't disagree.

Peter and James and Mary may have one will in the sense of agreeing about something, but they can also disagree. They can. Maybe they won't, but they can disagree. The three persons of the Trinity cannot disagree because they have only one will. They cannot act apart from each other. They cannot divide. They cannot be at loggerheads. They cannot be at war or conflict with one another because the three persons of the Trinity are one God.

All right. So let's look at the opposite side of it. If there is not three Gods, then three what? Three what? Not three Gods. Should we say perhaps three parts of God? Well, no, remember Augustine's seven statements: The Father is not part of God. The Father is God. The Son is not part of God. The Son is God. The Holy Spirit is not part of God, the Holy Spirit is God.

So in the Greek tradition of Christian theology, they needed a label for three what? And the Greek term for this is "hypostases." Hypostases. Three hypostases in the Trinity. Hypostasis is a fascinating word. It's the most abstract and colorless word you can get for three individual beings, three complete individual beings. A cat is a hypostasis. A table is a hypostasis. A human being is a hypostasis. A hand is not a hypostasis, because my hand is part of my complete individual being. And again, the Father, Son, and Holy Spirit, they're not parts of God. God does not have parts. The doctrine of the Trinity is not a doctrine about the three parts of God, because God doesn't have parts according to Christian theology.

God has three hypostases, three complete individual beings, each of which is God. Not part of God, but God. The Son is not part of God. He is God. The word "hypostasis" captures that sense in which the Son is God, not just part of God.

In the West, that is, the western part of the Roman Empire, where they speak Latin rather than Greek, the word that gets used is not "hypostasis" but "person." And, therefore, I have been talking about three persons of the Trinity. But it's very important to realize, the word "person" in Latin at that time did not have all of the meaning that the word "person" now has. The word "person" has had a history since then.

The word "person" in particular did not mean, sort of, someone with a separate personality, a separate consciousness, a separate will. That would be three Gods. If God were three persons in the modern sense of the word "person," three people like James and Peter and Mary, then there would be three Gods.

The word "person," it's funny, actually means "mask." It was used for roles in a drama, because the persons in a drama were all wearing masks in ancient drama. And so the list of characters in a drama is the *dramatis personae*, literally meaning the "masks of the drama."

There are three roles in salvation history, in the Bible, played by these three persons. But these three persons are one God. Three complete individual beings who are one God. The West, in order to explain what it meant by persons, in order to talk to the East and the Greek speakers, defined "person," the Latin *persona*, as a complete individual being—that is, a "hypostasis," with a rational nature. A complete individual being with a mind and thoughts. But again, the thoughts of God are not three separate centers of consciousness and will and action because that would be three Gods. So you've got three hypostases, three persons, and one God. And thus you get the standard language of trinitarian theology for the next several thousand years. Well, at least 1500 years or so. The language is, the Trinity is one essence, three persons, or, one essence, three hypostases.

As I mentioned by starting with Augustine, you don't actually have to use this language of hypostasis and *ousia* if you don't want to. If you want to make sure that you exclude the Arian heresy, you need this highly technical language about *ousia* and hypostasis, essence and hypostasis and person and so on. But all you really need to state the bare bones of the logical doctrine of the Trinity, the logical skeleton of the doctrine, is Father, Son, Holy Spirit. That name, and the word God, and the notion that the Father is not the Son and so on, so forth. Those seven statements, without the word "three," without the word "essence," without the word "hypostases" is all you need to explain, or at least to state, the doctrine of the Trinity. I don't think you can explain it, but at least you can formulate it.

Finally, one further question that the church fathers had to ask and answer: How is it that the Father and the Son and the Holy Spirit are different from each other, if they have the same will, the same essence, the same action, they always act together? What they said is, the difference is that the Father begets the Son, the Son does not beget the Father. The Father is, in fact, unbegotten, unoriginated. The Son originates from the Father, the Father does not originate from the Son. So that difference of origination distinguishes the Father from the Son, and likewise with the Holy Spirit, who proceeds from the Father, but the Father does not proceed from the Holy Spirit.

So that's different, and that difference establishes the difference between them. It also establishes a certain order in their actions. The Father originates the Son, and, therefore, the action of the Son carries out the will of the Father, as we see throughout the New Testament. The Son carries out the action of the Father, but his action is the Father's action in the Son. We rapidly get beyond our comprehension, here. But at least there is a sense in which the Christian doctrine of the Trinity can distinguish Father, Son, and Holy Spirit while affirming that there's only one God.

Last point, later on in the West, these relations of origination were called the Trinitarian Relations because the persons in the Trinity were not distinguished according to their essence or substance but according to their relations. That's a deep idea. The difference between Father, Son, and Holy Spirit is not a difference of essence or being but of relation, of relation like relation of Father to Son. So the Trinity is a community of persons in relationship to each other, and that relationship distinguishes the three but also binds them in one as one God. Three persons. One God: Father, Son, and Holy Spirit. One God. That's the doctrine of the Trinity.

Lecture Eleven
The Doctrine of the Incarnation

Scope:

After the Nicene doctrine of the Trinity was established, key developments in the doctrine of Christ's Incarnation could take shape. The key concept is that the same person who was eternally begotten from God the Father is born from the Virgin Mary, who is thus the mother of God, though not the originator of his divine essence. As Son of the Father, he is truly God, while as son of Mary he is truly human—and he did not cease to be divine when he became human, but "remaining what he was, he assumed what he was not." This means that just as God was born of the Virgin Mary, he also suffered and died on the cross. But this is said of the Son, one of the Trinity, not of the Father or the Spirit, who are beyond all suffering.

Outline

I. "Incarnation" in the Christian doctrine concerning who Jesus Christ really is.
   A. The doctrine is about Jesus and no one else.
      1. It has nothing to do with the concept of reincarnation, which comes from a whole different religion.
      2. It is not the same thing as embodiment, which happens to all humans.
      3. For Christian theology, there is only one Incarnation, and that is Jesus Christ.
   B. Trinity and Incarnation are the fundamental doctrines of orthodox Christianity.
      1. The Eastern church calls these two doctrines "theology" and "economy" (*theologia* and *oikonomia*), the doctrine of who God is and the doctrine of his plan or dispensation of salvation.
      2. In the West, the doctrine of the Incarnation is the centerpiece of the subdivision of Christian theology called "Christology," which concerns the person and work of Christ.

II. Two key points about the Incarnation were resolved within Nicene orthodoxy in the 4th century.
   A. In becoming incarnate, the divine word of God did not cease to be fully God. As Gregory of Naziansen put it, "remaining what he was, he assumed what he was not."
      1. The implication is that the Word retains all the divine attributes of eternity, impassibility, and immortality, even while he takes up human attributes of suffering and mortality.
      2. "Assumed" or "took up" becomes a key verb for the divine act of Incarnation.
   B. For Gregory, Christ was fully human, assuming a human soul as well as a human body.
      1. The view, rejected by the orthodox, that Christ did not have a human (rational) soul is called "Apollinarianism," after the Alexandrian theologian who espoused it.
      2. For Gregory, when the Word becomes flesh, this does not mean he merely assumed a human body, as if the Word took the place of the human soul.

III. The key points of the orthodox doctrine of the Incarnation were set forth by Bishop Cyril of Alexandria in the early 5th century.
   A. Following the narrative arc of the Nicene Creed, Cyril points out that the one who is "of the same essence with the Father" is the same one who is also "born of the Virgin Mary and made human."
      1. This means the same one has two births, of two different kinds: He is begotten from the Father in his divinity and he is born of Mary in his humanity.
      2. Because Mary gives birth to the same one who is "God from God," she is rightly called *theotokos*, "God-bearer" or "mother of God."
   B. Cyril introduced important technical concepts into Christology.
      1. The Incarnation is a hypostatic union, because it unites the divine and the human in one hypostasis or person.
      2. Because of this union there is a sharing of attributes, *communicatio idiomatum*, which means the divine Word has human attributes and the man Jesus has divine attributes.

3. On the one hand, for example, the divine Word is crucified.
4. On the other hand, for example, Christ's body is life-giving flesh.

C. Cyril's Christology was developed in opposition to Nestorius, archbishop of Constantinople.
1. Nestorius and his teachings were condemned as a heretical in the third ecumenical council at Ephesus in 431.
2. Henceforth "Nestorianism" became the label for Christologies that divided the humanity of Christ from his divinity, as if Christ were not one person but a combination of two separately-acting principles or persons.

IV. The Council of Chalcedon in 451 affirmed that in Christ there are two distinct natures, divine and human.

A. To emphasize the unity of Christ, Cyril spoke of his being "one incarnate nature of the Word."
1. He also spoke of "one nature after the union" and a "union of two natures." Christ is "out of two natures" not "in two natures" for there's only one Christ, and the two natures are not separate in him.
2. He was willing to speak of a union "in two natures" so long as it was clear that the two natures, divine and human, were inseparable and did not act apart from one another.

B. Chalcedon, by contrast, adopted a "two natures" formulation.
1. Because the same one is "complete in divinity and in humanity, truly God and truly man," he is "understood in two natures."
2. The Chalcedonian formula adds, "without confusion, without change, without division, without separation."

C. Chalcedonian vocabulary links the two doctrines of Incarnation and Trinity.
1. After Chalcedon, it becomes commonplace to speak of Christ as "two natures in one person," which provides a conceptual link with the doctrine of the Trinity, where there is "one nature in three persons."

2. "Nature" and "essence" (*ousia*) thus become equivalent terms in the doctrines of Trinity and Incarnation.
 D. Major schisms resulted in the East after Chalcedon.
   1. Partisans of Cyril's "one nature" formulation, called "Monophysites" (from the Greek term for "one nature") did not accept Chalcedon and eventually broke off from the mainstream Eastern Orthodox church of Byzantium.
   2. Both Monophysite and Nestorian churches were eventually excluded from Eastern Orthodoxy.
V. Two other councils also dealt with Christology in the early Christian church.
 A. The Second Council of Constantinople (the fifth ecumenical council) in 553 endorsed the *theopaschite* formula, "that one of the Trinity was crucified in the flesh."
   1. According to the doctrine of divine impassibility, universally accepted by the orthodox, the divine nature cannot suffer.
   2. But by the same logic which affirms that Mary gives birth to God in his humanity, it must be said that it is God who dies on the cross and suffers, not in his divine nature but in his humanity.
   3. Hence the orthodox tradition affirms that God suffers, but not that the Father suffers; for the Father is not human.
   4. In short, the tradition affirms Deipassionism but not Patripassionism.
 B. The Third Council of Constantinople (the sixth ecumenical council) in 681 teaches that Christ has two wills, divine and human.
   1. For if he is fully human, he must have a human will.
   2. But by the same token, if he is fully God, then his will must be the divine will.
   3. This point is illustrated in the Garden of Gethsemane, where he submits his human will to his divine will by praying, "Not my will, but Thine be done."

Suggested Reading:

"The Definition of Chalcedon" in Leith, *Creeds of the Churches*, 34–36; also in Schaff, *The Creeds of Christendom*, vol. 2, 62–65.

"The Second and Third Councils of Constantinople" in Leith, *Creeds of the Churches*, 45–53.

Kelly, *Early Christian Doctrines*, chaps. 11 and 12.

McGuckin, *Saint Cyril of Alexandria and the Christological Controversy*.

Pelikan, *The Christian Tradition*, vol. 1, chap. 5.

Questions to Consider:

1. Does the orthodox doctrine of the Incarnation appear to you as a faithful development of the early Christian view of Jesus?
2. Is it clear what orthodox Christian doctrine means when it affirms that God died on a cross?

Lecture Eleven—Transcript
The Doctrine of the Incarnation

After you get the doctrine of the Trinity right, then you can go on and get the doctrine of the Incarnation into proper focus. That's what actually happened in the history of Christian theology, and that's why after dealing with the doctrine of the Trinity in our last lecture, we go onto the doctrine of the Incarnation, the second of the great Christian doctrines of the patristic period, in this lecture.

To begin with, let me say a little bit about that word "Incarnation." It's actually a technical term in Christian theology. It comes from a Latin word meaning "flesh," *carnem*, related to "carnivore." But, as a technical term in Christian theology, it should not be confused with some related notions or even related words like reincarnation. It's a very similar word, entirely different idea, entirely different religion. It's a word for what happens in Hinduism and some other religions where souls get reincarnated in different bodies after they die. The Christian doctrine of Incarnation has nothing at all to do with that. Incarnation and reincarnation are two entirely different things. Incarnation is also not the same thing as embodiment. All of us human beings are embodied, but only one human being is the Incarnation of God. The Incarnation applies only to Jesus. In Christian theology, that word "Incarnation" is a word to describe Jesus and no other human being, no other creature; no one else is God incarnate. The Incarnation, in essence, is Jesus in Christian theology.

We start with the doctrine of the Trinity. It came before this doctrine of the Incarnation both historically and in our lectures, because the doctrine of the Trinity is the Christian doctrine about who and what God is. You've got to get the doctrine of God in focus before you can then go on to say how is it that Jesus is both God and human? First you get the doctrine of God in focus with the doctrine of the Trinity, then you talk about the relation of the divinity and humanity in Jesus, and that's the Incarnation.

The Eastern Orthodox Church will describe these two doctrines as the *theologia* and the *oikonomia*, or "theology" and "economy," "economy" being a word for sort of the divine plan. It originally meant household management. God has this plan for salvation for the world, and that plan is centered in Jesus Christ. For the Eastern Orthodox churches and Greek Orthodox especially, the word "economy" is almost equivalent with the word Incarnation. The point is that the Eastern Orthodox, like the West, needs some labels for the two fundamental doctrines of the Christian faith—Trinity, Incarnation. There are no doctrines in Christian theology more fundamental and important than those two. And the East has its own specific label for that—theology, economy. You could also use the label "Christology," meaning of course, the doctrine of Christ. But, Christology's a bit larger because it includes both the doctrine of Christ's person, which is the Incarnation, and the doctrine of his work or activity as savior. Incarnation is one aspect of this larger umbrella term, Christology.

Once you have Nicaea in focus, you can begin to get the Incarnation in focus. During the 4th century when the church was arguing about the Creed of Nicaea and the Council of Nicaea and trying to get Nicene trinitarian theology straight, a number of things also got straight already about Christology. There was one particular church father, Gregory of Naziansen, who is very influential in the second ecumenical council in Constantinople in 381, who put it very, very simply and very powerfully. It's a wonderful phrase; here's how it goes. Gregory of Naziansen says, "Remaining what he was, he assumed what he was not." The "he" here is the *Logos*, the eternal word of God, second person of the Trinity. "Remaining what he was"—that is, remaining God, unchangeable, impassable, eternal, remaining all those things—"he assumed [or "took up"] what he was not," namely humanity, mortality, changeability, the ability to die. God in himself can't die. He can't even change. He doesn't want to change. He's perfect. Why would he want to change? The unchangeability of God is one of his perfections, and he remains unchangeable. He retains all the perfections of God, and yet, he takes on our imperfections. He, as it were, adds our imperfections to his being—our vulnerability, our suffering, our death. He takes all that up and unites it to his eternal being. That's a formulation for the doctrine of the Incarnation. I think it captures a whole lot of what the Christian doctrine of the Incarnation is trying to get at. Let me repeat it one more time, because if you want to understand the Christian doctrine of the Incarnation, this one little saying will capture most of it for you. "Remaining what he was, he assumed what he was not."

Another thing that Gregory of Naziansen mentioned and dealt with in this period between Nicaea and Constantinople as the Nicene trinitarianism was getting sorted out, was what it was that Christ assumed. And he spent some time thinking about that because there was a Christian theologian in that time named Apollinarius, who said that the Word, the *Logos*, assumed a human body and a living soul, but not a rational soul. He did not assume our intellect or our rational faculties, the soul that makes us human, but rather it's as if the Word replaced our human reason with his own divine reason. It's as if the Word took up flesh, and the body and the livingness of the body, but not the human soul. The Word replaced the human soul.

Gregory of Naziansen said, no, that's not right. It's not like the eternal word of God simply took up our body, or even our body and its livingness. There's a biological soul. Quick note: There's a rational soul and a biological soul. Plants have souls in the ancient world. Animals have souls. Humans have rational souls; that's what makes us human. Apollinarius was saying that the Word took up this living human body with an animal soul, but no rational soul. The Word as the divine reason replaced the rational soul. Gregory of Naziansen said, no, that's wrong because—and here's another famous formulation—"Whatever is not assumed is not healed." The *Logos* assumes all of human nature including a rational human soul. Jesus has to be fully human, having all the features of human nature in order to redeem all of human nature. He's fully human and fully God, and that's a formulation that we get later in the Council of Chalcedon. But it's already implicit in what Gregory of Naziansen says.

Let's go on after Nicaea to some controversies that arose afterward, and I'm going to start with the most important figure in the history really of Christian theology dealing with Christology, probably the most influential theologian of the Incarnation in the Christian tradition. His name is Cyril of Alexandria. He's a bishop of Alexandria in the 5th century. His notion actually stems from the Nicene Creed—just as you would expect, the Incarnation is going to be based on Nicene trinitarianism And, he points out that in the Nicene Creed, you get this sort of story about one person or one's hypostases, to use that Greek term again. When you recite the Nicene Creed, or the Nicene-Constantinopolitan Creed of 381, here's part of what you say. "I believe in one Lord, Jesus Christ, the only begotten Son of God, begotten from the Father before all ages. God from God, Light from Light, true God from true God, begotten, not made, of one essence (or the same essence) with the Father." There's the divine being of Christ. But, then, of the same person or the same one, as Cyril will emphasize, you go on to say the following: "Who for us and for our salvation came down from Heaven. By the power of the Holy Spirit he was born of the Virgin Mary and became incarnate and became human." The same one who is begotten eternally from the Father, "God from God, Light from Light, true God from true God," the same one is "born of the Virgin Mary, suffers under Pontius Pilate, is crucified" and dead and buried. The same one. That same one is the key to Cyril's doctrine of the Incarnation, works just like Gregory of Naziansen. The same one who remains what he was, assumed what he was not.

Notice, if you trace this same one beginning up in heaven where he's begotten from God the Father, and down on earth where he is born of the Virgin Mary, you see that he has two births as it were. He's begotten from the Father in eternity; he's born from the Virgin Mary in time. He has a divine birth or divine begetting, begotten, not made, not a creature, but fully God, and then a second birth as a human being. A divine birth, a human birth. This human birth is, of course, the birth of the Word, the human birth of God. That's a deep and puzzling notion, and not everybody quite understood it or agreed with it, but Cyril insisted on it, and here's how he insisted on it. He said, "Mary is the mother of God," a phrase that, of course, becomes a favorite among Catholics in later centuries. His word for it in the Greek was *theotokos*, a famous little word. Sometimes it's translated "God-bearer." It's literally what it means, the one who gives birth to God, but "mother of God" is a good translation too, *theotokos*.

Of course, this does not mean that Mary is the origination of God, as if Mary originated God or created God or gave birth to God in the sense of being the origin of God. No, of course not. The Father is the origin of God, the Son, and the Holy Spirit, but she is the woman who bore in her womb the incarnate word of God who is God. If Jesus is truly God, and Mary bears him in her womb, then she is truly the mother of God, because the Jesus whom she has in her womb is God. She bears Jesus; therefore, she bears God. She's the mother of Jesus Christ; therefore, she's the mother of God. That's the logic of it. Not only Catholics, but Eastern Orthodox and indeed Protestants, accept this view. Even though Protestants don't particularly like the title "mother of God" very much, they accept the theology of it. Calvin, for instance, was very explicit on this.

Let me say a little bit about the terminology that Cyril introduces, some key technical terms and technical ideas. He speaks of a hypostatic union, or you could say a union of hypostases. Remember, hypostases is that word for what there are three of in the Trinity, and the second hypostases of the Trinity, the Son of God, is the one who is united to human flesh, united to a rational soul, united to a fully human being, and becomes one with that human being. The oneness is the union, the single person that results is the hypostases, so it's a hypostatic union. You could say, in more Western terms, personal union, but that's awfully misleading. Personal sounds like it's about your emotions or something like that, but no, it's one person is the idea. Jesus is one person, the same one, the same person who was begotten of the Father. The same hypostases, the same person, the same one who's begotten of the Father, is the man Jesus. That's the hypostatic union, the one person of Jesus Christ.

Because of this union, this oneness of person, oneness of the one person Jesus, the divine and the human in Christ belong together in that union. Cyril goes on to speak of what he calls a *communicatio idiomatum*. That's actually a Latin translation of a Greek phrase. You'll often see this Latin phrase if you read much theology, so I'll repeat it for you, a *communicatio idiomatum*. *Communicatio*, a communication or sharing. The original meaning of communication in Latin was "to share." *Idiomatum* means attributes or properties. The properties of the Divine Being are shared with the man Jesus because, after all, there's only one person there, and the properties of the man Jesus are shared with the divine Word. For instance, the man Jesus is crucified; therefore, the word of God is crucified. The eternal Word, unchangeable, impassable, there from the beginning, begotten of the Father, is crucified. You might think only a man could be crucified. God couldn't be crucified. But the implication is no, the eternal word of God is crucified. Likewise, the other way around, you've got this flesh, the flesh of Christ. This is flesh of a man, not the flesh of God. But no, because of the *communicatio idiomatum*, says Cyril, this flesh, the flesh of Christ, is God's own flesh. It is, therefore, as Cyril says, "life-giving flesh," picking up something from the Gospel of John—"life-giving flesh." Why? Because it's the very flesh of God. That's something, the very flesh of God, the Word.

That's the *communicatio idiomatum*. You can see why getting the concepts right about the Incarnation, very abstract concepts like *communicatio idiomatum*, hypostatic union, nonetheless result in some very concrete and powerful things to say about Jesus. The divine Word is crucified. The flesh of Jesus is divine flesh—the flesh of God himself, the flesh of God the Word, life-giving flesh. The religious power of the doctrine of the Incarnation stems from getting these abstract points right. The abstractions are only abstractions, but they give shape to a doctrine, which has deep religious power and obviously becomes a focus of religious devotion. There's a great deal of devotion to the life-giving flesh of Christ in the Christian tradition.

I'll say briefly that Cyril's Christology did run into opposition. In fact, he sought out some opposition in the archbishop of Constantinople, a man named Nestorius who denied that Mary was *theotokos*, the mother of God. That got sorted out in the third ecumenical council, the Council of Ephesus in 431, which Cyril presided over and ended up condemning Nestorius as a heretic. "Nestorianism" then, even afterward, is the name for the heresy that splits apart Christ, as if there's the divine person, the human person. They're kind of working together. They're united, but there's really two. There's God, there's the man Jesus, that are somehow conjoined, inseparable, but really you can't really just say that Jesus is the same as the Divine Person or the Divine Person is the same as the human person. Nestorius tends to split the two apart. That splitting is treated as a heresy. It has been condemned as a heresy since the Council of Ephesus, the third ecumenical council in 431. There's only one person there—only one God, one man, and they're the same one.

A further council occurred in 451, the fourth ecumenical council at Chalcedon. This is the council best known in the West. If you studied theology as a Protestant or a Catholic, this is the council that will define most of your views about the Incarnation. If you're Eastern Orthodox you'll know more about Cyril, and if you're a Western Christian, a Protestant or a Catholic, you ought to know more about Cyril. He's really important. But, in Chalcedon, this is after the death of Cyril, it's 451, there's a certain correction of Cyril's theology. There are actually some arguments among scholars about how much Cyril's theology needs correcting. But, here's something that Cyril said that the Council of Chalcedon didn't really accept. Cyril spoke of Christ as having "one nature after the union." There's the hypostatic union, one person, but also one nature once the two natures, the divine and the human, come together. "One nature after the union," or "a union of two natures," says Cyril. Cyril's willing to say Christ is a person "out of two natures," or even "in two natures," so long as you don't separate the two natures, but he preferred this formulation, "one nature." Chalcedon came along and insisted on a "two nature" formulation. I think it's actually true that Cyril was unfortunate in his choice of words when he talked about one nature. Because a nature can be shared by several persons—there's one nature in the Trinity, there's one human nature—it's best to use the word nature as something quite different from person. Thus Chalcedon, I think, helped us clarify what's going on in the Incarnation by speaking of one person, one hypostases, just like Cyril, but "two natures," divine and human, that remain distinct. That's what Chalcedon was insisting on.

The Chalcedonian definition of the faith—by the way, it wasn't a creed. There were no new creeds after Constantinople. It's a definition of the faith. The Chalcedonian definition talks about these "two natures," which remain distinct. It sort of pushes against the *communicatio idiomatum* by saying, all right, yes, there's this sharing of attributes, but the attributes do remain distinct. It's not like they get mixed up with each other. It's not like God turns into a man. It's not like God ceases to be unchangeable and changes into something changeable because he gets mixed up with humanity. We want to keep those two natures at least separate in terms of how we understand them. We don't want to mix them up and create something new, sort of like a horse and a donkey, and then you get a mule. Jesus is not like that. It's not like a mixing up of two things.

The Chalcedonian formulation in fact does follow a lot of Cyril's language. Some Westerners don't notice this, so let me read a little bit of it for you: "Our Lord, Jesus Christ is one and the same Son, [the same one] is complete in divinity, [the same one] is complete in humanity," That's Cyril's language, the same one. The same one "is truly God and truly man," and that's typical Chalcedonian language—truly God, truly man, fully God, fully man—that's the crucial contribution of Chalcedon. The same one "is truly God and truly man, of a rational soul and a body." That's rejecting that Apollinarian heresy. The same one "is the same essence as the Father in divinity," that's Nicaea, "and the same essence as us in humanity."

Christ is *homoousios* with us, the same essence as us as a human being. "Being like us in all respects except sin. From all eternity he was begotten of the Father in divinity and in these last days, [the same one] for us and for our salvation, was born of the Virgin Mary, [the *theotokos*, the mother of God] in humanity." There's that two births theme in Cyril. "One and the same Christ, Son, Lord, Only-begotten who is understood in two natures," and here's the distinctively Chalcedonian phraseology: "without confusion, without change, without division, without separation." The two natures are not confused with each other, mixed up with each other, but they're also not separated or divided from each other. I think Chalcedon, if read properly, affirms Cyril's Christology, but also qualifies it so you don't make the mistake of thinking that the two natures somehow get mixed up with each other and become a third kind of nature, which is neither divine nor human.

The other thing that Chalcedonian vocabulary does that's very helpful is it combines this language of nature and person in a way that links Trinity with Incarnation. In the Trinity, there are three persons or three hypostases, one nature, and one essence. What ended up in Chalcedon is that the notions of "nature" and "essence" ended up becoming equivalent with each other. There's one divine essence or *ousia*; there's one divine nature, three divine persons. And the second person of the Trinity is the very same person as Jesus Christ, the man, who has this one person, but two natures. You can use the words "nature" and "person" to relate Trinity and Incarnation in that way, and that's very handy for thinking through these issues in a clear way.

The problem was that Chalcedon did reject the formulation, "one nature," and there were many Eastern followers of Cyril. That is, people in the eastern half of the empire speaking Greek who followed Cyril of Alexandria and who liked that "one nature" formulation, unfortunate as it was. And there was a huge controversy about what was called Monophysitism. The Monophysites were those who affirmed one nature. *Monophysite* is a Greek term for "one nature." What ended up happening is that the [Eastern Orthodox] church rejected Monophysitism on the one hand, as confusing the two natures. And then Nestorianism, on the other hand, as separating the two natures. Chalcedon has been regarded ever since as sort of sailing down the middle. One person, two natures—

not one nature like the Monophysites, and not sort of two persons joined together like the Nestorians.

Let me run through a couple other councils. We have two more councils that deal with Christology in the early history of the Christian church, still during the time of the church fathers. The fifth ecumenical council is the Second Council of Constantinople in 553 under the Emperor Justinian. It endorsed what is called the *theopaschite* formula. That's the formula of the suffering of God. That becomes a very important issue. We've touched on it just a bit when we talked about the *communicatio idiomatum*. The *theopaschite* formula says this: "One of the Trinity was crucified in the flesh." There was some debate about this, but if you follow out the logic of Cyril's thought carefully, you're going to end up affirming this. "One of the Trinity," the same one who is eternally begotten of the Father, "was crucified in the flesh." People didn't want to say that the impassible, unchangeable, eternal God was hanging on a cross. They really sort of pulled back short of that. But the logic of the doctrine of the Trinity leads you exactly to that place. The man who suffered on the cross is God; therefore, it is God suffering on the cross. Remember, these church fathers have enough of Platonist philosophy in them that they want to say God is impassible. God by nature cannot suffer. He cannot change. He is too perfect to change. He can't change for the worst; he can't change for the better. He's already perfect. And he's eternal. He's outside of time. When you're outside of time, you can't change. You can't suffer. You can't die, except that the man on the cross is God, and he's suffering, and he's dying. The fifth ecumenical council ended up biting the bullet and saying, well, yes, one of the Trinity, who is God, suffered. The actual formulation that was incorporated into the statement of the council is this: "Our Lord Jesus Christ, who was crucified in the flesh, is true God and the Lord of Glory and one of the Holy Trinity."

Here's a label for it related to the label *theopaschite*, but I'm going to give it to you in a Latin form rather than a Greek form. The council affirmed Deipassionism. That is, God suffered—*Dei*, Latin for "God"; *passionism*, Latin for "suffering." God suffered on the cross. Cyril of Alexandria himself will actually say God suffers, or rather he avoids saying God suffers. Even he doesn't want to say that. He says the Word suffers, impassably. He suffers impassably on the cross because he remains what he was, namely impassible, while he suffers on the cross, assuming what he was not, our suffering. Remaining what he was, the impassable God, he assumes what he was not, which is our passability and suffering. There is double-sidedness; God really does suffer. But he remains God beyond all suffering and that actually ends up being how the patristic tradition in the tradition of these councils, parses out the relation of the divine and human in Christ. It's all about whether you can say God suffers, or how you can say God suffers. God, remaining impassable by his very nature, beyond suffering and death, suffers and dies on the cross. This is not an attempt to explain how that's possible. It is an attempt to get clear on what can be said and what can't be said.

Another thing that does have to be said is that God the Father does not suffer on the cross because, after all, God the Father is not incarnate. While the Christian theological tradition affirms Deipassionism, or the *theopaschite* formula that God suffers, it does not affirm Patripassionism—that would mean the Father suffers, *patri* from *patēr* in Greek. *Patērpassionism* would mean the Father suffers. But the Father isn't incarnate. The Father did not assume what he was not. The Father did not assume our suffering and death, therefore the Father, God the Father does not suffer. That preserved the sense of the impassability of God that these Christian theologians wanted to affirm. They didn't think it was a good thing for God to suffer.

I know that lots of modern folks want God to suffer; they think that that would help if we had a suffering God. Let me give you an image for why I think that doesn't help. If God the Father was suffering, it would be like we're drowning men or drowning women, drowning people. And he jumps into the water to save us, and we pull him down, and he dies. That doesn't help. According to the church fathers, we need an impassible God who is beyond suffering to rescue us from suffering. Imagine God the Father standing on the firm ground of eternity, while we're drowning, so he can pull us out of our drowning and put us with him in eternal life, everlasting life, life that doesn't die. But, with the Incarnation in mind, we have to enrich the picture by adding this point. The way he pulls us out of the water, God the Father standing on the firm ground of his eternity, is by throwing his own beloved son into the water with us. We do in fact pull him down with us to death. We're drowning; we make him drown with us. We kill him, but the Father, standing on the firm ground of his own eternity, pulls up the Son out of death, out of the waters of death and destruction, and we, clinging to that Son, come up out of the water with him and come to stand on the firm ground of everlasting life. That, I think, shows you why these church fathers wanted to affirm both God suffered, but the Father did not suffer.

One last little point: The sixth ecumenical council, very briefly, is the Third Council of Constantinople in A.D. 681. It settled the issue of how many wills there are in Christ. Monophysites were still there at this point, and so people who were sympathetic with the Monophysites said, here's one way of affirming the oneness of Christ, which is what we want to do in the tradition of Cyril. What we'll do is we'll affirm that there is only one will in Christ because he only has one nature, one will. The Council of Constantinople in 681, the sixth ecumenical council, rejected that view and affirmed two wills in Christ. The reason they did that is because they're thinking that, first of all, he's fully human so he has a human will. He's fully God; he has a divine will. This is illustrated in the Garden of Gethsemane in the famous scene where Jesus, sweating blood, prays to his Father and says, if it be your will Father, take this cup away from me. Now, the Father's will is God's will, and there's only one will in the Trinity—as we already learned in the doctrine of the Trinity—only one will in the Trinity, Christ as God has that will. When he submits himself to the Father's will, he's submitting himself to his own divine will. What does he mean when he says, "Not my will, but Thine be done"? What he's doing is he's submitting his human will to his divine will. He has two wills. His divine will is the same as the Father's will. His human will is the one that needs to submit to the divine will in obedience and that's what's happening when he says, "Not my will, but Thine be done." Two wills in Christ because two natures, fully divine, fully human, and that is the gist of the doctrine of the Incarnation.

Lecture Twelve
The Doctrine of Grace

Scope:

The crucial point made in the church father's doctrine of grace is that believers become children of God by grace, in contrast to Christ who is Son of God by nature. Augustine develops this doctrine further by treating grace as a gift of the Spirit to the soul, bestowing an inner delight which strengthens the will to love God. For Augustine, grace is necessary for salvation because of "original sin," which makes us guilty of Adam's sin and also corrupts our nature so that we cannot love God as we ought without the help of grace. Late in his career, he teaches that we cannot even pray in faith to receive the gift of grace unless grace is prevenient, which means it comes before any good will of ours, causing our free will to come to faith. This teaching leads Augustine to his controversial doctrine of predestination.

Outline

I. The patristic doctrine of grace was shaped by a contrast between nature and grace.

   A. Its prime concern was how believers in Christ became children of God: Only Christ is Son of God by nature, but believers become children of God by grace.

   B. A fundamental biblical metaphor for this was adoption: Whereas Christ is born Son of God, believers are adopted children of God.

   C. Adoption by grace was not just a change of status but a change in human nature, since it involved the gift of everlasting life, which is not natural to us.

   D. Since everlasting life means immortality, and an immortal is a god, it is not so surprising that this change came to be described as a kind of deification.

   E. Everlasting life therefore meant a "participation in the divine nature" (1 Peter 1:4).

   F. Hence the patristic formula: God became human so that humans could become divine.

- **G.** In Trinitarian terms, it arose from union with Christ, who is God.
- **II.** Augustine shifted the focus of the nature/grace distinction from overcoming death to overcoming sin.
  - **A.** He rejected Pelagianism because it meant that believers had no need of a transformative divine grace to be saved.
    1. Augustine found in Pelagius's writings the idea that human nature was capable of living without sin, so long as it was properly taught.
    2. Augustine's key claim was the necessity of grace: We cannot overcome sin without the help of an inner gift of divine grace which not only forgives past sin but gives our souls the power to love God and neighbor wholeheartedly.
  - **B.** Augustine's most widely-accepted argument for the necessity of grace is based on the practice of prayer.
    1. The basic premise is that Christians pray for God to help change their will and give them a deeper love for God and neighbor.
    2. This form of argument has been labeled *lex orandi, lex credendi* (roughly, "the rule for how you pray is the rule for what you believe").
  - **C.** Augustine's doctrine of "original sin" derives from a second argument he made for the necessity of grace, based on the widespread practice of infant baptism.
    1. Augustine argued that since baptism bestows forgiveness of sins, infants who are baptized must be guilty of some kind of sin, or they would not need to be baptized.
    2. Since infants have not committed any "actual sins" (a phrase which becomes a technical term), they must be guilty of Adam's "original sin."
    3. Augustine's doctrine of "original sin" means that every human being is born not just with a corrupted and sinful nature, but guilty of "original sin" and therefore deserving to be damned.

- **D.** A third argument Augustine makes for the necessity of grace is that Law without grace cannot help us but only terrify us.
  1. Telling us what to do doesn't help us do it, if what we are to do is not some outward act but an inward love of the heart.
  2. The grace we need is an inner gift of delight in God, "the love of God poured out in our hearts by the Holy Spirit which is given to us" (Romans 5:5).
  3. Hence, Augustine argues in his treatise *On the Spirit and the Letter*, the help we need is not the outward instruction of the letter but the inward grace of the Spirit.

III. Augustine's doctrine of grace led to deep issues that are still a matter of dispute in the Western Christian tradition.
- **A.** Augustine insisted with Paul that we are justified by faith, but does not teach the Protestant doctrine of justification by faith alone.
  1. For Augustine, our journey to God, our salvation really is like a journey along a road. When we're converted to the faith, that's like getting on the right road.
  2. What moves us along the road is love for God.
  3. But Christian faith is just the beginning of the journey, and is not sufficient to bring us home.
- **B.** Augustine insists on the necessity of grace if we are to do any good work, but does not teach the Protestant doctrine that we are saved by grace alone, because when our wills co-operate with grace our works of love have merit.
  1. By grace we come to love God, though we never do so perfectly in this life.
  2. Because believers pray for grace and forgiveness, their sins are not imputed to them.
  3. Gifts of grace, called "co-operative grace" work together with our good will to produce meritorious works of love.
  4. Although all our good works are outgrowths of grace, our salvation requires merit as well as grace.
  5. This is possible because the initial gift of grace, called "operative grace," works a change in our hearts, turning our wills toward the good.

- C. Augustine taught that grace and free will were compatible, but not everyone agrees that his doctrine of grace really is compatible with an adequate concept of free will.
    1. Augustine insists that this is not coercion, for it does not mean overcoming the unwilling but inwardly causing the unwilling to become willing.
    2. Hence on Augustine's view, God can cause us to will freely in a different way than we had before.
    3. This view of free will is deemed inadequate by those who think a truly free will is one that is ultimately in its own control.
- D. Augustine's notorious doctrine of predestination grows out of his doctrine of grace.
    1. Since the initial gift of grace does not depend in any way on our good will or merits, it is up to God who receives it.
    2. It is therefore God's choice that ultimately differentiates between the saved and the damned; this idea is known as the doctrine of "election."
    3. Augustine argues that this divine choice or "election" treats people unequally but not unjustly, because no one gets worse than they deserve (since all are born deserving damnation), and some get undeserved mercy.
    4. This divine choice is not made in response to unfolding events but is, like all God's choices, an eternal and unchanging plan that he carries out when the time comes.
    5. The name for this unchanging plan of God concerning how he will distribute the gifts of grace is predestination.
    6. Why God chooses to save one person rather than another is, by Augustine's own account, an unsearchable and frightening mystery.

IV. Augustine's view of grace is supported by his view of evil as a kind of nonbeing.
- A. Evil is a form of privation like darkness, lack, absence, or disorder.
    1. Augustine figures that since God created all things, whatever exists is good.

2. Since nothing God creates is evil, evil must not be a created thing, and therefore not a thing at all, but a lack of something.
   3. This does not mean evil is unreal, but that it has the reality of a privation, something lacking where it should be present, like a shadow or a hole or something twisted, broken, or disordered.
- **B.** Grace causes the will to fall in love with what makes us truly, eternally happy—our one true love.
   1. In healing the disorder of the will, grace restores true freedom of the will, which had been undermined by sin.
   2. Given his view of the nature of the will, evil, and grace, it makes perfect sense for Augustine to assume that grace and free will are always compatible with each other.

Suggested Reading:

Augustine, *On the Spirit and the Letter*, found in *Answer to the Pelagians I*.

Cary, *Inner Grace*.

Kelly, *Early Christian Doctrines*, chaps. 13 and 14.

Pelikan, *The Christian Tradition*, vol. 1, chap. 6.

Questions to Consider:

1. What is most attractive about Augustine's doctrine of grace?
2. What is least attractive about Augustine's doctrine of grace?

Lecture Twelve—Transcript
The Doctrine of Grace

We come now to the third of our series of three lectures on the great classic doctrines of early Christianity, the doctrines of the church fathers, the patristic doctrines. The first of them was the doctrine about who God is, the doctrine of the Trinity. The second, the doctrine about who Jesus Christ is, the doctrine of Incarnation. Now we come to a doctrine that's really about who we are as human beings. The overarching label for this is "soteriology," a technical term meaning the doctrine of salvation. The key concept we'll be discussing in this lecture is the concept of "grace," a New Testament term that has developed in all sorts of rich and powerful and fascinating ways in the history of Christian theology.

The concept of grace was used by the church fathers in the context of a contrast with nature. There's nature; there's grace. There's human nature, as it is in itself, then there's grace which transforms human nature. This is the part of the process of salvation; that's why it's soteriology. Human nature needs the grace of God to be saved. This grace of God, what it fundamentally does, is makes us children of God, sons and daughters of God. But, that's different from Christ who is the eternal Son of God; he is Son of God by nature. We've seen how these terms are used in the doctrine of the Trinity and the Incarnation. Jesus Christ, being fully God, has the divine nature; we don't. We are not God by nature; we are not sons and daughters of God by nature. We are sons and daughters of God by adoption. That's a crucial theological concept going back to the New Testament. We are sons and daughters of God by the grace of adoption. Jesus is the Son of God by nature. We are sons and daughters of God by the grace of adoption.

This adoption doesn't just change our status—although it certainly does that. We are now children of God. We are heirs of God. But it also changes our very nature because this gift of grace involves the gift of everlasting life. After all, we are by nature mortal. We all die. It's part of human nature. The gift of grace, which is a gift of everlasting life, transforms human nature, makes us more like God, who never dies. Indeed, the church fathers in the eastern part of the empire, the Greek-speaking part of the Roman Empire, were very happy to call this deification—meaning not that we become children of God by nature. We are not by nature gods. We cannot by nature be gods because we came into being. God never came into being. Nothing that was created and came into being could ever be, by nature, God. But we are by grace, gods, small "g" in the plural. And that's actually not a very surprising thing to say if you understand what the word "god" looked like in ancient Greek and Latin. The word god, *theos*, meant "immortal." They were pretty much interchangeable, equivalent terms. A god is an immortal. If we have an immortal life, everlasting life, then we are gods, small "g": It's the same thing with the Latin word *deus*. Even in the Old Testament in the Hebrew scriptures, you occasionally get the word gods used in this sense as the immortal beings, the angels. They're not gods that you worship, but they are immortals. We become immortals by the gift of the grace of adoption.

Another way of putting this, in the New Testament itself, in the second letter of Peter, chapter 1, is that we have "participation in the divine nature." We participate in the divine nature. "Participate" is one of those words like communicate that has an ancient meaning of sharing. We have a share in the divine nature. We have a share in immortality and everlasting life. How? By union with Christ. By faith in Christ we are united with Christ, and it's as if we get a share of who Christ is, his everlasting life, by union with him. By faith in Christ, we have union with Christ. We have the grace of adoption. We have everlasting life. We become gods, deified in that small sense, god, small "g": We are never gods by nature.

That's the common patristic doctrine of grace shared with the East and the West. I want to now focus on the development of the doctrine of grace that happens in the western part of the Roman Empire in the 5th century A.D., in the hands of the most influential of the western church fathers, Augustine, Saint Augustine for Catholics. He is the bishop of Hippo in North Africa. The Romans just called this Africa. It is where Algeria now is today; it's a town on the seacoast. He is the bishop of Hippo in North Africa. He is the most influential Christian theologian outside the Bible, although his influence is almost entirely among the offshoots of this western part of the Roman Empire, the Western church as it's called, meaning Protestants and Roman Catholics. He's not nearly so influential among Eastern Orthodox, Greek Orthodox, Russian Orthodox. But, in the West, among Protestants and Catholics, he is simply the most influential Christian writer outside the Bible, so his doctrine of grace is terribly, terribly important and influential. What he does is he applies the concept of grace not just to our mortal nature, not just to this notion that we have everlasting life and overcome death. But also he thinks very deeply about how grace changes our sinful nature. There's a fair amount of that sort of thinking in the Eastern church fathers also, but for Augustine it's particularly intense. He thinks very, very deeply about how the grace of God makes an inner change in our hearts, so that we overcome sin. God, by his grace, overcomes the sin in us.

Augustine's key argument was made against a man who ended up being labeled a heretic, a man named Pelagius. So Augustine's doctrine of Grace is often called an anti-Pelagian doctrine of grace. Augustine's argument was that Pelagius wasn't giving enough credit to grace. He wasn't clear enough about our need for grace, about the necessity of grace, about the fact that we cannot be saved without the grace of God. We can't just believe in Christ, believe in the teachings of Christ, and become better people. We can try, but that won't be good enough. Our efforts by themselves are not good enough to save us. Pelagius didn't seem to recognize that, or at least Augustine didn't think he did. It's possible that Pelagius got a bad rap. But for our purposes, we're going to follow Augustine's views here just to flesh out what Augustine is saying. He said, Pelagius, don't you understand, just trying to be a better person, trying to be a good Christian, trying to believe in love, God, and your neighbor, that's great, but it's not good enough. You're not going to be able to save yourself that way. You need the grace of God, an inward change in your heart that comes by the grace of God, which comes to us inwardly.

Augustine made three arguments against Pelagius to establish this necessity of grace for salvation. The first one is an argument from prayer. He says look, we Christians, we pray for the grace of God. We pray for God to change our hearts. We pray for God to give us the gift of love. We pray for God to cause us to love our neighbor more, to give us more love for God himself, and if we can pray for it, he can give it. This actually I think is the most powerful argument Augustine makes for the necessity of grace. This is, indeed, how Christians pray. They pray for such a gift. If they pray for it, then God can give it, wouldn't you think?

This kind of argument, by the way, which Augustine uses often and others do also, has a name. It's a Latin phrase, *lex orandi, lex credendi*, "the law of praying is the law of believing." If this is how Christians pray, then this is how Christians believe. If you pray for this kind of thing, especially in the liturgy of the church or in the psalms, well then this is something that God can give you. If you need help to learn to be a person who really, truly loves from the depths of your heart and you pray for that help from God, this is help that God can give, and that's grace, and that's necessary. You couldn't live without praying for such help. You couldn't be saved without such prayers. The prayer for grace is deeply important for Augustine.

The second argument for the necessity of grace that Augustine makes is more questionable and has caused a great deal more controversy and pain. Augustine noticed—he mentions this often in his sermons—women running with their infant children to the baptismal font, where their children can get baptized, because everyone assumed that if a child didn't get baptized before it died, there was a problem. By baptizing the baby, the people of North Africa figured they're keeping this child safe from damnation. Augustine says that's right; we baptize infants in the church. Why? After all, baptism is for the remission of sins. That's actually part of the Creed. I believe in one baptism for the remission of sins. What sin could an infant have? The infant hasn't done anything wrong with its own free will. The infant has no "actual sin." This becomes a technical term. The infant instead has, Augustine says, "original sin." Key phrase; you've probably heard it. It's the label for a doctrine that Augustine is the first to develop at great length. "Original sin," meaning the sin of Adam, is the same sin that this baby is born with. The baby is born guilty. Adam's sin is in some way the baby's own sin because somehow all of us were in Adam when Adam first sinned way back in Genesis, chapter 3. By the way, it's not Eve's sin. It's Adam's sin that's blameworthy here. We're born in Adam, partakers somehow in Adam's sin. Everyone of us not just sort of born with a bad nature prone to sin, not just born sort of corrupted and nasty, but already guilty. The day we're born, we're already guilty and deserving of damnation, and that's why it's so important to baptize your infant. Because if your infant's going to die, and of course lots of infants did in those days, then you want their sins washed away—the "original sin" of Adam. Baptism transfers you from death in Adam to life in Christ, and you want that for your child. That's Augustine's second argument. Baptism gives us this grace, which washes away our sin, and without this grace, we are damned. Baptism is necessary for salvation. Baptismal grace is necessary for the Christian life and for the salvation that follows, and that's what Pelagius doesn't seem to understand, Augustine says.

The third argument for the necessity of grace is more psychological. The other two are based on Christian practices, prayer and baptism. This is a psychological argument, although it's using the terms law and grace that come from Saint Paul in the New Testament. Paul often contrasts law and grace, although Paul was thinking primarily of the Law of Moses and the grace of Christ, and why you don't need to get circumcised in order to be a Christian if you're a Gentile. Augustine takes that set of terms and applies it to a psychology of grace. He takes the Law, grace terminology, out of the context of the issue about Jews and Gentiles, which is Paul's issue. And he reinterprets it as a psychological problem about how we come to obedience. This is an epochal change in how Christians read Paul. Ever afterward, the Western church reads Paul through Augustine's interpretation.

The Law commands us to love God with our whole heart, mind, and strength. What happens when we hear this law? Even when we're Christians, even when we're believers, we hear it and we obey it, right? That's what Pelagius seems to think, but Augustine says, of course not. When we get this law, what happens is we resent it. We'd rather not have to do it. If we had a choice, we would be disobedient. But we're afraid, so sometimes we try our best to obey God because we don't want to be, of course, roasting in hell for eternity. So out of fear we try to love God with our whole heart, mind, and strength. Out of fear, we try to love. It doesn't work. You can't love out of fear of punishment. That's a motivation that doesn't work. We need some different motivation. What we do, says Augustine, is we pray for grace, and God gives this grace so that our hearts are transformed, and we are delighted to love God. We find the love of God sweet. There's this inward transformation, this sweetness where we delight to love, and all things are easy if they are delightful. Even hard work is easy if it's delightful work. Likewise, the love of God becomes delightful to us and that leads us to our salvation.

That doctrine of grace about law and grace becomes absolutely crucial for Western theology. Let me mention, he works this out in a treatise called *On the Spirit and the Letter*, again, quoting that passage from Paul that we mentioned earlier, "The letter kills. The Spirit gives life." Augustine associates law with letter; it's external. All it can do is kill us. It says love God with your whole heart, mind, and strength, and if you don't you're going to hell. Oh, I'm so afraid. I'll love God. That doesn't work. Out of terror I'll love God. No. The law terrifies you so that you'll pray for grace. You'll flee to the grace of God. And that inward gift of grace, through baptism, through prayer, through the life of the church, will transform you inwardly so that you end up loving God with your whole heart, mind, and strength, and that's salvation.

This enormously influential doctrine of grace played a role both in Catholic theology and in Protestant theology. And I want to compare it now with some key points in Protestantism, which we will talk about later, because Augustine is not exactly a Protestant. In certain respects, he's not exactly a good Roman Catholic either; we'll talk about that later too. Augustine is not exactly a Protestant. He does not believe in justification by faith alone, which is the key Protestant belief. For Augustine, our journey to God, our salvation really is like a journey along a road, and faith is when we get on the road at the beginning. When we come to faith in Christ, when we're converted to the faith, that's like getting on the right road. But, then there's this long road to travel. How do we travel that road, the road to God?

We travel that road by love, by loving God with our whole heart, mind, and strength, and our neighbor as ourselves. That's the commandment of Jesus, which goes back to the Old Testament. And Augustine puts it at the heart of Christian ethics. Love is like a motive force, like a force of attraction—almost like a gravity. But it's a gravity that's pulling us upward. My love is my weight, says Augustine in a famous passage. My love is a gravity, in this case, that pulls us upward like fire going up to the stars. Love, love for God, attracts us to God, pulls us toward God, and it ultimately unites us with God. Faith alone isn't enough for Augustine. Faith is the beginning. It's indispensable; it's necessary. You can't even come to faith without grace, but then you need grace to carry you along in this journey of love toward God.

That also means that we are not saved by grace alone because what grace does is it causes us to love, strengthens our love, and by loving, we become more worthy of God, as well as closer to God. That worthiness is called merit, and Augustine is willing to say that by the love of God, which is instilled in us by grace, we become more meritorious. We become more worthy of God. Protestants say no, no, no, it's grace alone, no merit. Augustine is willing to talk about merit, although he doesn't think that we can simply earn our way to heaven. Protestants should not say that about Catholics; Catholics don't believe that. It's not in Catholic theology. It's not like we ever can come before God being perfect and saying, God, I love you so much, you have to send me to heaven. No, we are still sinners. Throughout our whole life, we still have sin. And Augustine will say our sins are not imputed to us because we pray for forgiveness. Every day Christians are supposed to be praying, forgive us our trespasses. All of the daily sins of our lives are forgiven, but we're never perfect. And that's all right. We're on the road. We don't get home, we don't get to God until after death, but all our lives we're on the road. We're getting better. We're not perfect. We need our sins forgiven, and God does forgive our sins when we pray for forgiveness. He doesn't impute our sins to us. Protestants are going to make a big deal out of that term, but they're going to make more of it than Augustine does.

Let me mention two aspects of grace that we can now fit into this picture. When we are on the road, when we're heading toward God by this power of love, this power of love is strengthened in us by grace. Augustine will say that grace strengthens and assists and helps us. He talks about assisting grace, which means helping grace. He also talks about grace healing our hearts because our hearts are wounded by our desires for things that are less than God, our desire for money or sex or drink or power, or any of the things that distract us from love of God and neighbor. That's like a disease, Augustine says. "Our diseased hearts want what is not actually good for us," like a sick man who wants what is not healthy for him. "And grace heals our heart so that we love what will make us ultimately happy," which is God and our neighbor with God.

That's what Augustine will call "assisting grace," "healing grace," and also "co-operative grace," because it co-operates with, it works with our own free will by stimulating, strengthening, and helping our free will to love. What our will does, by the way, for Augustine, what our free will is all about is how we love. Our free will sins, and we sin by our own free will. When we love say, money, more than our friends. Or, even when we love our friends more than God. When we love in the wrong order, then things go wrong, and we get off the road. We need to love God first with our whole heart, mind, and strength, our neighbors as ourselves, and then other things in order. We can even love money a little bit. It's useful, but only as something useful, not as something that's going to make you happy. Only God can make you eternally happy. That's why you should love God above all other things.

Grace gets into our will, into our free will, and strengthens it in loving the right things because what the will does is love. It can love the wrong way. It can love the right way. Grace helps it love the right way. But, there's also, in addition to this "co-operative grace" that works with our will—and remember "co-operation" is just Latin for "working with," so co-operative grace works with our will—in addition to that "co-operative grace," there is "operative grace" where God works in our will without our will, he'll say. Co-operative grace is God working in us without us, without our co-operation. It's God's grace coming deep into our heart and turning our will in a different direction. For instance, taking a wicked person and turning their will, converting them, so that they become a good Christian. Conversion, by the way, is a Latin word for "turning." What operative grace does is it turns our will without our will, not by coercion, not by force, but by this power of sweet delight, as if the thing that we love most in the world presents itself to us and says here is your true love. You've been seeking money or power or any of these other things, which can't make you eternally happy. But here is the true beauty, the true goodness, the true God, the true happiness that you have longed for all of your life. That's what operative grace does. It turns the will to take delight in what it had rejected, but to turn the will to take delight in God that will make you eternally happy.

Here's the problem. Lots of people think that if God's grace turns our free will without our co-operation, then that takes away our free will. Augustine says, no. Augustine says grace and free will co-operate. They are compatible with each other, even if sometimes it's grace that has the initiative. It's not just our free will responding to grace, it's grace turning our will, but it turns our will freely by this action of delight, not by coercion, not by force. Grace is never a kind of force. It's always a kind of delight. But it does have the power to turn our wills without violating our wills, without taking away our free will, so says Augustine. Lots of philosophers and even Christian theologians are not too happy about that formulation. Augustine is convinced that grace and free will are compatible, but not everybody is quite so convinced as Augustine.

That bears on the next crucial issue we need to talk about, Augustine's doctrine of predestination. Augustine's doctrine of predestination is built on this notion of "operative grace," a grace that can change our wills. His doctrine of predestination is famous; he's the one, really the first great Christian theologian, who had a fully developed doctrine of predestination. It didn't begin with Calvin. Calvin, the great Protestant theologian says I learned this from Augustine, and he pretty much did. Here's what Augustine's thinking. All of us are born in Adam with "original sin." All of us are born with a nature that is corrupted, attracted to the wrong things, attracted to good things like everything from food to money to sex to even power. All these things are good things, but they're not God. And we try to find our happiness in them, and that makes us miserable.

What can turn us around? We're all sinners. We're all included in what Augustine calls a mass of damnation. This comes from a metaphor in the letter of Paul to the Romans, chapter 9. He talks about a lump of clay. And God takes this lump or mass, and he separates it into two parts. And he's like a potter. He takes one lump of it, and he makes it into a beautiful vase for use in the temple, say. Another lump of it he makes into a chamber pot or something that's going to be thrown away. We are massive damnation, one lump of clay, all of us sinners born in Adam were one lump, one lump of damned sinners, sinners that deserve nothing but destruction and eternal death, eternal torture, damnation, hell. That's all of us, the whole human race, everyone who's a child of Adam. God is going to take that mass of damnation, all of which deserves destruction, and by his own grace, he's going to choose some, and he's going to pull some out of that mass, and say you I will give grace to. I'll give grace to you. Turn your hearts around. Change the direction of your love so that you come to me in salvation. Those other folks, well, they deserve damnation, and I'm not going to change that. I'm not going to give them the grace to save them; they can go get damned. This is called the doctrine of "election," or God's choice. God chooses. I'm going to save this part of the mass from damnation, but not that part. These folks get saved; these folks don't.

Notice, Augustine will say this is not unjust. Augustine does not believe God is unjust; he would never teach that. It's unequal, but that's not unjust. Here's how he says it: "It's unequal but not unjust because everybody in the mass of damnation deserves damnation. Those whom God does not choose just get what they deserve, which is damnation." That's just. There's nothing unjust about giving people what they deserve. Those who are pulled out of the mass of damnation by the grace of God, undeserved, unmerited grace, changing their will, well, they get better than they deserve. They get undeserved mercy; that's not unjust either. Some get underserved mercy. Some get deserved damnation. And both of this is just. Both of this is just, even though it's unequal. God can have mercy upon whom we wants to have mercy. Those upon whom he does not have mercy are justly condemned. That's justice. No one is being ill-treated. No one is being treated unfairly, even though they are being treated unequally. That's Augustine's argument. Again, lots of people don't like that argument at all. We're going to be revisiting it in a later context when we get to Protestant heirs of Augustine's doctrine of predestination.

One wonders why God chooses to save some rather than others, to save this person rather than that person. There's a famous passage in the same chapter of the letter to Romans: "Jacob have I loved, and Esau have I hated." This is what God says of Jacob and Esau, who are twins, even before they're born. Both of them, in Augustine's view, deserving damnation, but God is going to be gracious to Jacob and let Esau go to damnation. Why? Why does he choose the one rather than the other? Why choose Jacob rather than Esau? Augustine's answer comes from two chapters later in the letter to the Romans. When you press Augustine with that question, his answer is, "Oh the depths of the riches of the wisdom and the knowledge of God. How inscrutable are his judgments, how unsearchable his ways?" In other words, I have no idea why God chooses one rather than another. None of us could know. There is no reason that we know. There is a reason, Augustine thinks, because God chooses wisely. But it's a reason that we cannot possibly know, so it seems arbitrary. Out of sheer love, God chooses one, and he doesn't love the other. Why? Why does he choose one rather than the other, we cannot know. "Oh the depths of the riches and the wisdom of the knowledge of God. How inscrutable are his judgments." And terrifying, we might add. Augustine says, yes, these depths, we look into these depths of the judgment of God, the choice of God, the "election" of God, the predestination of God, and we shudder, shudder with horror. It's scary because this choice that God makes is made from before the beginning of Creation, before all time. It is predestined. The scary thing about it I think is not the predestination part, but the choice. God, for no particular reason that we know, differentiates between one part of the mass of damnation and another, choosing one rather than another for no reason we can possibly imagine. That's scary. It's the doctrine of "election" that's the scary part, I think. And again we'll get back to that in some later lectures.

Meanwhile, let me say just a little bit about a few other features of Augustine's thoughts that will help bring into focus why Augustine thinks that grace and free will are compatible because I don't want to leave us with simply the terror of Augustine and his doctrine of grace. There's a very optimistic side, oddly, of Augustine's doctrine of grace. Sometimes he's regarded as a pessimist. He believes in "original sin," the damnation of infants, where he actually believes that those infants who aren't baptized are damned. That's why later Catholics will have a doctrine of limbo, a place where the unbaptized infants don't go to heaven, but at least they're not punished. It all seems very pessimistic, doesn't it—predestination, infant damnation, "original sin."

In fact, Augustine will also say at one point in one of his writings in his book *Confessions*, chapter 7, that "Whatever is, is good," and that's a quote, "Whatever is, is good." Why? It's because God created everything that is. All that exists is God's creation, and God only creates good things. Literally, all being is good for Augustine. That's pretty optimistic you might say. It's ontological, metaphysical optimism. Evil can only take the form of an absence, of a lack of nonbeing. Evil is like darkness, which is the absence of light. By the way, it's not like blackness, which is a real color, but like darkness, which is the absence of light. Black and white are both real colors; darkness and light are different. Darkness is the absence of light. Evil is like absence, something missing, something unreal. Yet, it's real like shadows are real. Absences are real. A hole in my shirt is real, even if it's the absence of something that ought to be there. Evil is an absence in the good world that God created that has a real presence, a real effect on us, the way that darkness has when you stumble into a dark room. The darkness is real, in one sense, even though it's not got any substance to it. It's not got any reality of its own. It's just something missing.

Evil is always, for Augustine, a privation, a deprivation or lack of real being because the universe inherently is good. All things are inherently good because God made them that way, including human nature, which was made good at the beginning. Including even the devil, by the way, who was originally made an angel and who sinned by his own free will, turning away from God. The evil in the devil comes from the devil by his own free will, which is free to reject God. But the devil's nature is good. He's an angel. Even sinners have a good nature, and though they might want to reject God, they can't get away from the fact that they are God's good creatures. It must really bother the devil that he's God's good creature even though he hates God. At least that's an Augustinian thought to have.

Don't put Augustine down simply as a pessimist. In some deep philosophical sense, he's an optimist. But, he does leave a legacy of deep and sometimes terrifying thoughts in his doctrine of grace, some aspects of which I think are just deeply beautiful, this delight in God, this love for God, which grace instills in us. But, then, the doctrine of "election," there's something terrifying about that. And certainly the doctrine of "original sin" has something terrifying about it. There's a lot to sort out in the legacy of Augustine's doctrine of grace that will be important in the Middle Ages, and in the Reformation, and on into 20th-century theology. We're about ready to march onward into the Middle Ages, the Reformation, and eventually to modern theology.

Timeline

A.D.

c. 30	Crucifixion of Jesus.
50–64	Letters of the Apostle Paul, the earliest writings in the New Testament.
65	The earliest date suggested for the composition of the book of Mark, usually regarded as the first of the Four Gospels to be written (other scholars argue for a date after the destruction of the temple).
70	The Romans destroy the temple in Jerusalem at the culmination of the Great Jewish Revolt.
75–95	Most scholars date the composition of the Gospels of Matthew, Luke, and John to these decades.
144	Marcion excommunicated in Rome.
c. 145	Valentinus teaches in Rome, but his hopes of becoming bishop (that is, pope) go unfulfilled.
c. 150	Justin Martyr writes his *Apology* and *Dialogue with Trypho*.
180–200	Irenaeus, bishop of Lyons, writes his influential multi-volume treatise, *Against Heresies*.
c. 202	Origen begins his teaching career at age 17 by becoming head of the catechetical school in Alexandria.

325	The First Council of Nicaea (the first ecumenical council) condemns the teaching of Arius and approves a creed containing the *homoousios* clause.
381	The First Council of Constantinople (the second ecumenical council) approves an expanded version of the creed of Nicaea, which is today called the Nicene Creed.
385	Augustine, at age 31, begins his career as a Christian writer.
431	The Council of Ephesus (the third ecumenical council), led by Cyril of Alexandria, condemns Nestorius and his Christology; the council emphasizes the unity of Christ by teaching that Mary is *theotokos* (Mother of God), that the union of divine and human in Christ is hypostatic, and that Christ's body is life-giving flesh.
451	The Council of Chalcedon (the fourth ecumenical council), accepting the teaching of Pope Leo I, holds that there are in Christ two natures, divine and human, which remain distinct even in the unity of one person.
553	The Second Council of Constantinople (the fifth ecumenical council) gives a Cyrillian interpretation of the teaching of Chalcedon, re-emphasizing the unity of his person.

681	The Third Council of Constantinople (the sixth ecumenical council) rejects Monothelitism, the teaching that there is only one will in Christ, in favor of Dyothelitism, the teaching that he has both the divine will and a human will.
787	The Second Council of Nicaea (the seventh ecumenical council) rejects iconoclasm and teaches that icons are to be venerated, though not worshiped.
1054	Beginning of the official schism between the Western and Eastern churches, resulting in Roman Catholicism and Eastern Orthodoxy.
1093	Anselm becomes archbishop of Canterbury.
1215	The Fourth Lateran Council defines the doctrine of transubstantiation and requires Catholics to receive communion at least once a year at Easter.
1256	Thomas Aquinas begins his teaching career at the University of Paris.
1439	The Council of Florence defines the medieval sacramental system and all seven sacraments.
1517	Martin Luther posts the 95 Theses on the church door at Wittenberg announcing an academic disputation about the theology of indulgences; he has no idea that this would inaugurate the Reformation and lead to a split with the pope within five years.

1521	At the imperial Diet of Worms, Luther refuses to retract any of his writings, thus making the split between Protestants and Catholics inevitable in Germany.
1522	Ulrich Zwingli, parish priest and reformer in Zürich, begins publishing his writings and thus inaugurates the Reformed tradition of theology.
1525	Anabaptists in the environs of Zürich, rejecting the practice of infant baptism, begin "re-baptizing" (as their opponents think of it) those who have received baptism as infants; Thomas Müntzer, a Lutheran pastor in Germany convinced he is inspired by the Holy Spirit (for which Luther called him a "fanatic"), becomes a leader in the great Peasant War until he is defeated, captured, and executed.
1527	The Schleitheim Confesssion, the most important confessional document of the early Anabaptist movement, is published in Switzerland.
1529	Lutheran princes lodge a formal protest against a decision by the imperial Diet of Speyer, thus giving birth to the name "Protestant."
1530	Lutheran theologians led by Philip Melanchthon compose The Augsburg Confession and present it before Emperor Charles V at the Diet of Augsburg; it becomes the most important doctrinal standard of the Lutheran church.

1534	In the Act of Supremacy, Parliament declares King Henry VIII to be "supreme head on earth of the Church of England," thus breaking with the church of Rome and initiating the English Reformation.
1536	Menno Simons begins ministering among the surviving Dutch Anabaptists after the Anabaptist takeover of the city of Münster is ruthlessly suppressed; he leads them in a resolutely pacifist direction so successfully that they came to be called Mennonites; John Calvin begins his work as pastor, teacher, and theologian in Geneva, becoming the most influential theologian in the Reformed tradition; the first of five editions of his *Institutes* is published.
1545–1563	The Council of Trent meets—with numerous lengthy interruptions—and provides the official Roman Catholic response to Protestant theology as well as measures for the renewal of the Catholic church.
1549	The first edition of the *Book of Common Prayer* of the Church of England is issued under the authority of King Edward VI.
1559	The Act of Uniformity under Queen Elizabeth I establishes the Elizabethan Settlement, the mature form of the English Reformation.

1560s	In the Vestiarian controversy, Puritan theology begins to take shape, initially as the more Reformed wing of the Church of England.
1563	The *39 Articles*, the official confessional document of the Church of England, is issued under Queen Elizabeth I.
1567	Rome officially condemns the teachings of Catholic theologian Michael Baius ("Baianism").
1572	With John of the Cross as her confessor and spiritual director, Theresa of Avila comes to the ultimate state of inner union with God in this life, called spiritual marriage.
1577	Anabaptists are granted toleration under William I of Orange in the Netherlands.
1580	The *Formula of Concord* is published in the *Book of Concord* together with other Lutheran confessional documents such as The Augsburg Confession to settle a number of disputes among Lutheran theologians about free will, justification, and other issues.
1598–1607	Formal debates on the help of grace (*de Auxiliis*) are held in Rome between Molinists and Thomists; the issue is ultimately left unresolved by the pope, thus legitimizing both positions as acceptable theological opinions.

1609	Formation of the first English Baptist congregation from a Puritan Separatist congregation in exile in the Netherlands.
1616	Francis de Sales publishes his major work, *Treatise on the Love of God*.
1618–1619	Reformed theologians at the Synod of Dordt in Holland reject Arminianism and formulate five points of Calvinism.
1640	Posthumous publication of Cornelius Jansen's book *Augustinus*, which becomes the bone of contention in the Jansenist controversy.
1647	The Westminster Confession, the most important Reformed confessional document in English, especially important among Presbyterians, is accepted by authority of Parliament in the course of the English Civil War.
1648	In New England, the Cambridge Platform establishes the Congregationalist form of church governance.
1650	The Religious Society of Friends (Quakers) begins to form around the preaching of George Fox in England.
1653	Pope condemns five propositions attributed to Jansen's *Augustinus*, bringing the Jansenist controversy to a head in France.

1662	In New England, the Halfway Covenant allows baptized but unconverted Christians to be members of the Congregationalist (Puritan) church.
1675	Lutheran pastor Philipp Jakob Spener publishes his book *Pia Desideria* ("Pious Desires") in Germany, inaugurating the Pietist movement.
1687	Rome condemns Quietism.
1689	The Act of Toleration in England legalizes Protestant groups that dissent from the established Church of England.
1695	The French church condemns Madame Guyon's teachings for their Quietist tendencies.
1696	John Toland publishes the first major work of deism, *Christianity not Mysterious*.
1699	Rome condemns Fénelon's "semi-Quietist" teaching of "pure love."
1722	Protestants fleeing persecution in Moravia begin settling in Herrnhut, Germany, at the invitation of Count von Zinzendorf, who later becomes their bishop and the leading theologian of the Moravian church.

1734	A period of revival begins in Jonathan Edwards's congregation in Northampton, Massachusetts, which he describes in his influential book *A Faithful Narrative of the Surprising Work of God* (1737), one of the founding documents of *Revivalism*.
1739	John Wesley begins his career as itinerant preacher of revival and leader of the Methodist movement.
1740	The Great Awakening, a revival of religion whose most important theological advocate is Jonathan Edwards, begins to spread throughout New England.
1764	Voltaire publishes his *Philosophical Dictionary*, a collection of deist satirical essays highly critical of Christianity.
1794	Thomas Paine publishes the first part of *The Age of Reason*, the most important work of American deism.
1799	Friedrich Schleiermacher takes an initial step toward the founding of liberal Protestant theology by publishing his book, *On Religion: Speeches to Its Cultured Despisers*.
1811	Schleiermacher becomes the first professor of theology at the new University of Berlin, soon to become one of the most influential universities in the world.

1824	Charles Finney begins applying "new measures" in revival preaching, based on a much greater emphasis on free will than in Jonathan Edwards's Revivalist theology.
1832	John Nelson Darby, a founding figure in the Plymouth Brethren, begins teaching Dispensationalist theology.
1836	Methodist teacher Phoebe Palmer begins leading the Tuesday Night Meetings for the Promotion of Holiness in her home in New York City, inaugurating the Holiness tradition.
1854	In *Ineffabilis Deus* ("The Ineffable God"), Pope Pius IX defines the Blessed Virgin Mary's Immaculate Conception as a doctrine to be believed by all the faithful.
1864	Pope Pius IX promulgates the *Syllabus of Errors*, denouncing a large number of modern beliefs.
1867	The National Camp Meeting Association for the Promotion of Holiness begins spreading Holiness teachings.
1870	Pope Pius IX, with the approval of the First Vatican Council, defines the doctrine of papal infallibility as well as the doctrine that God can be known by natural reason.

1875	A meeting of Presbyterians and Anglicans in Keswick, England, begins the Keswick movement, which adapts Holiness teachings to non-perfectionist (that is, non-Methodist) traditions.
1879	Pope Leo XIII's encyclical *Aeterni Patris* promotes "the restoration of Christian philosophy according to the mind of Saint Thomas Aquinas," thus giving a major boost to neo-Thomism.
1906	Albert Schweitzer publishes *The Quest of the Historical Jesus*, arguing that the quest was a failure because the historical Jesus was an eschatological prophet belonging to his time, not ours; The Azusa Street Revival begins in Los Angeles; it lasts several years and gives birth to Pentecostalism.
1910–1915	Publication of *The Fundamentals*, a series of books from which the Fundamentalist movement later took its name.
1917	Publication of the second edition of the *Scofield Reference Bible*, which becomes the most important text of the Dispensationalist movement.
1922	Harry Emerson Fosdick's sermon "Shall the Fundamentalists Win?" defines the key issues on the modernist side of the Fundamentalist-modernist controversy.

1923	J. Gresham Machen's book *Christianity and Liberalism* defines the key issues on the Fundamentalist side of the Fundamentalist-modernist controversy.
1925	The Scopes "Monkey Trial" results in the cultural discrediting and marginalization of Fundamentalism, and spurs anti-intellectualism within the Fundamentalist movement.
1950	The papal bull *Munificentissimus Deus* (The Most Munificent God) defines the Assumption of the Blessed Virgin Mary, her being taken body and soul into heaven, as doctrine to be held by all the faithful; The papal encyclical *Humani Generis* condemns theologies which deny that God could have created human nature without directing it to a supernatural happiness.
1962–1965	The Second Vatican Council provides measures for the renewal of the Roman Catholic church as well as ecumenical openings toward non-Roman churches.

Glossary

absolution: From a Latin verb meaning "to loose" (related to the word "dissolve"), in a broad sense this term is another word for forgiveness of sins, while in a narrow sense it means specifically the priest announcing forgiveness of sins to the penitent in the sacrament of Penance by saying, "I absolve you of your sins in the name of the Father, the Son, and the Holy Spirit."

actualism: A technical term for the emphasis on revelation as an event, characteristic of the neo-Orthodox theologians, especially Karl Barth.

adiaphora: A Greek term meaning "indifferent things," *adiaphora* is a technical term in theology referring to church practices which are not necessary to obtain salvation or required by Christian faith, for example, kneeling in church, use of special vestments, and making the sign of the cross. Controversies often arose among Protestant groups (especially in state churches like the German Lutherans and the Church of England) about whether regulations requiring such practices could legitimately be made by the church or enforced by the government.

aeons (Sometimes spelled "aions"): Gnostics used this Greek term to refer to other-worldly spiritual principles making up the divine realm of the Pleroma.

aggiornamiento: (See **Vatican, Second Council**.)

agility: In medieval theology, a quality of glorified human bodies after the resurrection, which means they can freely and instantaneously (or nearly so) move to whatever place the soul wishes to be. (See **clarity**, **impassibility**, and **subtlety**.)

agrapha: From the Greek word for "unwritten," a technical term in contemporary scholarship for sayings of Jesus not written down in the New Testament but found in other writings, such as those of the church fathers.

alien immersion: In Landmarkism, baptism in any non-Baptist church—which, even when it is adult baptism by immersion, as required by Baptist teaching, is not a true baptism because it is alien to the true church.

allegory: A form of reading, first used by pagan writers, in which religious texts are understood as having hidden, usually philosophical, meaning. In early Christian theology this is often combined inextricably with typology.

Alumbrados: Spanish for "the illuminated ones," a mystical movement in 15th- and 16th-century Spain, which was rejected by Rome and may have contributed to the late 16th-century theology of Quietism. (See *dejamiento*.)

Amish: (See **Anabaptists**.)

Amyraldianism: Named after Moses Amyraut or Amyraldus, and also called "hypothetical universalism" or "four-point Calvinism" (or "moderate Calvinism" by its advocates), according to which Christ died for the redemption of every human being (thus rejecting the doctrine of limited atonement). However, this redemption is available only on condition that Christ be accepted in faith, which is done only by those to whom God chooses to give the gift of faith (thus affirming the doctrine of unconditional election). Richard Baxter was its most important advocate among the English Puritans.

Anabaptists: From the Greek term for "rebaptizers," a name given them by their opponents. This Protestant movement originated mainly in German-speaking lands in the 16th century, known for rejecting infant baptism (which means they did not think people baptized as infants received true Christian baptism, and thus they did not think it was "rebaptism" when they baptized adults who had been baptized as infants). They are not to be confused with Baptists, who also rejected infant baptism but who arose in England in the 17th century. The best known Anabaptist groups today are the Mennonites and the Amish.

anfechtung: German for "assault," the word Luther used to translate the Latin word *tentatio*, that is, "temptation." This is the characteristically Lutheran concept of temptation, which means that the devil assaults the conscience by making you aware of your sin and weakness of faith, thus tempting you to doubt that Christ will keep his promise to you.

Anglicanism: From the Latin phrase *anglicana ecclesia*, meaning "English Church," the worldwide communion of churches stemming from the established Protestant Church of England led by the archbishop of Canterbury including, for instance, the Episcopalian church in the United States.

anhypostasis: Literally "without hypostasis," the orthodox applied this term to the humanity of Christ, which for all its completeness (including both a body and a rational soul) is not a person in its own right, for the person of the man Jesus Christ is the divine Word. This doctrine arose because the humanity of Christ cannot be a person in its own right without making Christ into two persons, one divine and one human, which is contrary to orthodox Christology.

anthropology: In theology, this refers to theories of human nature. Anthropology is what theology or philosophy has to say about the meaning of human existence. This should not be confused with the discipline of cultural anthropology as represented in the anthropology departments of American universities.

antinomianism: Literally "anti-law-ism," the teaching that the Law of God no longer matters to Christians. This is almost always an accusation made by one theologian against another, who denies the accusation. No major theologian teaches an explicit antinomianism, but some Protestant theologians are arguably in danger of falling into antinomianism when they emphasize the free grace of justification at the expense of the obligation of sanctification and holy living (a charge Calvinists have sometimes made against Lutherans, and Wesleyans have sometimes made against Calvinists).

Apollinarianism: The view, named after the 4th-century Alexandrian theologian Apollinarius, that in the Incarnation the divine Word replaced the rational human soul, so that Jesus was the Word united with a human body, not with a whole human being. Apollinarianism is rejected as a heresy because it implies that Jesus, not having a human soul, is not fully human.

apophatic: From the Greek word for "denial" or "negation," apophatic theology is the characteristically Eastern Orthodox approach of refusing to describe God directly but only to say what God is not. When such an approach is used in the West it is called the *via negativa* (Latin for "way of negation").

Apostle's Creed: This Western baptismal creed is the earliest creed known to us.

apostolic succession: The historical continuity of bishops being consecrated by bishops, who were themselves consecrated by bishops, etc., going back to the original twelve apostles of Christ. For Eastern Orthodox, Roman Catholics, and Anglicans, apostolic succession is a necessary feature of the episcopate, which means that no one who is consecrated outside the apostolic succession is really a bishop.

archon: The Greek word for "ruler" or "prince," used by the Gnostics as a term for the enemy spirits of the visible heavens who block the soul's escape from this world. The chief of the archons is the God of the Jews, who in his ignorance created the evil, physical world and in his arrogance thinks he is the only God.

Arianism: The theology attributed to 4th-century Alexandrian presbyter Arius, a radical form of subordinationism in which the preexistent word of God (prior to the Incarnation) is regarded as a creation of God the Father, so that "there was once when he was not." The Council of Nicaea 325 condemned this view.

Arminianism: A Protestant theology in the Reformed tradition, derived from the work of Jacobus Arminius (d. 1609), which assigns a larger role to free will in salvation than was accepted by the Calvinists, who rejected Arminianism at the Synod of Dordt in 1619. Arminian theology became widespread though not dominant among both Anglicans and Baptists, and was wholeheartedly adopted by John Wesley and the Methodists.

Ascension: The doctrine that after his resurrection from the dead, Jesus ascended to heaven, to be seated in exaltation at the right hand of God the Father.

Assumption of the Blessed Virgin: The Roman Catholic teaching, defined infallibly as doctrine by Pope Pius XII in 1950, that at the end of her natural life the Virgin Mary was assumed, that is, taken bodily into heaven.

atonement: Term for expiation or reconciliation, that is, doctrines of atonement (of which there are several in the Christian tradition) which answer this question: How did Christ's suffering and death on the cross take away sins and reconcile human beings to God?

attrition: Fear of God and his judgment; proposed by some medieval theologians as a sufficient substitute for contrition in the sacrament of Penance.

Augustinianism: A theological tradition derived from the work of Augustine, which did not form a distinct school of theology like Thomism or Calvinism but rather became the mainstream of theological opinion through most of the history of Western theology, including both Catholicism and Protestantism. However, it was also controversial because of Augustine's strong view of sin (including original sin) and grace (including the doctrine of predestination). Thomas Aquinas, Martin Luther, and John Calvin are all strongly Augustinian theologians; Arminius, Molina and Wesley are less Augustinian, especially about predestination.

Azusa Street: The location in Los Angeles of an ongoing revival, beginning in 1906 and lasting several years, from which arose Pentecostalism.

baptism: From a Greek verb meaning "to dip" or "immerse;" a ritual washing marking Christian beliefs of death of sin with Christ and rising to newness of life in him, and also their incorporation as members of the Church, which is the Body of Christ.

Baptists: Originating as 17th-century congregations of English Puritan Separatists who rejected infant baptism, the Baptists became a family of denominations emphasizing congregational self-government and regenerate church membership.

beatific vision: Roman Catholic concept of seeing the essence of God with the intellect, called "beatific" because it confers beatitude or ultimate happiness, and thus constitutes the ultimate goal of human existence.

beatitude: From the Latin term for happiness, *beatitudo*, used especially in Roman Catholic theology to refer to the ultimate fulfillment of human beings in God, which is thus equivalent to the biblical term "eternal life."

bishop: (See **episcopate**.)

Book of Common Prayer: The official prayer book of the Church of England and many of its offshoots in the Anglican communion (often called simply "the prayer book"). First published under King Edward VI in 1549, revisions were issued under Edward (1552), Elizabeth (1559), James I (1604), and Charles II (1662), and in the United States in 1789, 1892, 1928, and 1979.

Calvinism: Central theological trend of the Reformed tradition, defined not just by relation to the work of John Calvin but also by the Synod of Dordt and the Westminster Confession.

canon: From a Greek term for "rule" (in the sense of ruler or measuring rod), in early Christian theology the canon was a list of books approved for reading aloud in the church service, which thus eventually formed the content of holy scripture.

Cappadocians: Collective term for 4th-century Greek-speaking Christian theologians from Cappadocia in ancient Asia (modern Turkey), including Basil of Caesarea, his brother Gregory of Nyssa, sister Macrina, and friend Gregory Naziansen, who were important in the development of ascetic practice in the East as well as the Nicene doctrine of the Trinity. The Cappadocians came to the fore in the generation after Athanaisus, and their theology had a predominant influence on the Council of Constantinople 381.

catechesis: (See **catechumens**.)

catechumens: In the ancient church, people undergoing catechesis (Greek for "instruction" and the root of the modern term "catechism") in preparation for baptism. By the 4th century this was an official designation for a kind of half membership in the church, which could last for years if people wished to delay baptism, which they frequently did.

cathedra: A Latin term taken from a Greek word for "chair," used in theology to refer to the seat of a bishop's authority. (Hence a cathedral church is the home church of a bishop.) In Roman Catholic theology, the pope is infallible when he defines doctrine *ex cathedra*, which means "from the chair" of Peter, that is, by exercising his unique authority as the successor of the apostle Peter. (See **pope**.)

catholic: From a Greek word meaning "universal," this term originally referred to beliefs and practices that were accepted by all churches worldwide and was used in effect as a synonym for "orthodox." In this sense the Eastern Orthodox and Protestant churches join Roman Catholics in believing in one holy Catholic church.

character: A Latin word meaning roughly "indelible mark" (such as a tattoo). In Roman Catholic sacramental theology, this is a technical term for an indelible mark on the soul. The sacraments of Baptism, Confirmation and Holy Orders each imprint their own distinctive sacramental character on the soul.

Charismatic movement: Once known as "neo-Pentecostalism," this is a widespread movement among mainline Protestant and Catholic churches in the West arising from and influenced by, but no longer directly connected to, Pentecostalism. It emphasizes divine healing and speaking in tongues as gifts of the Holy Spirit (from the Greek word *charisma*, the New Testament word for "gifts"), as well as lively ("Spirit-filled") worship services.

charity: From the Latin term *caritas* (used to translate the New Testament term *agape*), it is the form of love which consists of obedience to the commandment to love God and neighbor. (Note: In Christian theology, giving money to the poor is not called charity but "alms," which of course can be one form of love of neighbor, but is not the only one.)

chrism: (See **confirmation**.)

chrismation: (See **confirmation**.)

Christology: Branch of Christian theology concerned with the person and work of Christ, including especially the doctrine of the Incarnation (the person of Christ) and the atonement (the work of Christ).

church fathers: The orthodox Christian theologians up to about A.D. 500, including Jerome, Ambrose, and Augustine in the West and Athanasius, Gregory Naziansen, Gregory of Nyssa, and Cyril of Alexandria in the East.

clarity: From the Latin word for "brightness," a quality of glorified human bodies after the resurrection, which means they shine with a beautiful light derived from the blessedness of their souls. (See **agility**, **impassibility**, and **subtlety**. For the clarity of scripture, see **perspicuity**.)

close communion: In Baptist theology, this means the practice, advocated most insistently by Landmarkism, of allowing only members of the local congregation (not visitors, even from other Baptist churches) to participate in the Lord's Supper.

communicatio idiomatum: Latin for "the sharing of characteristics," the phrase refers to a Christological doctrine developed most importantly by Cyril of Alexandria, who taught that because of the Incarnation, divine characteristics belong to the man Jesus (for example, he does miracles; he is worshiped) and human characteristics belong to God (for example, he has a mother; he suffers and dies).

communion: From the Latin word *communio*, which can be translated "sharing," "partaking," or "fellowship" (the root idea is found in the English phrase "to have in common"). It is a theological term with many meanings, including a fellowship of churches (such as the Anglican communion) and the act of partaking in the Eucharist, a sacrament which is therefore often called "Communion."

confession: A word with many theological uses. It can mean the act of confessing the faith (for example, by reciting the creed) or a written confession of faith adhered to by a particular group of churches (such as The Augsburg Confession, which is the standard of faith for the Lutheran churches). It can also mean the act of confessing one's sins, including especially private confession of sins to a priest in the sacrament of Penance, which is why the sacrament itself is often called "Confession."

confessor: A priest who hears confessions in the sacrament of Penance.

confirmation: From a Latin term for "strengthening," one of the seven sacraments of Roman Catholicism (also in Eastern Orthodoxy, where it is usually called chrismation, after the consecrated oil that is used, which is called chrism). This sacrament includes anointing with oil and laying on of hands (in Roman Catholicism, this must be done by a bishop) for the purpose of bestowing the Holy Spirit upon the baptized, strengthening them in faith, and bestowing a sacramental character upon the soul. Usually this is done when young people are entering early adulthood. In other high church traditions, such as Anglicanism and Lutheranism, confirmation is an important practice but is not regarded as a sacrament.

conformity: (See **nonconformist**.)

Congregatio de Auxiliis: A series of formal debates about the help of divine grace (*de Auxiliis* means "about the help") held in Rome from 1598–1607, to settle the controversy between Jesuits, who advocated Molinism, and Dominicans who advocated the Augustinian doctrine of grace as developed by Thomism. In the end the pope declared both viewpoints legitimate, prohibited either side from calling the other heretics, and forbade further discussion.

congregationalism: (See **polity**.)

contrition: Hatred of one's own sin, which produces sorrow of heart and the intention not to sin again. It is one of the four parts of the sacrament of Penance.

conversion: From a Latin word meaning "turning," as a theological term this refers to a turning of the will from evil to good, typically by coming to Christian faith and joining the church.

corporeal: An adjective formed from the Latin word *corpus*, meaning "body." In ancient philosophy, this is a word that could be translated "bodily," referring not just to the human body but to anything that we would now call "physical." (See **materialism**.)

Councils of the Church: (See **ecumenical**.)

covenant theology: A major element in Reformed theology, beginning with Calvin's contention that the Old Testament promulgated the same covenant of grace as the New Testament, but under a different form of administration. This covenant of grace is contrasted with the covenant of works which God made with Adam.

created grace: Catholic concept of grace as an inherent quality or habit of the soul, distinct from uncreated grace, which is the action of God, the Holy Spirit. (See **sanctifying grace**.)

creature: In theology, a technical term meaning "something God created." The term designates absolutely everything that has being other than God, who is not creature but Creator.

creed: From *credo*, "I believe," the word with which the Latin creeds begin, it is a verbal formula of Christian faith originally used as a confession of faith at Baptism. (See **Apostle's Creed**.) It was later used as a way of excluding heretical teaching and included in the regular Sunday liturgy. (See **Nicene**.)

dark night: Term used by John of the Cross to describe the stages in the soul's ascent to God when its powers are emptied of all that is not God, like an eye emptied of light.

decrees: In Calvinist theology, the eternal resolution of God's will to bring about some specific thing in time. For Calvinists, all things are ordained to happen by divine decree, but evil is decreed permissively—allowed rather than ordained—but in the very act of allowing them to happen God determines that they shall inevitably happen.

Deipassionism: From a Latin phrase meaning "God suffers," an implication of the orthodox doctrine of the Incarnation, according to which the same word of God who is "God from God" and eternally begotten of the Father, is also born of Mary and crucified under Pontius Pilate. (Contrast **Patripassionism**, which the orthodox deny.)

deism: An 18th-century Enlightenment theology in which critiques revealed religions (including especially Christianity) in light of natural religion, which is understood to be the religion of reason.

__dejamiento__: Spanish for "letting" or "letting go," sometimes translated "abandonment." This is a key concept among the *Alumbrados*, which seems to have influenced Quietism, that is, the idea that the highest form of spiritual life consists not in doing anything but in letting God do all things in you.

Dispensationalism: A theological movement originating in the late 19th century based on biblical interpretation that divides history into different periods or dispensations in which God relates to humanity differently. It is characterized by premillenialism, the expectation of the imminent return of Christ, and the belief that the people of Israel would enjoy an earthly kingdom prior to the end in fulfillment of God's promise.

dissenter: An English Protestant who is not a member of the Church of England; hence the term includes Presbyterians, Methodists, Baptists, and Quakers, among others.

Docetism: From the Greek word for "appearance," the view characteristic of many Gnostic groups that the physical body of Christ is not real but an illusion or mere appearance.

doctrine: From a Latin term *doctrina*, meaning "teaching," it is a prime concern of Christian theology, because teaching about Christ is the basis of Christian faith.

dominical institution: From the Latin word *dominus*, meaning "lord," it is the requirement that every sacrament, in the strict sense of the term, be instituted by the Lord Jesus.

Donation of Constantine: A document purported to be by the Emperor Constantine (280–337), donating all the lands of the West to the pope. It was exposed as a fraud in 1440 by the humanist scholar Lorenzo Valla, who showed that it was written in 8th-century Latin.

Dordt, Synod of (Sometimes spelled "Dort"): A conference of Dutch Reformed pastors and theologians in 1619 which rejected Arminianism and formulated the famous five points of classic Calvinism, represented in English by the acronym TULIP: T = total depravity; U = unconditional election; L = limited atonement; I = irresistible grace; and P = perseverance of the saints.

double predestination: A version of the Augustinian doctrine of predestination, originating with Calvin but arguably found in some passages of Augustine, teaching that God not only predestines some people for salvation but predestines others for damnation. (See **reprobation**.)

double procession: (See *filioque*.)

Eastern Orthodoxy: (See **orthodox**.)

ecclesiology: From the Greek word for "church" (*ecclesia*), the branch of theology that considers the nature, government, and mission of the church. (See **polity**.)

economy: From a Greek word, *oikonomia*, meaning literally "household management" or "stewardship" (hence the related word *oikonomos* or "steward"), is used in the New Testament to refer to the divine dispensation or plan of salvation in Christ. In Eastern Orthodox theology, the term "economy" (sometimes spelled "oeconomy") becomes almost synonymous with the Incarnation of Christ. (See **theologia**.) As a side note, theological uses of this term have nothing to do with the modern study of economics, though both come from the same Greek word. The ancient discipline of economics was concerned with managing the wealth of a household; hence the modern discipline of economics was originally called political economy, as it was concerned with managing the wealth of nations.

ecumenical: From a Greek word meaning "worldwide," this term refers both to recent discussions aimed at restoring unity between the various Christian churches (that is, ecumenism) and also to ancient church councils representing the worldwide church. There is disagreement about which councils were truly ecumenical and thus speak for the whole church. Eastern Orthodox and Roman Catholics agree on the first seven ecumenical councils (whose names include the year the council occurred), which were the First Council of Nicaea 325, the First Council of Constantinople 381, the Council of Ephesus 431, the Council of Chalcedon 451, the Second Council of Constantinople 553, the Third Council of Constantinople 681, and the Second Council of Nicaea 787. But thereafter councils called ecumenical by the Roman Catholic church (for example, Trent, the First Vatican Council, and the Second Vatican Council) are not regarded as truly ecumenical by other churches. Also, many Protestants do not accept all seven early councils as ecumenical. For example, most Protestants reject the Second Council of Nicaea, which taught the veneration of icons, and other Protestants do not accept the authority of church councils at all. For the issues discussed at these councils, see the timeline.

ecumenism: (See **ecumenical**.)

effectual call: Calvin's teaching, based on Romans 8:28–30, that there is a specially effective call of the Gospel, when God by the Holy Spirit works in a sinner's heart to produce true saving faith—the kind of faith which is sure, by the grace of God, to persevere to the end and thus to result in eternal salvation.

election: From the Latin word for "choice," the doctrine concerning God's eternal choice about who will ultimately be saved, often called "predestination." "Unconditional election" is the Calvinist label for the doctrine taught by Augustine, Aquinas, and Luther, as well as Calvin, that God eternally chooses (that is, predestines) those whom he will save, without considering any of their foreseen merits or faith. (See **Dordt, Synod of**). "Conditional election" by contrast is the doctrine of Arminianism, that God eternally chooses to save those who he foresees will accept Christ in faith. In conditional election, human faith is the basis or "condition" of God's choice; in unconditional election human faith is a "result" of God's choice. (See **reprobation**.)

Elizabethan Settlement: The mature form taken by the English Reformation under Queen Elizabeth I, rejecting Roman Catholicism but not reforming the church as thoroughly as the Puritans thought necessary, it was characterized by the *Book of Common Prayer* (re-issued in 1559) as well as the *39 Articles* (1563) and enforced by the Parliament's Act of Uniformity (1559).

encyclical: From the Greek word for "circular" (because an encyclical was originally a letter circulated among the bishops by the pope), it is a type of papal document used in modern times as a venue for major teachings, though not usually declared infallible.

energies: From a Greek word for "activities" or "workings" (or "operations," from *operationes*, the usual Latin translation of this word), a technical term in Eastern Orthodox theology that refers to the uncreated activities and glory of God, distinct from his essence.

Enlightenment: A broad term for 18th-century European intellectual developments, including deism and other movements critical of orthodox Christianity, that are characteristically modern, emphasizing reason against tradition and authority.

enthusiasm: Originally a pejorative term suggesting religious fanaticism and self-deception, applied by opponents to Quakers and others who believed they received direct inner revelation from God or his Spirit.

epiclesis: Greek for "invocation," a calling upon the name of God; specifically it is the part of the eucharistic liturgy in which the priest prays for God to send his Holy Spirit to make Christ's body present in the sacrament.

Epicureans: (See **hedonism**.)

episcopacy: (See **episcopate, polity**.)

episcopate: From the Greek term *epi-scopos*, literally "overseer" or "supervisor," but translated "bishop" (a corrupted English form of the word *episcopos*), this term refers to the network of bishops which governed the worldwide church from the 2nd century onward. This arose from the "monarchical episcopate" which prevailed within a century after the New Testament, a structure of local church governance in which there was only one bishop per town, under whom the presbyters (priest or elders) of the church served.

Erastianism: From a now obscure Swiss theologian named Erastus (d. 1583), the view of an influential party within the Anglican tradition that the government (especially the crown) is properly supreme over the church in matters of discipline and ecclesiastical appointments.

eschatology: Greek for teaching about "the end" (*eschaton*), in New Testament studies this term refers to early Christian understanding of the drama of the world between the "already" (Christ is already raised from the dead) and the "not yet" (Christ has not yet returned in the Parousia). In later theology, eschatology means the doctrine of the four "last things," namely death, the last judgment, hell, and heaven.

essence: Translation of the Greek term *ousia*, sometimes translated "being" or "substance" (because the Greek term was usually translated into Latin as *substantia*). In ordinary philosophical usage, it refers to what makes something what it is (for example, the essence of a human being is human nature). In Nicene trinitarianism it refers to the unique divinity that the Father, Son, and Holy Spirit have equally in common. (See ***homoousios*** and **energies**.)

established church: A state church, such as the Church of England, the Lutheran churches in Scandinavia and parts of Germany, and the Congregationalist churches in Connecticut and Massachusetts until the early 19th century. (The United States Constitution forbids a nationally established church and was not to interfere with established churches in the states). Established churches are typically supported by taxes (which pay ministers' salaries), are usually under some degree of government control (for example, in the appointment of ministers), and often subject other churches in the territory to various penalties and sometimes persecution.

Eucharist: From the Greek word for "thanksgiving" (because the words of institution grow out of the Jewish rite of thanksgiving over bread and wine at the passover meal), it is the central Christian rite of a sacred meal in which bread and wine are used to signify or present the body and blood of Christ. Also called, in various traditions, "the sacrament of the altar," "Communion" or "the Lord's Supper."

evangelicalism: In English-speaking countries, this term refers broadly to low-church movements beginning in the 18th century with an emphasis on conversion and revival (for example, Methodism and various branches of Calvinism and Anglicanism), and more narrowly to the movement beginning in the 1950s, led by figures like Billy Graham in the United States and John Stott in England, in which Christians who have previously called themselves "Fundamentalist" turned to engage modern culture rather than separate from it. Note, in Germany and elsewhere in Europe, "evangelical" or *evangelische* simply means Protestant.

ex cathedra: (See *cathedra*.)

excommunication: A church's act of refusing communion to a person, which means not allowing him or her to share in the church's celebration of the Eucharist.

Existentialism: A 20th-century movement in philosophy and theology which makes use of a concept of human existence derived from Kierkegaard, for whom existence is a task, a concern that inevitably involves guilt, anxiety, and despair, which can only be honestly faced by the free decision of faith.

Extreme Unction: Derived from a Latin phrase which is more literally translated, "final anointing," it is the sacrament now called "Anointing of the Sick," which in the Middle Ages was performed only for those thought to be dying.

extrinsicism: A criticism often leveled against neo-Thomism that it separated the supernatural order from the natural order so sharply that it made the life of grace extrinsic and irrelevant to normal human life and experience.

federal theology: From the Latin word *foedus*, meaning "covenant," another term for covenant theology. (It has nothing to do with the United States federal government.)

filioque: Latin term meaning "and of the Son," from a clause in the Western version of the Nicene Creed saying that the Holy Spirit "proceeds from the Father and the Son." This doctrine of "double procession" is rejected by the Eastern Orthodox and became the cause of the schism between the Eastern and Western churches in 1054, resulting in the formal separation of Eastern Orthodox from Roman Catholic.

forensic justification: The predominant form of the doctrine of justification in Protestantism, according to which believers, being united to Christ by faith, are declared righteous by God in view of the merits of Christ that are imputed to them. (See **imputation**, **four-point Calvinism**, and **Amyraldianism**.)

Fundamentalism: A 20th-century religious movement which originated in the Fundamentalist-modernist controversy in the United States beginning about 1920, although rooted in Anglo-American evangelicalism of the 19th century and characterized by a high view of scriptural infallibility and the concern that liberal Protestantism was abandoning the fundamentals of the faith. Also typically (though not always) involving Keswick or Holiness piety and Dispensationalist theology.

glossolalia: Term used by non-Pentecostals to describe "speaking in tongues." In fact it comes from a Greek phrase which means "speaking in tongues," a phenomenon of ecstatic worship attributed to the Holy Spirit in which believers give utterance to what sounds like language but is not any recognizable human tongue. (Contrast *xenolalia*.)

Gnosticism: A broad label for a wide variety of non-orthodox forms of Christianity which proliferated in the early centuries A.D., which is discussed at length in Lecture Six. The Gnostics' central conviction is that there is a special higher knowledge (Greek *gnosis*) which the human spirit needs in order to escape this evil world and go to a heaven that is above the stars and beyond the material world.

Gospel: English translation of the Greek (New Testament) term *evangelion*, meaning "good news." This is a central term in the theology of Luther, who insists on a strong contrast between Law and Gospel because Law can only tell people how to be righteous, and thereby condemn them for not doing what they're told, whereas the Gospel makes them righteous by giving Christ to all those who receive him by faith.

grace: A New Testament term for the unmerited mercy of God used by Christian theologians as a label for the power of God to redeem and transform human beings, it is an especially important term in Augustinian theology. (See **created grace**, **infused**, **irresistible grace**, **prevenient grace**, **sanctifying grace**, and **supernatural**.)

Great Awakening: A period of religious revival in the early 1740s in colonial America, in which Jonathan Edwards was a leading theologian.

Great Church: A name that mainstream Christianity gave itself in the first few centuries, in contrast to sects and heresies.

Halfway Covenant: Policy agreed upon by most of the Puritan (Congregationalist) churches in New England in 1662, allowing the baptized children of church members to join the church without being converted.

Harrowing of Hell: The traditional teaching that after his death the soul of Jesus descended into hell, rescued the souls of those who believed in him, and later brought them to heaven.

hedonism: From the Greek word for "pleasure," *hedone*, the view in ancient philosophy that happiness is a feeling, that is, a good feeling—pleasure. (It does not mean living a wild party life. In fact, the most important hedonist philosophers, the Epicureans, believed that a quiet and tranquil life was the most pleasant and therefore the happiest.)

heresiologists: Church fathers writing against heresy, typically by producing a book cataloguing the views of a large number of diverse Christian groups, such as Irenaeus's treatise *Against Heresies*. These books are often our main source of information about forms of Christianity that have since disappeared.

heresy: From a Greek term meaning "sect," theologians of the Great Church applied this term to doctrines they rejected as not catholic or orthodox.

Herrnhut: Town in the lands of Count Nicholas von Zinzendorf, where he offered asylum to Moravians and became their bishop. Hence a "Herrnhuter" means a Moravian, and it was to this that Schleiermacher referred when he called himself "a Herrnhuter of a higher order."

hierarchy: From a Greek word meaning literally "rule by priests," this term refers to churches with an episcopal polity. (See **episcopate**). The Roman Catholic and Eastern Orthodox churches are hierarchical, whereas Baptist and Presbyterian churches are not.

high church: Originally an Anglican term, this describes churches that have a high view of the sacraments (for example, baptismal regeneration and Real Presence in the Eucharist). Also typically involving a hierarchical polity. It emphasizes learned ministry (pastors need to go to seminary and learn Greek and Hebrew), accepts religious art in churches (for example, stained glass, statues, or icons), and uses formal liturgy and ritual. (Contrast **low church**.)

Holiness movement: A Wesleyan perfectionist movement founded in the 1830s in America by Methodist teacher Phoebe Palmer and advocating a special act of consecration (which Palmer calls "laying all upon the altar") to acquire the "second blessing" of entire sanctification or Holiness.

Holy Saturday: The day between Good Friday, when Christ was crucified, and Easter Sunday, when he was raised from the dead. Accordingly, it is the day when the eternal Son of God descended among the dead, and for that reason is of particular importance in the theology of von Balthasar.

homoousios: Key term used in the Nicene Creed to describe the relation of the Son to the Father, translated into English in various ways: consubstantial (from *consubstantialis*, the standard Latin translation of the term), "of one substance," "of one essence" or "of one being," it means that the Son has the same divine essence as the Father.

hyperousios: A technical term meaning literally "above essence" or "above being" and sometimes translated "superessential" (since the Latin preposition *super* is the equivalent of the Greek preposition *hyper*, both of which mean "above"). Pseudo-Dionysius used this term to express the transcendence of the Trinity, which is beyond all being and knowing.

hypostasis: A Greek term for "complete individual being" (a tree, a star, a dog, an angel, and a human being are all hypostases. A hand, an eye, and human nature or essence are not). This is a technical term for what is three in the Trinity and one in Christ, which Eastern Orthodox theologians use to designate what Western theology typically calls "persons."

hypostatic union: A technical term for the unique unity between the two natures, divine and human, in the one person or hypostasis of Christ.

icon: The Greek word for "image" (for example in the biblical phrase "image and likeness of God"), used to describe the holy images of Christ, saints, and angels venerated by the Eastern Orthodox and also by Roman Catholics.

iconodules: Those who venerate icons, in contrast to iconoclasts (which means literally those who break icons). The word "iconodule" incorporates the key defense of icons made in the Second Council of Nicaea 787, which is that icons are not worshiped like an idol (with the worship called in Greek, *latreia*) but only venerated (with the veneration called in Greek, *dulia*).

Immaculate Conception: The Roman Catholic doctrine, defined by Pope Pius IX in 1854, that the Blessed Virgin Mary was conceived without original sin—thus her conception was immaculate (literally "spotless") because it was free from any spot or stain of original sin.

impassibility: An attribute of God, according to Platonism and the church fathers, which means that he suffers no passions. That is, nothing is done to him that moves him or causes him to change, to suffer, or to respond emotionally. According to Western medieval theology, a similar freedom from suffering is one of the four qualities of glorified bodies in the resurrection, along with clarity, subtlety, and agility. (See **passion**.)

imputation: From a Latin word which translates a Greek word in the New Testament whose basic meaning is to credit something to a person's account, to reckon or "count as." It is a fundamental term in doctrines of forensic justification, according to which the righteousness that justifies believers in God's sight is not acquired by their efforts nor infused in them as created grace, but imputed to them when the merits of Christ are credited to their account.

Incarnation: Literally "en-flesh-ment" (from the Latin for "flesh," *carnem*), the doctrine concerns how Christ is both God and man. In Christian theology, the term "Incarnation" refers only to Christ, not to human embodiment in general or to theories of "re-incarnation," as in Hinduism.

incomprehensibility: From a Latin term meaning literally "ungraspability." In Nicene Christian theology, God is typically described as incomprehensible, which means beyond the understanding of any created mind.

indulgence: In Roman Catholicism, a formal promise by the church (in Luther's day, typically in a written document that could be purchased) that someone meeting certain criteria (for example, participating in a crusade, going on a specified pilgrimage, or purchasing a written indulgence) will receive a reduction in the amount of time one suffers in purgatory.

infralapsarianism: From the Latin phrase *infra lapsum* meaning "after the Fall." In the Calvinist theology of the decrees of God, this is the view that the eternal decree of double predestination logically follows the decrees to create the world and permit the Fall. (Contrast **supralapsarianism**.)

infused: From the Latin word for "poured in" (derived from Romans 5:5, "The love of God is poured out in our hearts by the Holy Spirit which is given to us"). This term is used in Roman Catholic theology, in contrast to "acquired," to describe graces, virtues, and activities of the soul that are not acquired by effort and practice but bestowed by God and poured into the soul by the grace of God. This Catholic concept of infused virtue is often contrasted with the Protestant doctrine of forensic justification, in which believers receive the righteousness of Christ by imputation, not infusion.

intelligibility: From the Latin term *intellectus*, which originally meant "understanding." This concept originated in Platonist philosophy, which insisted on a fundamental contrast between sensible and intelligible things, that is, things perceptible to the senses and things perceptible to the intellect by a kind of intellectual vision or insight (as when we suddenly understand a difficult mathematical concept and say, "Aha! Now I see it!"). In neo-Platonism, intelligibility is also contrasted to the incomprehensibility of the highest divine principle.

irresistible grace: The Calvinist teaching of the Synod of Dordt, that when God chooses to give grace to sinners, that choice is effective, in such a way that even sinners who do not want grace are made willing to accept it, by the power of grace itself. (See **praevenient grace**.)

Jansenism: A 17th-century French religious movement within Roman Catholicism, centered in the Port-Royal convent near Paris and advocating the highly Augustinian theology of sin, grace, and predestination developed by Cornelius Jansen, which was condemned by Rome because of its affinities with Calvinism yet survived for generations until it was effectively suppressed by King Louis XIV.

Jew: This word comes into English from a Greek word used in the New Testament, *Ioudaios*, which literally means "Judean." After the fall of the Northern Kingdom consisting of ten tribes of Israel in 722 B.C., this term, originally referring to people of the Southern Kingdom of Judah or Judea ruled by kings in the lineage of David, became the term for all the surviving people of Israel, that is, all 12 tribes descended from the 12 sons of Jacob or Israel (which is another name for Jacob). Hence Jesus, coming from the northern area of Galilee, is in one sense a Jew (that is, an Israelite) but in another sense not, because he does not come from Judea, the region around Jerusalem. This is important for understanding why the Gospel of John often contrasts Jesus with "the Jews," meaning the Judean establishment in Jerusalem.

justification: The doctrine about how God makes human beings just or righteous. (See **righteousness**, **sanctification** and *sola fide*.)

Kerygma: Greek for "proclamation," based on the Greek word for "herald," someone who proclaims official news, for example , of the king. The verb formed from this noun can be translated "proclaim," but is usually translated "preach" when it appears in the New Testament. Biblical scholars often use this New Testament term to emphasize that early Christian preaching was understood to be the proclamation of the kingdom of God and Jesus, the Messiah, as its king.

Keswick: Named after annual meetings held in Keswick, England, beginning in 1875, it was a British-American theological movement influential to later Fundamentalists and evangelicals, incorporating themes from the Holiness movement in a non-perfectionist (that is, non-Methodist) theology, typically including such teachings as: the importance of being filled with the Holy Spirit as an enduement of power for service, continually yielding to the influence of the Spirit so as to obtain ongoing victory over sin, and the motto "let go and let God."

Landmarkism: A radical separatist and primitivist movement among Southern Baptists beginning in the 1850s, taking as its watchword a biblical admonition not to remove old landmarks of the faith. The Landmarkists rejected alien immersion, insisted on closed communion, rejected missionary societies, and promoted a successionist history of Baptist faith and practice.

lex orandi, lex credendi: Latin for "The law of praying [is the] law of believing," the phrase is a label for a form of theological argument used, for example, by Augustine in his doctrine of grace, in which what we pray for informs us of what we should believe about the help God can give us.

liberalism: Not to be confused with political liberalism with which it is sometimes but not always in alliance with theology, liberalism is rooted in developments in German universities of the 19th century led initially by Friedrich Schleiermacher. It is characterized by criticism of ancient orthodox dogmatic formulas (such as "two natures" Christology) and by the attempt to find a new basis of Christian faith in a turn to inner experience.

light of Tabor: (See **Tabor**.)

limited atonement: Also called, more accurately, "particular redemption," the most controversial point in the "five-point Calvinism" taught by the Synod of Dordt, according to which Christ died to redeem only those whom he actually does redeem, which does not include everybody.

liturgy: A form of worship, characteristic of the high churches, using an ancient and venerated written text (such as the Roman Rite in the Catholic church, the Liturgy of Saint John Chrysostom among the Eastern Orthodox, or the *Book of Common Prayer* in the Anglican Communion).

logos: A Greek word meaning, among other things, "word" and "reason." *Logos* is a central term in trinitarian and Christological discussions because of the opening chapter of the Gospel of John, which identifies Christ as the "divine *Logos* made flesh."

low church: Originally an Anglican term, this describes churches that have a low view of the sacraments (for example, teaching that baptism and the eucharist are not means of salvation) and typically also having a strong emphasis on conversion. Among non-Anglicans, this is often joined by a suspicion of liturgy and a rejection of hierarchy. (Contrast **high church**.)

maranatha: An Aramaic term meaning "O Lord, come," which Paul used in 1 Cor. 16:22, it was probably a familiar piece of liturgy calling upon the exalted Lord Jesus in the Jewish Christian church. (Aramaic was the common spoken language of 1st-century Israel.)

Mariology: Teachings concerning the Blessed Virgin Mary, Jesus's mother—an important branch of Roman Catholic theology.

materialism: From the word for "matter," in ancient philosophy, this means the view that all things, including God and the soul, are made up of some kind of bodily or corporeal stuff—the material or matter out of which they are made. In ancient philosophy, matter consists of four elements: earth, water, air, and fire, and perhaps a fifth element in the heavens, called "ether" or "quintessence."

Mennonites: Named after Menno Simons (1496–1561), who led Dutch Anabaptists in a resolutely pacifist direction after the failure of the violent Anabaptist revolt in the Dutch city of Münster, they are the most widespread group of Anabaptists today, of which the Amish are an offshoot.

Messiah: From a Hebrew term for "anointed one," referring to the king of Judaea (since ancient Israelite kings were anointed with oil rather than crowned), translated into Greek as *Christos*, whence the term "Christ." To call Jesus "Messiah" or "Christ" is to say he is the King of the Jews, the legitimate successor to the lineage of King David.

Methodism: Revival movement begun by John and Charles Wesley with others in 18th-century England, characterized by Arminian theology and a strong emphasis on practical Holiness, including the expectation of entire sanctification or Christian perfection. (See **perfectionism**.)

Molinism: A theology of grace based on the writings of the Spanish Jesuit Luis de Molina, who argued that the effectiveness of divine grace depends on the will's prior consent, which means that the decision about who is to be saved or not is ultimately up to the human will.

Monarchy of the Father: From a Greek word meaning "one principle" or "one source" (the Greek word *arche*, like its Latin translation *principio*, means source or beginning), it is the doctrine that the Father is the sole source of the being of the Son and the Holy Spirit. Both Eastern and Western churches affirm this doctrine, but in light of the doctrine of double procession they may have different understandings of what it means.

Monophysitism: From the Greek phrase for "one nature," the teaching, rejected by the orthodox, that Christ incarnate has only one nature.

Monothelitism: From the Greek phrase for "one will": the teaching, rejected by the orthodoxy, that Christ incarnate has only one will.

Montanism: A Christian movement, calling itself "the New Prophecy," founded in Phrygia (in modern Turkey) in the late 2nd century by Montanus, who designated himself the Paraclete, that is, the Holy Spirit. Its rejection by the Great Church as a heresy meant that prophecy was no longer part of the authority structure of the church as it had been in the New Testament.

Moravians: A Protestant group from Moravia (in what is now the Czech Republic) who, fleeing from persecution in the 1720s, settled on the lands of Count Zinzendorf and accepted him as their pastor, bishop, and theologian. Their missionary work was widespread and has resulted in churches in America, England, and elsewhere.

mysticism: Originally called "mystical theology," a term taken from the treatise of that name by Pseudo-Dionysius, referring to aspects of God that are hidden from human understanding because God is incomprehensible. "Mystical theology" became an important term in medieval devotional theology and eventually came to refer (for example, in the writings of Theresa of Avila) to the theology of states of prayer that involve a supra-intellectual experience of God. Later, the term "mysticism" was taken over in 19th- and 20th-century theories of religion and was used to describe paranormal states of religious experience that need not be specifically Christian.

neo-orthodoxy: A trend in 20th-century theology originating in the dialectical theology of the early Karl Barth and including such theologians as Rudolf Bultmann, Paul Tillich, and Emil Brunner. It rejects the 19th-century liberal theology of consciousness in favor of a focus on how the divine-human encounter affects human existence (typically conceiving the latter in existentialist terms). The later Barth rejected this existentialist focus and thus broke with other Neo-Orthodox theologians.

neo-Thomism: (See **Thomism**.)

Nicene: Having to do with the Council of Nicaea 325 or the trinitarian theology that stems from it. Nicene theology is the orthodox theology of the Trinity on which Catholics, Orthodox, and Protestants agree. What is commonly called the "Nicene Creed" was actually formulated at the Council of Constantinople 381, incorporating key elements of the original creed promulgated by the Council of Nicaea, including the famous *homoousios* clause. (For a listing of these councils, see the timeline.)

Nonconformist: Originally a term for Puritan ministers who did not conform to the church practices and ceremonies mandated by the Act of Uniformity under the Elizabethan Settlement. It was later a label for all Protestants who were dissenters.

oikonomia: (See **economy**.)

ontology: From a Greek term meaning "theory of being," a branch of metaphysics or philosophy that is concerned with the nature of being. Hence, for example, Augustine's teaching that all being is good can be labeled "ontological optimism."

original sin: The doctrine, advocated most powerfully by Augustine, that every human being is born not only with a corrupt and sinful nature but guilty of Adam's sin and deserving damnation.

orthodox: From a Greek term meaning both "right belief" and also "right worship." When capitalized, it refers to Eastern Orthodoxy, the mainstream of the Christian tradition in the East, rooted in the Greek-speaking half of the ancient Roman Empire, developing in the Byzantine Empire, and later spreading to the Slavic peoples (thus including not only Greek Orthodox but Russian Orthodox, Serbian Orthodox, etc.). When not capitalized, the term typically includes Catholics and Protestants as well as Orthodox. The opposite of "orthodox" is "heretical."

ousia: (See **essence** and *homoousios*.)

Paraclete (Sometimes spelled "Paraklete"): Greek for advocate, counselor, or comforter. Jesus used the term in the Gospel of John to refer to the Holy Spirit.

parousia: Greek term meaning "presence" or "arrival," which is used in the New Testament to refer especially to the presence of Christ at his Second Coming, when the exalted Christ returns to establish the kingdom of God on earth.

passion: In ancient thought, this means a form of passivity (since "passion" is related to passivity as "action" is related to activity) associated both with emotion (that is, being moved by passions) and suffering (for example, the "passion of Christ" means his suffering). All ancient writers assume that passion is at best a form of weakness, at worst a form of irresponsibility or vice. For it is better to act than to be acted on, to move than to be moved, to form than to be formed, and so on. Ancient moralism focused as intently on the problem of passion as modern moralism focuses on the problem of selfishness. (See **impassibility**.)

Patripassionism: From a Latin phrase, "the father suffers," which claims the God the Father suffered. But orthodox maintains the inviolability of God by asserting that it is the incarnate word of God (the Son) who is crucified and suffers, not God the Father. (See **Deipassionism** and **theopaschite formula**.)

patristic: Having to do with the church fathers (from the Greek word *pater*, "father").

Pelagianism: The view ascribed to Pelagius and rejected as heretical that believers are capable of overcoming sin and living meritorious lives without the inner help of grace.

penance: An old word for "repentance," often used specifically to designate the sacrament of Penance or Confession, in which a penitent confesses sins to a priest and receives absolution.

penitent: A person engaged in repentance, especially by participating in the sacrament of Penance and confessing his or her sins.

Pentecost: From the Greek word for "fifty," the name for the Jewish harvest festival or "feast of weeks," held seven weeks and a day after the festival of Passover. (See Leviticus 23:15 ff.). Christian theology celebrates the birth of the church and the outpouring of the Holy Spirit on Pentecost, as narrated in the New Testament book of Acts, chapter 2. Christians now celebrate their feast of Pentecost fifty days after Easter.

Pentecostalism: Evangelical religious movement named after the outpouring of the Holy Spirit on Pentecost, and originating in the United States at the beginning of the 20th century (especially at the Azusa Street revival in Los Angeles beginning in 1906). Its distinctive teaching is that speaking in tongues is the necessary evidence of the baptism of the Holy Spirit. (See **glossolalia**.)

perfectionism: The doctrine of various Protestant groups, most notably the Methodists and the Holiness tradition derived from them, that the attainment of perfect or entire sanctification (Holiness) is not only possible but normative for Christians.

perseverance: In Western theology after Augustine, this is a technical term for the "gift of grace," which causes those who have begun the life of faith to persevere in faith (and works of love) to the end of their lives. The Calvinist doctrine of the perseverance of the saints, taught at Dordt, is that all who truly have faith in Christ are given this gift (which implies that anyone who gives up the Christian faith never really had true saving faith to begin with). The crucial consequence is that if you know you have true faith, then you know you are saved for eternity. This Calvinist doctrine is sometimes known by labels such as "eternal security" or "once saved, always saved."

person: A technical term for what there are three of in the Trinity (that is, Father, Son, and Holy Spirit are each persons of the Trinity) and one in Christ (who is one person in two natures). This is a translation of the Latin term *persona* or the Greek term *prosopon*. (See **hypostasis** and **hypostatic union**.)

perspicuity of scripture: The Protestant doctrine that in matters necessary for salvation, the words of the Bible are clear enough that any devout and attentive believer can properly interpret them.

Pietism: A 17th- and 18th-century reform movement, primarily among Lutherans in Germany, emphasizing the need for true Christianity, based on true faith, repentance, conversion, and rebirth, as opposed to the kind of scholastic theology that does not touch the heart. Methodism is often regarded, with reason, as an offshoot of Pietism.

Pleroma: A Greek term meaning "fullness," and in Gnosticism, the divine realm of the *aeons*.

polity: A technical term for the various forms of church government. For example, episcopacy means the church is governed by bishops (that is, an episcopate); Presbyterianism means it is governed by synods of elders or presbyters; and congregationalism means that each congregation is self-governing.

pope: The Roman Catholic bishop of Rome, understood to be the successor of the apostle Peter, who was the first bishop of Rome and thus the first occupant of the Apostolic. (See ***cathedra***.)

postmillennialism: The view of biblical prophecy, characteristic of early 19th-century American evangelicals, which holds that a golden age (the millennium mentioned in the book of Revelation, 20:4) will be brought about by the progress of Christian civilization and missions before the end of the world. (Contrast **premillennialism**.)

postmodernism: A term with many disputed meanings. In these lectures, it refers to the view that traditions are the inevitable context of thought and that modern thought, which regards tradition as irrational, cannot survive the recognition that modernity itself is a tradition. In Dr. Cary's terminology, *left wing postmodernists*, such as Derrida and Foucault, draw skeptical or deconstructive conclusions from this recognition (for example, suggesting that claims of rationality are really disguised bids for power) while *right wing postmodernists*, such as Gadamer and Alasdair MacIntyre, draw the conclusion that tradition is the necessary context for learning, rationality, and wisdom.

prayer book: (See ***Book of Common Prayer***.)

predestination: Originating with Augustine's interpretations of New Testament usage of the verb "to predestine" (in Romans, Ephesians, and Acts), this doctrine is specifically about God's eternal plan, choice, or decree to bestow the grace of salvation on some unworthy sinners rather than others. Since the doctrine of predestination is always part of the doctrine of grace, it should be distinguished from the more general doctrine of God's sovereignty or providence over all events that happen, as well as from philosophical theories of determinism. (See **election**, **double predestination**, and **reprobation**.)

prelate: A high-ranking member of a hierarchical church, such as an abbot, an archbishop, or the pope. Both the pope and the (Anglican) archbishop of Canterbury are prelates. The Puritans rejected prelates.

premillennialism: The view of biblical prophecy characteristic of Dispensationalism, which teaches that the Second Coming of Christ is imminent and will occur before the millennium, in which the saints reign with Christ in a golden age (book of Revelation, 20:4). (Contrast **postmillennialism**.)

Presbyterian: (See **polity** and **presbyters**.)

presbyters: From the Greek word *presbyteroi*, usually translated "elders" when it occurs in the New Testament. Originally this term referred to the leadership of local churches, then to a group of leaders under one bishop (the monarchical episcopate). This group later came to be called "priests" (an English word derived from *presbyteroi*). In the 17th century, Presbyterians were the mainstream of English Puritanism, who aimed to revive the New Testament form of church government based on a council of elders or presbyters, whom the Presbyterians did not think of as priests. (See **polity**.)

prevenient grace: From the Latin word *praevenire*, meaning "to come before," it is grace that comes before the human choice to accept grace in faith, as opposed to grace that comes as a result of such faith. Questions about exactly what role grace plays in a person's initial conversion to faith are thus always questions about the role of prevenient grace. The key disagreement is between the Augustinian view prevenient grace causes us to have faith and the Arminian view prevenient grace is an offer or incitement or preparation that leaves it ultimately up to us whether to believe or not. In the Calvinist version of the Augustinian view, prevenient grace is called "irresistible grace." In the Thomistic version of the Augustinian view, it is called "efficacious in itself."

procession: Technical term in trinitarian theology for the divine origination of the Holy Spirit, in contrast to the begetting of the Son, which is a different mode of divine origination. The Western doctrine of double procession teaches that the Holy Spirit proceeds from the Father "and the Son." (See *filioque*.)

Protestant: Term now used for the Western churches that broke with Roman Catholicism beginning with the 16th-century Reformation, including Lutherans, Reformed, and Anabaptists. The term does not refer to any kind of protest against the church, but to a formal protest lodged by Lutheran princes against an unfavorable decision made by the imperial Diet of Speyer in 1529.

providence: From a Latin verb meaning both "foresee" and "provide," the doctrine concerning God's benevolent sovereignty over the events of history.

pure nature: Technical term in modern Roman Catholic theology designating human nature as considered apart from the effect of the supernatural.

purgatory: In Roman Catholic doctrine, the realm of temporal punishment and purification after death for redeemed souls who are not yet perfect in holiness.

Puritanism: English religious movement beginning in the reign of Queen Elizabeth I (1558–1603) and seeking to push the Church of England further in the direction of Reformed theology and practice throughout the 17th century. Outgrowths of Puritanism include Presbyterians, Congregationalists, and Baptists. (See **Vestiarian controversy**.)

Quietism: Roman Catholic theological term for a form of mystical theology originating in 17th-century Spain and influential in France and Italy, which focused on passive contemplation and letting God work in the soul, denying the importance of the active pursuit of virtue, holiness, salvation, and even the desire for beatitude.

Real Presence: The doctrine that Christ's body and blood are really present in the Eucharist, in such a way that they are literally eaten by those who partake of it (whether or not they believe it or partake worthily). Transubstantiation is the Roman Catholic version of this doctrine, according to which the substance of bread and wine are removed from the Eucharist and changed into the substance of Christ's body and blood. Whereas Lutherans teach that the bread and wine remain and the body and blood of Christ are present in them.

Reformation: A 16th-century movement for church reform beginning with Luther in Germany and Zwingli in Switzerland, from which arose the Protestant churches.

Reformed: The form of Protestantism originating in Switzerland, predominant in Holland, and represented in the English speaking world by Puritans, Presbyterians, Congregationalists, and many Baptists, its most important founding figures are Zwingli and Calvin. It takes its name from the conviction that the church needs to be reformed according to the word of God. It is important to note that, despite the similarity of words, the Reformed do not represent the whole of the Reformation, which includes non-Reformed movements such as the Lutherans and Anabaptists.

regeneration: From a Latin term meaning "born again," any theological doctrine describing an individual's passage from birth in Adam, which means a life subject to sin, to rebirth, and new life in Christ. Baptismal regeneration, for example, is the doctrine that one is born again through baptism—a doctrine shared by Roman Catholics, Eastern Orthodox, Lutherans, and Anglicans, but rejected by most other Protestants, who associate rebirth with the experience of conversion.

reprobation: The doctrine that God predestines some people for damnation. (See **double predestination**.)

resurrection: In Christianity, the doctrine that God will bring the dead to life and has done this already with Jesus. This is not to be confused with the doctrine of the immortality of the soul, according to which the soul lives on after being separated from the body in death. Most Christian theologians combine the two doctrines but do not confuse them.

Revivalism: Religious practices focused on preaching that aims at bringing about the experience of conversion, characteristic of Wesleyan and Methodist churches beginning in the 18th century as well as certain Reformed circles in the United States, especially those indebted to Jonathan Edwards (of whom Charles Finney is representative).

righteousness: Until the 20th century this word was the standard English translation for the terms for "justice" in Latin *justitia* or Greek *dikaiosyne*. In theological usage, therefore, it is simply equivalent to the word "justice." (It is important to be aware that the word "righteous" was never used theologically as an equivalent to "self-righteous," though that has become its primary usage in contemporary English.)

sacrament: From the Latin term *sacramentum*, which translates the Greek term *mysterion* or "mystery," originally referring to any secret or hidden meaning. By the Middle Ages this term came to have a specialized meaning referring to seven sacred rites of the church (Baptism, Eucharist, Penance, Confirmation, Extreme Unction, Ordination, and Matrimony), which were authorized by dominical institution to serve as outward signs conferring the inner grace they signified and hence were called as "means of grace." Protestants typically reduced the number of rituals to two (baptism and eucharist), while still practicing most of the others but not calling them sacraments. And they often rejected the notion that sacraments were a means of conferring grace. Many Protestant groups reject the term "sacrament" altogether and prefer to call baptism and Eucharist "ordinances."

sanctification: From *sanctus*, the Latin word for "holy," the process by which a person becomes holy. In Protestant theologies, this is contrasted with justification, which is typically treated as a once-in-a-lifetime event, an act of God, which takes place at conversion, in which God forgives people's sins, imputes to them the merits of Christ, declares them righteous, and bestows salvation (hence later Protestants often equate justification with salvation), but does not make a real inward change in their hearts. Sanctification is the name for the process of real inward transformation that begins immediately at conversion and results in holy living. In the Holiness traditions stemming from Wesley, the term typically refers to the stage of Christian perfection or entire sanctification.

sanctifying grace: Standard English translation of the Roman Catholic theological term *gratia gratum faciens*, literally "grace that makes [a person] acceptable," it is the supernatural but created form or habit that is infused into the soul so as to make it righteous before God and capable of the theological virtues of faith, hope, and charity.

sanctus: The Latin word for "holy," the name of a prayer early in the eucharistic liturgy which begins, "Holy, holy, holy, Lord God of hosts."

satisfaction: From a Latin verb meaning "to do enough" (the basic idea being to "make up for" some wrong or injustice you have done to someone else). In Anselm's theory of atonement, the term refers to the payment of an infinite debt which sinners incur by their offense against the infinite majesty of God—a payment that no one is capable of making except God-made-man. This term is also a technical term in the sacrament of Penance, meaning what penitents must do after absolution to make up for their sins.

Schleitheim Confession: The most important doctrinal statement of the early Anabaptist movement, published in Switzerland in 1527.

scholasticism: University-based theology in the west from the Middle Ages to the 18th century. Aquinas is a medieval scholastic theologian, in contrast to Anselm, who is a medieval monastic theologian (you find Aquinas at universities and Anselm in monasteries). In the 17th century there also arose a Protestant form of scholasticism, against which Pietism was a reaction.

Scopes "Monkey Trial": Trial of a biology teacher, John Scopes, in rural Dayton, Tennessee, in 1925 for defying a state law forbidding the teaching of Darwinism in public schools. With the help of skeptical journalist H. L. Mencken, Fundamentalists suffered a cultural disaster, which drove them from the north and east to the south and west.

scriptures, holy: Theological term for the Bible, used not just to indicate this particular set of writings but to stress their divine authority.

see: From Latin *sedes*, meaning "seat," the location of a bishop's authority (for example, the see of the bishop of Venice is Venice). The see of Rome, that is, the papacy, is called the Apostolic See because Rome's first bishop, and thus the first pope, was the apostle Peter. (See *cathedra*.)

semper reformanda: Latin for "always needing to be reformed," a Protestant motto about the need for continual reformation of the church.

***Shepherd* of Hermas**: An early Christian book, written in Greek in Italy in the late 1st or early 2nd century, read with appreciation by many in the Great Church, some of whom regarded it as part of the canon.

simplicity: A philosophical concept used in theology to describe God. To say God is simple is to say he has no parts and is not composed of many things.

simul justus et peccator: Latin for "at the same time righteous and a sinner," this term is a key doctrinal formulation of Luther, stemming from his conviction that even the good works of someone who is justified by faith in Christ are in themselves (that is, apart from Christ) mortal sins.

Socinianism: A Unitarian theology that arose in the radical Reformation of the 16th century and became widely influential in the 18th century, affecting both Deist and Enlightenment thinkers.

sola fide: Latin for "by faith alone," this term is a catchphrase for distinctively Protestant doctrines of justification after Luther, according to which people become righteous simply by believing the Gospel of Christ, quite apart from any good works.

sola gratia: Latin for "grace alone," this term is a catchphrase for the characteristic Protestant insistence that believers are saved simply by God's grace, without any contribution of their own merits.

sola scriptura: Latin for "scripture alone," this term is a catchphrase for the Protestant conviction that no teaching is binding on the conscience as necessary for salvation except what is taught (explicitly or by clear implication) in scripture.

soteriology: From the Greek word for "salvation," this technical term refers to the part of theology concerned with the nature of salvation.

Stoics: An ancient school of philosophy which taught that the life of wisdom and happiness consisted of living by reason without passions—a radical version of the most common form of moralism in the ancient world. The Stoics were also materialists, believing that both God and the soul were made of living fire.

subordinationism: This view of the Trinity was widespread before the Council of Nicaea, according to which the preexistent *Logos* or word of God (prior to the Incarnation) is a divine intermediary between God and the creation, an intelligible image of the incomprehensible God, but existing at a lower and more understandable level.

subtlety: In medieval theology, a quality of glorified human bodies after the resurrection, which means they can enter or pass through another body like fire or air. (See **agility**, **clarity**, and **impassibility**.)

successionism: The view of Baptist history advocated by Landmarkism, according to which the Baptist churches of today can trace their roots through an unbroken succession of Baptist churches going back to the Baptism of Jesus.

superessential: (See *hyperousios*.)

supernatural: In Roman Catholic theology, especially Thomism, the concept of grace as not only assisting, healing, and restoring human nature but also elevating it so as to make it capable of a happiness or beatitude beyond the natural capacity of any created being. In this Catholic context, the term has nothing to do with ghosts, demons, or miracles. When used in later Protestant contexts, it usually refers to miracles, understood as acts of divine intervention in nature that contravene natural law, such as the virgin birth of Jesus.

Supernatural Existential: Advocated by Roman Catholic theologian Karl Rahner, a concept of a supernatural, graced component of human existence meant to explain how all people can experience a divine call to supernatural happiness or beatitude, even though that call does not belong to pure human nature.

supralapsarianism: From the Latin phrase *supra lapsum* meaning "prior to the Fall." In the Calvinist theology of the eternal decrees of God, this is the view that the decree of double predestination logically precedes and determines the decree to create the world and permit the Fall. (Contrast **infralapsarianism**.)

Sursum Corda: Latin for "lift up your hearts," it is the name of the opening prayer of the eucharistic liturgy, which includes these words.

synod: A regional meeting of clergy from more than one local church.

Synoptic Gospels: The Gospels of Matthew, Mark, and Luke, so called because they tell the story of Jesus's life in roughly the same order, so that making a synopsis covering all three is relatively easy. The Gospel of John tells the story differently, and is not one of the Synoptics.

Tabor, light of (Sometimes spelled "Thabor"): In Eastern Orthodox theology, the light of the glorious energies of God shining from the transfigured body of Christ on the Mount of Transfiguration, traditionally identified as Mount Tabor; this is the light of the beatific vision, as the Eastern Orthodox understand it.

teleology: From the Greek word *telos*, meaning "end" in the sense of goal, completion, or perfection. Teleology is a philosophical view of nature typical of ancient philosophy, according to which everything acts and moves in accordance with a goal inherent to its nature. For instance, human nature is inherently oriented toward the ultimate goal of happiness.

temporal: A technical theological term meaning the opposite of eternal, equivalent to "in time" as opposed to in eternity. Not to be confused with the ordinary, non-technical term "temporary."

theologia: Greek for "theology," the Eastern Orthodox often use this term as a synonym for the doctrine of the Trinity. It is paired with the term *oikonomia*, which refers to the Incarnation; thus, *theologia* and *oikonomia* designate the two prime concerns of Christian doctrine. (See **economy**.)

theopaschite formula: The formula "one of the Trinity was crucified in the flesh," an expanded version of which was accepted by the Second Council of Constantinople 553, that is, "our Lord Jesus Christ who was crucified in the flesh is true God and the Lord of glory and one of the holy Trinity." (See **Deipassionism**.)

theotokos: A Greek term meaning literally "God-bearer" (the translation preferred by Protestants) or more loosely translated, "Mother of God" (the traditional Roman Catholic term). This title was given to Mary by orthodox Christians not because she originated God—for of course she didn't—but because the baby Jesus to whom she gave birth is the Word, which is God incarnate. Nestorius was condemned for denying that Mary was *theotokos*.

Thomism: Roman Catholic thought based on the work of medieval theologian and philosopher Thomas Aquinas, especially prominent in 19th and 20th centuries, when it is often called "neo-Thomism."

total depravity: This term is a Calvinist label for a doctrine shared with Lutheranism, according to which every aspect of human life is corrupted by sin, including not just free will but also reason. Total depravity thus does not mean humans are pure evil (for like all Augustinians, Calvinists teach that there can be no such thing as pure evil, because everything that exists is God's good creation), but that no part of human nature is free from the evil of sin and the corrupting effect it has on God's good creation. (See **Dordt, Synod of.**)

tradition: From a Latin verb meaning "to hand down," this term originally referred to the teaching of the apostles as handed down in the churches they founded. Later it came to be paired (and sometimes contrasted) with scripture, which contains the written record of apostolic teaching.

transcendence: From a Latin verb meaning "to go beyond," modern theologians use this term to describe God's being beyond the natural world.

Transfiguration: Name for the event narrated in the Synoptic Gospels in which Jesus is transfigured or transformed by a glorious light (in Matthew 17, Mark 9, and Luke 9), which the Eastern Orthodox tradition regards as the uncreated and beatifying light of the divine energies.

transubstantiation: Roman Catholic doctrine, developed in the 13th century, that explains the eucharistic change of bread and wine into the body and blood of Christ as a change of substance but not of accidents, so that the substance of Christ's body and blood is present under the appearance of bread and wine.

transverberation: From a Latin term meaning "to pierce all the way through," this was a visionary experience Theresa of Avila had, in which an angel pierced her heart several times with a long golden spear tipped with fire, setting her heart aflame with a love of God both painful and sweet.

Trent, Council of: The council of Roman Catholic bishops meeting in the city of Trent (on the border of Austria and Italy) with interruptions during nearly two decades (1543–1547, 1551–1553, 1562–1563), that formulated the definitive Roman Catholic response to Protestantism, as well as initiated reforms in the Roman Catholic church itself.

Tridentine: Having to do with the Council of Trent (taken from the Latin form of the name of the city of Trent).

Trinity: The Christian doctrine that God is Father, Son, and Holy Spirit. The orthodox version of this doctrine is called Nicene theology.

typology: From the Greek word *typos* or *type*, often translated into Latin as *figura* and hence into English as "figure," a form of Christian reading in which persons, things, and events in the Old Testament are taken as prefiguring Christ, Christians, the Church, or Christian life.

uncreated: This technical theological term designates what is in the strictest sense divine, by contrasting it with all the things God has created. (The meaning of the term is thus parallel to "not made" rather than "unmade." The word "uncreated" does not imply that God ever "unmakes" anything.) The underlying idea is that everything that exists is either created by God or is God the creator, who is uncreated. Hence it is an important question whether grace (or one kind of it) is created or uncreated.

unitarianism: This is a label for Christian theologies that deny the doctrine of the Trinity (unitarianism being opposed to trinitarianism), including an American church denomination espousing unitarian theology, now called the Unitarian Universalist church.

Vatican, First Council: A council of Roman Catholic bishops in 1869–1870, presided over by Pope Pius IX, known for its definition of the doctrine of papal infallibility and also for the teaching that the existence of God can be known by natural reason.

Vatican, Second Council: A council of Roman Catholic bishops in 1962–1965, presided over by Pope John XXIII and then Pope Paul VI which, in a move called in Italian *aggiornamento* or "updating," envisioned a new and more positive relation between the church and the modern world, other religions, and other Christian groups, including a powerful emphasis on *ecumenism*.

Vestiarian controversy: Debate in the Church of England beginning in the 1560s and marking the emergence of Puritan theology, which objected to the continued use of Catholic vestments, such as cope, surplice, and stole.

via media: Latin for "middle way," often used to describe Anglican theology and practice as a middle way between Catholicism and Protestantism.

via negative: Latin for "way of negation." (See **apophatic**.)

Vincentian Canon: The widely accepted principle in the Great Church, articulated by Vincent of Lerins in 433, that the criterion of orthodox doctrine is its catholicity, in the sense that it is what is taught "everywhere, always, and by all" (*ubique, semper, et ab omnibus*).

Westminster Confession: A Reformed confession of faith composed by the Westminster Assembly of Divines, a group of Puritan theologians called together by Parliament and meeting from 1643–1647. It is frequently used as a doctrinal standard by Presbyterian churches.

Words of Institution: The words of Jesus, "This is my body [etc.]" and "This is my blood [etc.]," repeated as part of the liturgy of the Eucharist.

xenolalia: Greek phrase meaning "foreign speaking," which means speaking in a foreign language that the speaker has never learned or studied, a phenomenon which Pentecostals call "missionary tongues" because it is highly useful in missionary preaching; unlike glossolalia, the evidence that this actually occurred is not compelling.

Biographical Notes

Note: Ancient and medieval figures, as well as popes, are typically listed by first name. For ancient theologians, where exact dates of birth and death are often unknown, "c." (Latin for *circa*) means "approximately" and "fl." (for "flourished") refers to the period at which time this person was known to be active.

Amyraldus: (See **Amyraut**.)

Amyraut, Moses (1596–1664): Also known by a Latinized version of his name, Amyraldus, was a French Protestant (a Huguenot) who advocated a modified form of Calvinism which came to be known as Amyraldianism, hypothetical universalism, or four-point Calvinism, because it accepted all the teachings of the Synod of Dordt except limited atonement.

Anselm (c. 1033–1109): Monk, then abbot of Bec in Normandy, then archbishop of Canterbury (1093–1109); the first great medieval theologian of the West who is famous for his account of how Christ's death made satisfaction for human sin in the treatise *Why God Became Man*.

Aquinas, Thomas (c. 1225–1274): Dominican friar, teacher at the University of Paris, central figure of medieval scholasticism, and the most authoritative theologian of the Roman Catholic tradition; known for his use of Aristotelian philosophy and his conception of supernatural grace.

Aristotle (384–322 B.C.): Greek philosopher, student of Plato, founder of the sciences of logic, physics, and biology, whose writings were a major conceptual resource for medieval scholastic theologians, especially Aquinas.

Arius (c. 256–336): Alexandrian presbyter whose teaching on the Trinity was condemned at the Council of Nicaea 325.

Arminius, Jacobus (c. 1560–1609): Dutch pastor and originator of the form of Protestant theology rejected by the Calvinists at the Synod of Dordt and now called "Arminianism."

Arndt, Johann (1555–1621): German Lutheran pastor and author of *True Christianity* (1606–1609), the most important precursor to the German Pietist movement.

Athanasius (c. 293–373): Bishop of Alexandria and early proponent of the Nicene doctrine of the Trinity.

Augustine (354–430): Bishop of Hippo in North Africa, the most influential theologian of the West, known especially for his doctrine of grace, including related doctrines of original sin and predestination.

Baius, Michael (1513–1589): Also called Michael du Bay, professor at the University of Louvain. The Vatican in 1567 condemned this Catholic theologian for his denial of the supernatural and radical doctrine of the corruption of human nature. Baius submitted to the condemnation and later became chancellor of the University.

Balthasar, Hans Urs von (1905–1988): Swiss priest and Roman Catholic theologian, friend of Henri de Lubac, Karl Barth, and Adrienne von Speyr, is known for his emphasis on beauty as the theme of theology. Balthasar proposed a controversial new theology of Holy Saturday, which is connected with a hope for universal salvation.

Barth, Karl (1886–1968): Swiss Reformed pastor and professor, founding figure of Neo-Orthodoxy and probably the most influential Protestant theologian of the 20th-century. He was known for a Christocentric theology highly critical of Protestant liberalism.

Basil of Caesarea (c. 330–379): Older brother of Gregory of Nyssa and leader of the Cappadocian Fathers, who advocated a reformulation of Nicene theology that prevailed at the Council of Constantinople 381.

Baxter, Richard (1615–1691): English Puritan, advocate of Amyraldianism or "four-point Calvinism."

Benedict XVI (1927–): Born Joseph Ratzinger, German priest and theology professor, archbishop of Munich (1977–1982), cardinal (1977–2005), and pope beginning in 2005.

Brunner, Emil (1889–1966): Swiss Reformed pastor and theologian, advocate of a neo-Orthodox theology of divine-human encounter that requires a "point of contact" between God and human nature, a point famously and fiercely rejected by Karl Barth.

Bultmann, Rudolf (1884–1976): German New Testament scholar, neo-Orthodox theologian, advocate of "demythologizing" the language of the New Testament and interpreting it using Existentialist concepts.

Calvin, John (1509–1564): French Protestant theologian who lived most of his adult life in Geneva. He was the most influential figure in Reformed theology and author of the *Institutes*, the most important systematic theology text of Protestantism.

Cyril of Alexandria (c. 378–444): Nestorius opponent, Bishop of Alexandria, dominant figure at the Council of Ephesus 431, known for his Christology of hypostatic union, which emphasizes the unity of the person of Christ, and his defense of the title *theotokos* (Mother of God) for the Virgin Mary.

Dante Alighieri (1265–1321): Italian poet and author of the *Divine Comedy*, an epic poem in which Dante portrays himself journeying through hell, purgatory, and heaven. He's an important source for the Christian imagination of the afterlife.

Darby, John Nelson (1800–1882): Anglo-Irish theologian, leader of the Plymouth Brethren, and founder of Dispensationalist theology.

Dionysius (fl. c. 500): Pseudonymous Christian neo-Platonist theologian, in the west called Saint Denys (or Denis), and by modern scholars labeled Pseudo-Dionysius because his identification with Dionysius the Areopagite, mentioned in Acts 17:34, is not credible. An author of an extremely influential little treatise on the incomprehensibility of God called *Mystical Theology*, as well as a treatise about concepts used to describe God called *On the Divine Names*, and a treatise on the nine orders of angels called *Celestial Hierarchy*.

Eckhart, Meister (c. 1260–c. 1327): Dominican priest and mystical theologian, the most prominent figure in German mysticism, whose teachings were under investigation for heresy at the time of his death.

Edwards, Jonathan (1703–1758): Puritan minister, Calvinist theologian, the first American theorist of revival, and leader of the Great Awakening in New England.

Fénelon, Francois (1651–1715): Archbishop of Cambrai in France, known for teachings about "pure love," which Rome condemned as "semi-Quietism" in 1699.

Finney, Charles Grandison (1792–1875): Presbyterian minister, theological heir of Jonathan Edwards, and the most prominent American *Revivalist* in the first half of the 19th century.

Fosdick, Harry Emerson (1878–1969): American Baptist minister, leading spokesman for theological liberalism, noted especially for his 1922 sermon, "Shall the Fundamentalists Win?"

Franck, Sebastian (c. 1499–c. 1542): Leading spiritualist theologian of the radical Reformation.

Francke, August Hermann (1663–1727): German Lutheran pastor and theology professor at the University of Halle, protégé of Philipp Jakob Spener, organizer and proponent of Pietism.

Gregory Naziansen (c. 330–c. 390): Sometimes known as Gregory of Naziansen, one of the Cappadocian Fathers. Among the Eastern Orthodox he is called "Saint Gregory the Theologian" because of the importance of his *Theological Orations* in formulating the orthodox trinitarian theology that prevailed after the Council of Constantinople 381.

Gregory of Nyssa (c. 335–c. 394): One of the Cappadocian fathers, brother of Basil of Caesarea, and author of important works on the Trinity, including a brief but influential treatise explaining why the orthodox do not say there are three Gods.

Guyon, Madame Jeanne (1648–1717): Mystic, writer, and spiritual director, a major inspiration for the "semi-Quietist" theology of Fénelon and influential for a time at the court of Louis XIV. Her writings were rejected by the French church but admired by Wesley and later evangelicals.

Heidegger, Martin (1889–1976): German philosopher whose early work, *Being and Time* (1927), which owed a great deal to Kierkegaard's analysis of human existence, was one of the most important sources of existentialism and thus highly influential on 20th-century theology.

Hooker, Richard (c. 1554–1600): Anglican theologian, author of the multi-volume treatise *The Laws of Ecclesiastical Polity*, which defended the Elizabethan settlement from Puritan criticisms.

Hopkins, Samuel (1721–1803): New England Puritan pastor and theologian; student and rigorous advocate of Jonathan Edwards's theology.

Irenaeus (c. 120–200): Bishop of Lyon, the most important Christian theologian of the 2nd century; author of a large work, *Against Heresies*.

Jansen, Cornelius (1585–1638): Catholic bishop of Ypres in Belgium, and author of the posthumously published *Augustinus* (1640), which argued for a doctrine of grace that Jansen believed was truly Augustinian but which was rejected by Rome as too close to Calvinism.

John XXIII (1881–1963): Born Angelo Giuseppe Roncalli, Italian priest, archbishop of Venice (1953–1958), then pope (1958–1963), who summoned the Second Vatican Council with the aim of *aggiornamiento*, bringing the church up to date.

John of the Cross (1542–1591): Spanish monk, mystical theologian, Roman Catholic saint, and friend of Theresa of Avila; known for his concept of the dark night of the soul.

John Paul II (1920–2005): Born Karol Wojtyla, Polish priest, philosophy professor, archbishop of Krakow (1963–1978) then pope (1978–2005) in the second-longest pontificate in history, important theologically for his theology of the body, his defense of long-standing Catholic doctrines and practices (such as not ordaining women to the priesthood) and his advocacy of a philosophically-informed Christian humanism.

Justin Martyr (c.100–c. 165): Born in Palestine early in the 2nd century, Justin was educated as a philosopher and converted to Christianity, retaining many of his Platonist convictions. He wrote an important *Apology* (meaning a defense of Christianity against the pagans) and the *Dialogue with Trypho*, trying to convince a Jew of the truth of Christianity.

Kant, Immanuel (1724–1804): German philosopher and founder of the idealist tradition of German philosophy, in which the structure of consciousness gives structure to the world.

Kierkegaard, Søren (1813–1855): Danish philosopher and theologian, who adapts Hegel's dialectic to describe the role of anxiety, guilt, and despair in an individual human existence facing the task of becoming Christian. His focus on human existence as a task makes him a founder of Existentialism.

Lindbeck, George (1923–): American Lutheran theologian whose influential work, *The Nature of Doctrine* (1984), positioned him at the forefront of postliberal theology. He was the Pitkin Professor of Historical Theology at Yale University until his retirement in 1993, and is widely respected for his commitment to ecumenical dialogue.

Lubac, Henri de (1896–1991): French Jesuit theologian, patristic scholar, and leading critic of neo-Thomism. His views led to the church silencing him in the 1940s, though he was in effect vindicated after the Second Vatican Council, when he was made cardinal.

Luther, Martin (1483–1546): German theologian, pastor, professor at the University of Wittenberg, ex-monk, and founding figure of Protestantism. He was known for his doctrine of justification by faith alone and his insistence on distinguishing between Law and Gospel.

Machen, J. Gresham (1881–1937): Presbyterian minister, New Testament scholar and advocate for the Fundamentalist side of the Fundamentalist-modernist controversy, most notably in his book *Christianity and Liberalism* (1923).

Marcion (fl. early 2nd century): Early Christian opponent of orthodoxy, known for his sharp distinction between the good God and the God of the Jews.

Maximus the Confessor (c. 580–662): Early Byzantine monk and theologian, advocate of the orthodox view that Christ has two wills, divine and human.

Melanchthon, Philipp (1497–1560): German theologian, reformer, and professor at the University of Wittenberg, Martin Luther's colleague and best friend, and principal author of The Augsburg Confession (1530), the most important Lutheran confessional document.

Mencken, H. L. (1880–1956): Controversial American journalist and critic renowned for his biting critiques of provincialism and prudery in American society. His scathing portrayal of fundamentalists during the Scopes "Monkey Trial" generated a cultural stereotype that persists to this day.

Molina, Luis de (1535–1600): Spanish Jesuit whose theology of free will was opposed by the Dominican Thomists represented in the *Congregatio de Auxiliis* debates.

Montanus (fl. 2nd century): Founder of a "New Prophecy" in Phrygia (in modern Turkey), which advocated stricter moral discipline—for example, no remarriage of widows or widowers and the veiling of unmarried women—on the basis of statements alleged to be made by the Holy Spirit through himself and several followers.

Moody, Dwight L. (1837–1899): The most prominent American *Revivalist* of the second half of the 19th century, influencing and influenced by the Keswick movement.

Mullins, E. Y. (1860–1928): Southern Baptist pastor, professor, theologian, denominational leader, and advocate of "soul competency."

Müntzer, Thomas (c. 1490–1525): A pastor and Luther's former student who became a leader in the Peasant Revolt of 1525, claiming authority from the Spirit to preach the violent overthrow of the wicked in the end times.

Nestorius (fl. early 5th century): Archbishop of Constantinople who denied that Mary was *theotokos* or Mother of God. His Christology was accused of splitting Christ into "two sons" and was condemned at the ecumenical Council of Ephesus 431.

Origen (c. 185–254): Alexandrian theologian famous for his commentaries and homilies on the scriptures, which established a long-lasting tradition of Christian allegorical exegesis. Long after his death, his speculations about the preexistence and the Fall were a cause of intense controversy and were officially rejected by the church.

Osiander, Andreas (1498–1552): Lutheran pastor, professor, and theologian, in whose doctrine of justification believers are united to the essential righteousness of God. The forensic doctrine of justification, developed as both Reformed and Lutheran, rejected Osiander's doctrine.

Owen, John (1616–1683): English Puritan, classic advocate of the high Calvinism represented by the Synod of Dordt and the Westminster Confession, especially known for his defense of the doctrine of limited atonement or "particular redemption," as he called it.

Paine, Thomas (1737–1809): American political writer, author of *Common Sense* and *The Rights of Man*, but also author of the most famous work of American deism, *The Age of Reason*.

Palamas, Gregory (1296–1359): Byzantine theologian, known for his articulation of characteristic Eastern Orthodox doctrines, especially the distinction between the divine essence and divine energies, the latter of which include the deifying light of the Transfiguration of Christ.

Palmer, Phoebe (1807–1874): American Methodist and Bible teacher, whose "shorter way" to the blessing of entire sanctification, "laying all on the altar," made her the founding figure in the Holiness movement.

Paul (c. 4 B.C.–c. A.D. 64): Apostle and early Christian missionary, whose letters are the earliest documents contained in the New Testament and thus the first extant writings in Christian theology.

Pelagius (fl. 410–420): British monk, spiritual advisor, and theologian whose teaching gave rise to Pelagianism, the view against which Augustine's doctrine of grace was developed.

Philo of Alexandria (c. 20 B.C.–A.D. 50): Jewish philosopher and exegete who used an allegorical method to interpret the scriptures that was influential on ancient Christian writers, especially in Alexandria.

Pius IX (1792–1878): Also known by the Italian form of his name, "Pio Nono," pope from 1846–1878, the longest reigning pope in history, who defined the doctrine of the Immaculate Conception in 1854, promulgated the Syllabus of Errors in 1864, and presided over the First Vatican Council, which defined the doctrine of papal infallibility in 1870.

Plato (c. 427 B.C.–c. 348 B.C.): Greek philosopher, Socrates's student, Aristotle's teacher, and founder of the only rigorously non-materialist philosophical tradition in the West and, therefore, a major philosophical resource for Christian theology.

Plotinus (c. A.D. 205–270): Pagan philosopher and founder of neo-Platonism, one of the major sources of Christian Platonism (for example, Augustine and Pseudo-Dionysius).

Pseudo-Dionysius: (See **Dionysius**.)

Rahner, Karl (1904–1984): German Jesuit theologian, known especially for his concept of the "supernatural existential," a major theological influence at the Second Vatican Council and subsequently in liberal Catholic theology.

Sales, Francis de (1567–1622): Roman Catholic bishop, French author of the highly influential devotional writings, *Introduction to the Devout Life* and *Treatise on the Love of God*.

Schleiermacher, Friedrich (1768–1834): German theologian and philosopher, minister in the Reformed church, professor at the University of Berlin (1811–1834), and founding figure of Protestant liberalism.

Scofield, C. I. (1843–1921): Minister, Bible teacher, Dispensationalist theologian, and editor of the *Scofield Reference Bible*, whose 2nd edition (1917) is the most influential book in the Dispensationalist movement.

Servetus, Michael (c. 1511–1553): Anti-trinitarian theologian, arrested and executed in Geneva on evidence Calvin presented.

Simons, Menno (1496–1561): A former Catholic priest in Holland who became a leader in the Dutch and North German Anabaptist communities, which were later called "Mennonites" because of him.

Spener, Philipp Jakob (1635–1705): German Lutheran pastor who became one of the founders of Pietism when, in 1675, he published *Pia Desideria* ("Pious Desires"), calling for reform of the Lutheran church.

Speyr, Adrienne von (1902–1967): Swiss physician and Roman Catholic theologian whose visionary experiences were a major inspiration for the theology of von Balthasar.

Stoddard, Solomon (1643–1729): Puritan minister in Northampton, Massachusetts (and grandfather of Jonathan Edwards), who allowed unregenerate church members under the Halfway Covenant to take communion.

Teresa of Avila (1515–1582): Also known as Saint Teresa of Jesus; Spanish nun and mystical theologian known for her descriptions of the various levels of mystical experience, including the Prayer of Quiet and Spiritual Marriage.

Tertullian (c. 160–225): North African priest and theologian, the first major Latin Christian author. Despite the large number of his writings that have survived, his influence was limited because at the end of his life he joined the Montanist heresy.

Tillich, Paul (1886–1965): German Lutheran minister, neo-Orthodox theologian, and Existentialist philosopher, who had an influential teaching career in the United States beginning in 1933.

Valentinus (c. 100–c. 175): Author of an influential and philosophically sophisticated version of Gnosticism. He was active in Rome in the 140s, and even hoped to become bishop of Rome.

Voltaire (1694–1778): Pen name of François-Marie Arouet, a French Enlightenment writer, satirist, and critic of Christianity.

Wayland, Francis (1796–1865): Baptist minister, president of Brown University (1827–1855), and advocate of congregational autonomy and the right of individual judgment in religion.

Wesley, John (1703–1791): Anglican priest, revival preacher and organizer, and together with his brother Charles, a founding figure of Methodism, whose theology combines Arminianism and Pietism and is known for a strong emphasis on sanctification, including the expectation that believers will seek and sometimes attain Christian perfection.

Zinzendorf, Count Nikolaus Ludwig von (1700–1760): Lutheran minister, Pietist theologian, godson of Philipp Jakob Spener, and leader of the Moravian religious community based in Herrnhut, Germany that was known for "heart Christianity," which emphasizes the wounds of the Savior.

Zwingli, Ulrich (or Huldrych) (1484–1531): Swiss pastor and theologian based in Zurich, a founding figure of the Reformed Protestant tradition, most famous for his low view of the Eucharist.

Bibliography

General

Ante-Nicene Fathers. 10 vols. A series of 19th-century translations, reprinted by various publishers (most recently Eerdmans and Hendrickson) containing the most extensive English collection of writings by Justin Martyr, Tertullian, Origen, and others. (See *Nicene and Post-Nicene Fathers* series below.)

The Bible, English Standard Version. Wheaton, IL: Good News Publishers, 2001. I recommend this translation over any other English version of the past century. It avoids paraphrase and translates "word for word," which gives readers a better grasp of the verbal echoes that are essential to the artistry of the original. Quotations of the Bible in these lectures are usually taken from this version, although often modified to bring them even closer to the original.

Buschcart, W. David. *Exploring Protestant Traditions*. Downers Grove, IL: InterVarsity Press, 2006. Excellent and sympathetic introduction, both historical and theological, to the Lutheran, Reformed, Anabaptist, Anglican, Baptist, Wesleyan-Holiness, Dispensational, and Pentecostal traditions.

Foster, Richard J. *Streams of Living Water: Celebrating the Great Traditions of the Christian Faith*. San Francisco: HarperSanFrancisco, 1998. A beginner's guide to the variety of spiritual practices in the Christian tradition.

González, Justo. *A History of Christian Thought*. 3 vols. Nashville: Abingdon Press, 1970–1975. Both readable and thorough.

Kelly, J. N. D. *Early Christian Doctrines*. 5th ed. New York: Continuum, 2000. The best one-volume introduction to the doctrines of the ancient orthodox church.

Leith, John H. *Creeds of the Churches*. 3rd ed. Louisville: John Knox Press, 1982. The best one-volume collection of creeds, confessions, and official documents of the ancient church and various modern denominations.

Livingston, James C. *Modern Christian Thought*. 2nd ed. Minneapolis: Fortress Press, 2006. Everything you wanted to know about 19th century European theology with some of the 18th century background.

Marthaler, Berard L., ed. *The New Catholic Encyclopedia*. 2nd ed. Detroit: Gale, 2003. Indispensable reference source for all things Catholic, including details of doctrinal controversies about such things as Jansenism, Molinism, etc.

Nicene and Post-Nicene Fathers. Together with the *Ante-Nicene Fathers*, its companion series (see above), this is still the most complete collection of English writings by the church fathers, containing 19th-century translations. It is broken into two series, the first consisting solely of writings by Augustine and Chrysostom (14 vols.) and the second covering everybody else (14 vols.). For more recent translations with up-to-date scholarly introductions and notes, look for individual volumes in the *Ancient Christian Writers* series, which unlike these two series does not come as a set. For Augustine's writings, look for publications by New City Press, which is in the process of publishing the first complete edition of his works in English (look for Hill's translations; avoid Boulding's translations).

Olson, Roger E. *The Story of Christian Theology*. Downers Grove, IL: IntraVarsity Press, 1999. Highly readable, though weak on modern Roman Catholic theology.

Pelikan, Jaroslav. *The Christian Tradition: A History of the Development of Doctrine*. 5 vols. Chicago and London: University of Chicago Press, 1971–1991. The most comprehensive recent history of Christian doctrine in English. Volumes cover the ancient church (*The Emergence of the Christian Tradition 100–600*, the Eastern Orthodox tradition (*The Spirit of Eastern Christendom 600–1700*), the Western church until shortly before the Reformation (*The Growth of Medieval Theology 600–1300*, the Protestant Reformation and Catholic Counter-Reformation (*Reformation of Church and Dogma 1300–1700*, and the history of modern theology (*Christian Doctrine and Modern Culture since 1700*.

Schaff, Philip. *The Creeds of Christendom*. 3 vols. Grand Rapids: Baker, 1990. Affordable reprint of a 19th-century classic, containing a more extensive set of documents than Leith, including a history of the creeds in vol. 1 and the full text of the decrees of Trent and the First Vatican Council in vol. 2.

United States Catholic Conference. *Catechism of the Catholic Church*. Libreria Editrice Vaticana, 1994. A translation of the official catechism authorized by the Vatican under Pope John Paul II, this is the first place to go to find out what the Roman Catholic church currently teaches.

Willis, John R., S.J. *The Teachings of the Church Fathers*. San Francisco: Ignatius Press, 2002. A systematic presentation of Roman Catholic doctrine based on a rich selection of excerpts from the church fathers—a fine introduction to the deeper roots of the tradition.

More Specialized

Anselm. *The Major Works*. Oxford and New York: Oxford University Press, 1998. The best one-volume collection of Anselm's works in English, which includes the great treatise on the doctrine of atonement, *Why God Became Man*.

Aquinas, Thomas. *Introduction to St. Thomas Aquinas*. Edited by A. Pegis. New York: Random House, 1945. A selection of representative texts from Aquinas's major writings, the *Summa Theologica* and the *Summa contra Gentiles*. Aquinas's writing is dense and demanding, but extraordinarily lucid and instructive once you "get it." For beginners, it is best to read it together with a guide like Davies's guide below.

———. *Summa Theologica*. 5 vols. Westminster, MD: Christian Classics, 1981. A complete edition of the greatest masterwork of medieval thought, for those who wish to pursue in-depth study of Roman Catholic theology.

Arndt, Johann. *True Christianity*. Mahwah, NJ: Paulist Press, 1979. Edited and translated by P. Erb. One of the main inspirations for the Pietist movement, this edition includes a translation of Book 1 (from the original 1-volume corrected edition of 1606) and selections from later books.

Augustine. *Answer to the Pelagians I*. pt. 1, vol. 23, *The Works of St. Augustine: A Translation for the 21st Century*. New York: New City Press, 1997. Contains Augustine's most important treatises on original sin and the necessity of grace, including *On the Spirit and the Letter*.

———. *Answer to the Pelagians IV: To the Monks of Hadrumentum and Provence*. pt. 1, vol. 26, *The Works of St. Augustine: A Translation for the 21st Century*, New York: New City Press, 1999. Contains treatises written late in Augustine's life dealing with the topics of grace and predestination, including *Grace and Free Choice* and *Rebuke and Grace*, which are the most illuminating of Augustine's writings on the topic of predestination and free will.

———. *City of God*. Translated by H. Bettenson. New York: Penguin, 1984. The most important statement on the meaning of Christian philosophy by a church father.

———. *Confessions*. 2nd ed. Translated by W. Sheed. Indianapolis: Hackett, 2007. Of the many English translations of the *Confessions* available, this one does the best job of capturing the poetic power of the original without sacrificing theological accuracy.

Avis, Paul. *The Identity of Anglicanism*. Edinburgh: T. & T. Clark, 2008. An up-to-date introduction to Anglican theology.

Bainton, Roland. *Here I Stand: A Life of Martin Luther*. New York: Penguin, 1995. Originally published in 1950 but still a favorite, this biography of Luther is also a great introduction to the Reformation.

Balthasar, Hans Urs von. *Dare We Hope "That All Men Be Saved"?* San Francisco: Ignatius Press, 1988. Balthasar's "yes" answer to the question in the title is controversial but very influential in contemporary Catholic theology.

———. *First Glance at Adrienne von Speyr*. San Francisco: Ignatius Press, 1981. An introduction to the life and work of the mystical theologian who inspired Balthasar's radical thinking about Holy Saturday, with a brief selection from her writings.

Barth, Karl. *Church Dogmatics*. Edinburgh: T. & T. Clark, 1956–1973. Barth's major work is a multi-volume masterpiece. Most influential are vol. 1, pt. 1, on the word of God and the doctrine of the Trinity, vol. 2, pt. 2, on the doctrine of election (that is, predestination), and vol. 4, pt. 1, on the atonement. Some readers find Barth's style impenetrable; others find it exhilarating.

———. *Dogmatics in Outline*. Translated by G. T. Thomson. New York: Harper & Row, 1959. A good place to start for a brief introduction to Barth's mature theology.

———. *The Epistle to the Romans*. Translated by E. Hoskyns. London: Oxford University Press, 1968. When this commentary on the biblical book of Romans came out in German in 1919, it was a bombshell that began Barth's theological career and generated the movement called "dialectical theology" and later, "neo-Orthodoxy." This English translation of the second and substantially revised edition of 1922 conveys the vividness and power of Barth's writing, but the book should not be taken as a mature statement of his theology.

Bauckham, Richard. *God Crucified: Monotheism and Christology in the New Testament*. Grand Rapids: Eerdmans, 1998. A leading scholar argues that the earliest Christians understood Jesus, in both his suffering and his exaltation, as belonging to the identity of the one God of Israel.

———. *The Testimony of the Beloved Disciple: Narrative, History and Theology in the Gospel of John*. Grand Rapids: Baker Academic, 2007. A challenging new argument that high Christology and firsthand historical memory go together in this most unique Gospel.

Bettenson, Henry. *Documents of the Christian Church*. 2nd ed. New York: Oxford University Press, 1963. A useful collection of historical documents from the early church to the 20th century.

Book of Common Prayer. New York: The Church Pension Fund, 1928. The old American edition of the most important theological book in the Anglican tradition. Revisions undertaken in the 1970s in the United States and other countries have substantially altered the prayer book, so those with an interest in the history of Anglicanism need to go back to older editions.

Braaten, Carl E. and Robert W. Jenson, eds. *Union with Christ: The New Finnish Interpretation of Luther*. Grand Rapids: Eerdmans, 1998. An introduction to the most important alternative to purely forensic interpretations of Luther's doctrine of justification. According to recent Finnish scholars, justification for Luther does not mean simply that God imputes Christ's righteousness to us, but that he gives us Christ so that we are united with him in heart and made partakers in his divine attributes, such as righteousness.

Brown, Raymond. *An Introduction to New Testament Christology*. Mahwah NJ: Paulist Press, 1994. A widely-respected Catholic scholar provides an introduction to the scholarship on early Christian views of Christ, including especially helpful discussions of the meaning of Christological titles such as "Christ," "Son of God" and "Son of Man."

Bultmann, Rudolf. *New Testament and Mythology and Other Basic Writings*. Philadelphia: Fortress Press, 1984. Contains Bultmann's most influential essay of those famous on demythologizing the New Testament.

Calvin, John. *Institutes of the Christian Religion*. 2 vols. Edited by John T. McNeill. Philadelphia: Westminster, 1960. Calvin's major work, the most influential systematic theology text in the history of Protestantism, in a contemporary translation with excellent scholarly annotations and extensive indexes.

Caputo, John D. *Philosophy and Theology*. Nashville: Abingdon Press, 2006. A brief popular introduction to what I call "left wing" postmodernism, with particular focus on the intertwining of faith and reason in the Western tradition.

Cary, Phillip. *Augustine: Philosopher and Saint*. Audio CD or Audio Cassette. Chantilly, VA: The Teaching Company, 1997.

———. *Augustine's Invention of the Inner Self*. New York: Oxford University Press, 2000. Includes material on the contrast between Augustine and Denys on the intelligibility and incomprehensibility of God.

———. *Inner Grace: Augustine in the Traditions of Plato and Paul*. New York: Oxford University Press, 2008. Provides a detailed account of the development and theological motives of Augustine's doctrine of grace.

———. *Philosophy and Religion in the West*.

———. "*Sola Fide*: Luther and Calvin," *Concordia Theological Quarterly* (July/Oct. 2007): 265–281. Also available online at http://www.ctsfw.edu/events/symposia/papers/2007.php. Explains where I stand in agreement with Luther's theology.

Catherine of Genoa. *Purgation and Purgatory, The Spiritual Dialogues*. Mahwah, NJ: Paulist Press, 1979. Writing at the end of the 15th century, Catherine gives a humane and deeply spiritual account of souls in purgatory motivated by love for God to embrace their sufferings because of their desire to be purified and their joy in God's will. Quite different from the scare-tactics found in most popular treatments of Purgatory at the time, it received papal approval in 1683.

Chadwick, Henry. *The Early Church*. rev. ed. New York: Penguin, 1993. Good brief history of the ancient church until the fall of the Roman Empire.

Colson, Charles and Richard John Neuhaus, Richard, eds. *Evangelicals and Catholics Together: Toward a Common Mission*. Nashville: Thomas Nelson, 1995. The initial statement of the most important ongoing theological dialog between Catholics and evangelicals.

Crossan, John Dominick. *Jesus: A Revolutionary Biography*. San Francisco: HarperOne, 1995. Crossan, a member of the Jesus Seminar and one of the most radical and interesting scholars on the revisionist end of the spectrum of historical Jesus research, provides a popular summary of his lengthier work, *The Historical Jesus* (1993).

Crouzel, Henri. *Origen: The Life and Thought of the First Great Theologian*. San Francisco: Harper & Row, 1989. The best one-volume introduction to this enormously important, controversial, and often poorly-understood figure.

Cyril of Alexandria, Saint. *On the Unity of Christ*. Translated by John McGuckin. Crestwood, NY: St. Vladimir's Seminary Press, 1995. This little book contains a translation of one of Cyril's major treatises on Christology; the translator also provides a detailed and helpful scholarly introduction to the issues.

Dante Alighieri. *The Divine Comedy. vol. 1, Inferno*. Translated by Mark Musa. New York: Penguin, 1985. In the first part of Dante's medieval Christian epic, he is taken on a journey through hell while still alive so that he may understand the nature of God's eternal justice. This is one of the best of many translations of what is perhaps the greatest poem ever written. It is accompanied by extensive notes and explanations, which modern readers need.

———. *The Divine Comedy. vol. 2, Purgatorio*. Translated by Mark Musa. New York: Penguin, 1985. Dante's journey through purgatory shows the medieval understanding of purgatory at its best, both poetically vivid and theologically deep.

———. *The Divine Comedy. vol. 3, Paradiso*. Translated by Mark Musa. New York: Penguin, 1986. Dante's journey up to the height of heaven culminates in a powerful attempt to represent what Catholic theology calls beatific vision.

Davies, Brian. *The Thought of Thomas Aquinas*. Oxford: Clarendon Press, 1992. A lucid explanation of Aquinas's key concepts, more in-depth than Pieper (below).

Dionysius. *Pseudo-Dionysius: The Complete Works*. Translated by Colm Luibheid. Mahwah, NJ: Paulist Press, 1987. Includes *Mystical Theology, The Celestial Hierarchy* and other works.

Dünzl, Franz. *A Brief History of the Doctrine of the Trinity in the Early Church*. Edinburgh: T. & T. Clark, 2007. Combines a readable narrative (in less than 150 pages) with adequate attention to detail, giving the bulk of its attention to the development of Nicene theology in the 4th century.

Edwards, Jonathan. *A Jonathan Edwards Reader*. Edited by J. E. Smith, H. S. Stout, and K. P. Minkema. New Haven: Yale University Press, 1995. A judicious selection of Edwards's writings, including the famous sermon, "Sinners in the Hands of an Angry God," and long excerpts from Edwards's most important books, including *A Faithful Narrative of the Surprising Work of God*, *A Treatise concerning Religious Affections*, and *Freedom of the Will*.

Erb, Peter. *The Pietists: Selected Writings*. Mahwah, NJ: Paulist Press, 1983. Includes selections from Spener's *Pia Desideria*, as well as writings by Francke and Zinzendorf.

Eusebius. *The History of the Church from Christ to Constantine*. Translated by G. A. Williamson. New York: Penguin, 1989, rev. ed. Originally completed about A.D. 325, this is the most important source of information we have on the first centuries of Christian history.

Evans, Craig. *Fabricating Jesus: How Modern Scholars Distort the Gospels*. Downers Grove, IL: InterVarsity Press, 2006. A scholar on the conservative side of mainstream historical Jesus scholarship argues against scholars on the revisionist side (including the Jesus Seminar) and also provides antidotes to really silly views of Jesus, such as those in the best-selling novel *The Da Vinci Code*.

Finney, Charles G. *Lectures on Revival*. Minneapolis: Bethany House, 1989. A theology of revival from America's great Revivalist, originally published in 1835.

Flannery, Austin, ed. *Vatican Council II: Constitutions, Decrees, Declarations*. Northport, NY: Costello Publishing, 1996. Updated translation of the 16 basic documents of the Second Vatican Council.

Fosdick, Harry Emerson. "Shall the Fundamentalists Win?" Though out of print, this famous 1922 sermon is available in an abridged version online at http://historymatters.gmu.edu/d/5070.

Fox, George. *The Journal*. New York: Penguin, 1998. Autobiographical account of the early years of the Quakers by their founder, originally published posthumously in 1694.

Hardy, Edward R. *Christology of the Later Fathers*. Philadelphia: Westminster, 1954. A useful anthology of texts including Athanasius's *On the Incarnation of the Word*, Gregory of Naziansen's *Theological Orations*, Gregory of Nyssa's important little essay *That We Should Not Think of Saying There Are Three Gods*, Cyril of Alexandria's 3rd Letter to Nestorius with 12 "chapters" or anathemas against Nestorian teaching (decisive documents at the Council of Ephesus 431) and the Tome of Pope Leo I (a crucial document in the Council of Chalcedon 451).

Heppe, Heinrich. *Reformed Dogmatics, Set Out and Illustrated from the Sources*. Translated by G.T. Thomson. Grand Rapids: Baker, 1978. The indispensable guide to Reformed scholasticism, that is, Calvinist theology after Calvin, in its continental (Dutch and German) form. Original published in 1861. (For Lutheran scholasticism, see Schmid.)

Hurtado, Larry. *At the Origins of Christian Worship*. Grand Rapids: Eerdmans, 2000. A leading scholar traces the worship of the exalted Jesus back to the earliest days of Jewish Christianity.

Jefferson, Thomas. *The Jefferson Bible*. With an introduction by F. Church and an afterward by Jaroslav Pelikan. Boston: Beacon Press, 1989 (reissued). A fascinating document, the product of a few evenings after work at the White House when Jefferson literally took scissors and paste and produced a volume he called "The life and morals of Jesus of Nazareth," shorn of miracles, messianism, and anything else a Deist would find offensive in the Bible.

John of the Cross. *The Collected Works of St. John of the Cross*. Translated by Kieran Kavanaugh and Otilio Rodriguez. Washington DC: ICS Publications, 1991. Includes *The Ascent of Mount Carmel*, *The Dark Night*, *The Spiritual Canticle*, and *The Living Flame of Love*.

Jonas, Hans. *The Gnostic Religion*. 2nd ed. Boston: Beacon Press, 1963. A classic and still the deepest introduction to how the Gnostics thought.

Klaassen, Walter. *Anabaptism in Outline*. Kitchener, ON: Herald Press, 1981. A collection of 16th-century documents written by Anabaptists, covering the whole range of their theology.

Layton, Bently. *The Gnostic Scriptures*. New York: Doubleday, 1995. Contains translations of the most important and best-preserved of the ancient Gnostic texts, including the Gospel of Thomas and other major finds from Nag Hammadi, with helpful scholarly notes and introductions.

Liardon, Roberts. *The Azusa Street Revival*. Shippensburg, PA: Destiny Image Publishers, 2006. A history of Pentecostalism from a theological advocate of the movement, including biographies of key figures, sermons and articles, and eyewitness testimony of the Azusa Street revival.

Lossky, Vladimir. *The Mystical Theology of the Eastern Church*. Crestwood, NY: St. Vladimir's Seminary Press, 1976. Originally published in French in 1944, this is a classic treatment of the doctrines of Eastern Orthodoxy, emphasizing (perhaps over-emphasizing) the difference from the doctrines of the Western church as represented by Catholicism.

Luther, Martin. *Martin Luther: Selections from His Writings*. Edited by John Dillenberger. Garden City, NY: Anchor, 1961. A handy one-volume selection of Luther's most important writings, including "Preface to the Epistle of St. Paul to the Romans," the sermon on "Two Kinds of Righteousness," and *The Freedom of a Christian*.

Machen, J. Gresham. *Christianity and Liberalism*. Grand Rapids: Eerdmans, 1923 (often reprinted). The book that, more than any other, defined the original position of Fundamentalism in the Fundamentalist-modernist controversy in the United States.

MacIntyre, Alasdair. *Whose Justice? Which Rationality?* Notre Dame, IN: Notre Dame University Press, 1988. A big, dense, difficult, and original book, the founding document of "right wing" postmodernism (see Lecture Thirty-Two), containing a history of Western moral thinking which culminates (in chap. 28, titled "The Rationality of Traditions") in an argument that narrating the history of intellectual traditions is the only way to understand how rationality really works.

Marsden, George. *Fundamentalism and American Culture*. New York: Oxford University Press, 1980. The best single volume on the history and theological sources of Fundamentalism, including an overview of late 9th century *Revivalism*, the Holiness, Keswick movement, and Dispensationalism.

McGuckin, John. *Saint Cyril of Alexandria and the Christological Controversy*. Crestwood, NY: St. Vladimir's Seminary Press, 2004. The best single-volume introduction to Cyril of Alexandria, the Christian tradition's most important theologian of the

Incarnation, together with a very illuminating selection of Cyril's shorter writings.

McNeill, John T. *The History and Character of Calvinism*. Oxford: Oxford University Press, 1954. Includes a biography of Calvin and a history of the Reformed tradition from Zwingli through the Puritans.

Miller, Ed. L. and Stanley Grenz. *Fortress Introduction to Contemporary Theologies*. Minneapolis: Fortress Press, 1998. Very brief introductions to neo-Orthodox and other 20th-century theologians, good for those wanting to get an initial idea about how Tillich, Bultmann, Barth, et al., think.

Noll, Mark and Carolyn Nystrom. *Is the Reformation Over? An Evangelical Assessment of Contemporary Roman Catholicism*. Grand Rapids: Baker Academic, 2008. One of American evangelicalism's premier historians gives a sympathetic but not uncritical account of the move toward ecumenical rapprochement between evangelicals and Catholics.

O'Keefe, John and R. R. Reno. *Sanctified Vision: An Introduction to Early Christian Interpretation of the Bible*. Baltimore: Johns Hopkins University Press, 2005. A brief and accessible introduction to early Christian reading, including typology and allegory.

Origen. *Origen*. Edited by Rowan Greer. New York: Paulist Press, 1979. A judicious selection of Origen's writings with a very illuminating introduction by the editor.

Ouspensky, Leonid and Vladimir Lossky. *The Meaning of Icons*. Crestwood, NY: St. Vladimir's Seminary, 1976. In-depth explanation of the meaning of the Eastern Orthodox practice of veneration of icons, profusely illustrated with breathtaking color prints.

Owen, John. *The Death of Death in the Death of Christ*. Carlisle, PA: Banner of Truth, 1959 (frequently reprinted). This defense of Dordt's doctrine of limited atonement (or "particular redemption," as Owen more aptly calls it) is perhaps the best place to go to get acquainted with the "high Calvinism" of the English Puritans.

Pagels, Elaine. *The Gnostic Gospels*. New York: Random House, 1989. A sympathetic popular introduction to ancient Gnosticism, with particular attention to the "lost gospels" found at Nag Hammadi.

Palamas, Gregory. *Gregory Palamas: The Triads*. Edited by John Meyendorff. Mahwah, NJ: Paulist Press, 1983. Selections from

Palamas's major theological work on the knowledge of God, the light of Tabor, and the distinction between the divine essence and energies, with a learned and helpful introduction by the editor.

Palmer, Phoebe. *Phoebe Palmer: Selected Writings.* Edited by Thomas C. Oden. Mahwah, NJ: Paulist Press, 1984. An introduction to the thinking and spirituality at the foundation of the Holiness movement.

Pelikan, Jaroslav. *Christianity and Classical Culture.* New Haven and London: Yale University Press, 1993. Informative study of how ancient Greek philosophy was used and transformed in the theology of the Cappadocian Fathers.

Pieper, Josef. *Guide to Thomas Aquinas.* Notre Dame: University of Notre Dame Press, 1962. An introduction both to Thomas Aquinas and to his medieval scholastic environment.

Plotinus. *The Enneads.* Edited by John Dillon. New York: Penguin, 1991. A generous selection of writings of the founder of neo-Platonism, with extremely helpful editorial notes and introductions. Includes Plotinus's treatise on "The Three Initial Hypostases," which is important for understanding the philosophical background against which Nicene trinitarianism was working.

Pritz, Ray A. *Nazarene Jewish Christianity.* Leiden: Brill, 1988. Scholarly study of the little-known and poorly-documented history of Jewish Christianity after the New Testament, which is important for clarifying the distinction between Nazarenes and Ebionites.

Rahner, Karl. *Foundations of Christian Faith.* New York: Crossroad, 1987. A big book that provides the most comprehensive introduction to Rahner's theology—but not easy reading.

Sales, Francis de. *Treatise on the Love of God.* Rockford, IL: Tan Books, 1997. Reprint of an 1884 translation. De Sales's major work, in which he incorporates concepts of mystical theology from Theresa of Avila into the devotional life for all Christians.

Sanders, E. P. *Paul, the Law and the Jewish People.* Minneapolis: Fortress Press, 1983. One of the founding documents of the "New Perspective on Paul."

Schleiermacher, Friedrich. *Friedrich Schleiermacher: Pioneer of Modern Theology.* Edited by K. Clement. Minneapolis: Fortress Press, 1991. Key selections from Schleiermacher's works, together with a substantial introduction to his life and work by the editor.

Schmid, Heinrich. *Doctrinal Theology of the Evangelical Lutheran Church*. 3rd ed. (1899). Translated by C. Hay and H. Jacobs. Minneapolis: Augsburg, 1961 (reprint). The indispensable guide to Lutheran orthodoxy or scholasticism, the shape of Lutheran theology in the two centuries after Luther. (For Reformed scholasticism in the same period, see Heppe.)

Scofield, C. I., ed. *The Scofield Reference Bible*. Rev. ed. New York: Oxford University Press, 1917. This edition of the King James Version of the Bible was first published in 1909 with Scofield's notes presenting in great detail his Dispensationalist reading of the text. The 1917 edition, which is Scofield's own revision (mainly an expansion) of his notes, became the single most influential book for Dispensationalist theology. Those interested in the history of Dispensationalism should be aware that recent revised editions of the Scofield Bible are by later editors who tone down some of Scofield's more controversial views. The notes from the 1917 edition can now be found online at http://www.studylight.org/com/srn.

Spong, John Shelby. *Why Christianity Must Change or Die*. San Francisco: HarperSanFrancisco, 1998. A introduction to what the church's teaching might look like without theism, that is, without belief in a creator-God existing independent of the world.

Stead, Christopher. *Philosophy in Christian Antiquity*. Cambridge: Cambridge University Press, 1994. Knowledgeable and scholarly study of how the church fathers used philosophy, together with a helpful introduction to the ancient philosophy they used.

Sweeney, Douglas A. and Allen C. Guelzo. *The New Haven Theology*. Grand Rapids: Baker Academic, 2006. A selection of writings from Jonathan Edwards and his followers, including Charles Finney. The best single volume for understanding how New England *Revivalism* developed from Edwards's Calvinism to Finney's near-Pelagianism.

Teresa of Avila. *The Interior Castle*. Translated by Kieran Kavanaugh and Otilio Rodriguez. Mahwah, NJ: Paulist Press, 1979. Contains her most important descriptions of the spiritual marriage of the soul and God.

———. *The Life of Theresa of Jesus: The Autobiography of Theresa of Avila*. Translated by E. Allison Peers. New York: Doubleday, 1991. Contains vivid descriptions of the variety of her mystical states as well as the four levels of mental prayer.

Tillich, Paul. *Dynamics of Faith*. San Francisco: HarperOne, 2001. Originally published in 1957, this short book is an accessible introduction to Tillich's fundamental theological commitments.

Tull, James E. *Shapers of Baptist Thought*. Reprint. Macon, GA: Mercer University Press, 1984. The most helpful single volume I have found for purposes of understanding the shape and intent of Baptist theology.

Voltaire. *Philosophical Dictionary*. Translated by T. Besterman. New York: Penguin, 1984. Not really a dictionary or very philosophical, this is actually a collection of short essays, written in Voltaire's inimitably vigorous satirical style, providing a vivid introduction to the later Deists' critique of revealed religion and especially of the Bible.

Watt, Jan van der. *An Introduction to the Johannine Gospel and Letters*. Edinburgh: T. & T. Clark, 2008. A brief introduction both to the theology of the Gospel and Letters of John and to recent scholarship on them.

Wesley, John. *John Wesley*. Edited by Albert C. Outler. New York: Oxford University Press, 1964. The best single-volume selection from Wesley's writings, including "The Scripture Way of Salvation" and "Thoughts on Christian Perfection" and a very illuminating conversation with Zinzendorf.

Williams, Daniel H. *Retrieving the Tradition and Renewing Evangelicalism: A Primer for Suspicious Protestants*. Grand Rapids: Eerdmans, 1999. How Protestantism might benefit from taking the Christian tradition more seriously, as suggested in Lecture Thirty-Two.

Williams, George Huntston. *The Radical Reformation*. 3rd ed. Kirksville, MO: Sixteenth Century Journal Publishers, Inc., 1992. A big, informative book, including not only the best history of the Anabaptist movement available but also a lucid account of the social unrest of 16th-century Europe.

Wills, Garry. *Papal Sin: Structures of Deceit*. New York: Doubleday, 2000. A progressive American Catholic's diagnosis of the ills of his church by pointing to its inability to admit past errors.

Wright, N. T. *The Challenge of Jesus: Rediscovering Who Jesus Was and Is*. Downers Grove, IL: InterVarsity Press, 1999. A leading scholar gives an illuminating and readable summary of his research on the historical Jesus. Wright, an Anglican bishop who sometimes publishes popular work under the name "Tom Wright," is the most eminent scholar on the conservative end of the spectrum of historical Jesus scholarship.

———. *Surprised by Hope: Rethinking Heaven, the Resurrection, and the Mission of the Church*. New York: HarperCollins, 2008. In a popular summary of the massive scholarship of his *The Resurrection of the Son of God* (Minneapolis: Fortress, 2003), Wright explains the difference between New Testament eschatology and the notion of immortal souls going to heaven.

———. *What Saint Paul Really Said*. Grand Rapids: Eerdmans, 1997. A brief and accessible presentation of the theology of Paul, in line with the "New Perspective" inaugurated by E. P. Sanders (above).

Notes

Notes